D0090305

Code
of
Silence

Olsen, Lise, 1964-
Code of silence : sexual
misconduct by federal judges,
2021.
33305250003229
sa   12/20/21

Code
of
Silence

SEXUAL MISCONDUCT
BY FEDERAL JUDGES,
THE SECRET SYSTEM
THAT PROTECTS THEM,
AND THE WOMEN
WHO BLEW
THE WHISTLE

LISE OLSEN

BEACON PRESS
BOSTON

Beacon Press
Boston, Massachusetts
www.beacon.org

Beacon Press books
are published under the auspices of
the Unitarian Universalist Association of Congregations.

© 2021 by Olsen Writing Projects LLC

All rights reserved
Printed in the United States of America

24 23 22 21   8 7 6 5 4 3 2 1

This book is printed on acid-free paper that meets the uncoated paper
ANSI/NISO specifications for permanence as revised in 1992.

Text design and composition by Kim Arney

"Appointed Forever," lyrics 1997 by the Bar & Grill Singers, used by
permission. See https://www.singers.com/group/Bar-Grill-Singers.

Library of Congress Cataloging-in-Publication Data

Name: Olsen, Lise, author.
Title: Code of silence : a federal judge, a reluctant whistleblower, and a
    culture of cover-ups in our nation's courts / Lise Olsen.
Description: Boston : Beacon Press, 2021. | Includes bibliographical
    references and index.
Identifiers: LCCN 2021012855 (print) | LCCN 2021012856 (ebook) |
    ISBN 9780807008676 (hardcover) | ISBN 9780807008997 (ebook)
Subjects: LCSH: Judges—United States—Discipline. | Judicial
    corruption—United States. | Judges—Sexual behavior—United States. |
    Sexual harassment of women—Law and legislation—United States.
Classification: LCC KF8779 .O47 2021 (print) | LCC KF8779 (ebook) |
    DDC 347.73/2034—dc23
LC record available at https://lccn.loc.gov/2021012855
LC ebook record available at https://lccn.loc.gov/2021012856

To whistleblowers everywhere,
who speak out and right wrongs

CONTENTS

The Tip

Houston is a humid, heavy-breathing city where news takes no break even when quitting time approaches on a Friday. I was absorbed in notes for another investigative story in our bustling *Houston Chronicle* newsroom in March 2007, when Deputy Managing Editor George Haj waved me inside his private office and shared one of the most improbable tips I'd ever heard. Haj told me that Harvey Rice, another senior staff reporter, had just called with a tale of something strange that a source witnessed inside the federal courthouse on Galveston Island. That afternoon, a woman had run, crying, from the chambers of US District Judge Samuel Bristow Kent with her clothing in disarray.

The tipster identified her as the judge's top assistant, Cathy Mc-Broom, known as a normally unflappable court employee and Judge Kent's longtime case manager. After leaving chambers, McBroom never returned to her own office. Instead she detoured to another floor, apparently to hide from the judge. Some coworkers believed Kent had sexually assaulted her.

Perhaps if I'd worked elsewhere, I might have automatically rejected the rumor that a man sworn to uphold our laws would violate them inside a so-called palace of justice. But I was an investigative reporter in Texas, a place where the improbable often occurs. Houston is home to the moon men of NASA, and to Joanne Herring, the glittering socialite and heiress who allied with a Texas congressman to finance a secret CIA war in Afghanistan. Skyscrapers near our downtown newsroom had formerly housed the swaggering swindler kings of Enron, before their pipeline empire fell to fraud. Already focused on the story, I navigated back through a maze of metal cabinets loaded with newspapers, maps, dictionaries, and bulging manila file folders. I plopped down at my desk and kept my voice low as I called Rice to follow up. This was such a sensitive subject that I didn't want even colleagues to overhear.

Harvey Rice lived on Galveston Island and was well connected both there and in the federal courts. Before coming to Texas, Rice had worked for the *Clarion-Ledger* in Mississippi. During his time in Jackson, Rice told me, he'd been assigned to investigate rumors involving another powerful federal jurist named Walter Nixon—no relation to the former US president. Nixon, rumor had it, had quietly accepted a bribe to help a business associate's son beat drug charges. Rice tracked down sources and ferreted out documents. Nixon later beat the rap for bribery, but was convicted of perjury for lying to investigators and went to prison. Then Nixon refused to resign and continued to collect his judicial pay as a prisoner, Rice said.

Rice had just alerted me to the unusual level of power we were confronting. Federal circuit and district judges such as Kent and Nixon are appointed for life under Article III of the Constitution. They cannot be removed from office by anything less than impeachment by the US House of Representatives and removal by the US Senate. Nixon was one of three federal judges who were impeached and removed back in the 1980s. No other federal judge had been impeached or removed since.

Even if Kent had sexually assaulted an employee, I wondered, how could we possibly confirm that? It was a classic he said, she said situation. Kent certainly wasn't going to talk. And McBroom seemed to have vanished.

Rice and I began making cold calls and knocking on doors, but McBroom and all federal court employees in Galveston and Houston, where McBroom had been transferred, had been ordered not to speak. Sources said that McBroom had made a formal complaint and that a top secret judicial misconduct investigation was underway. Very slowly one source led to another, though most people we contacted were nervous and willing to speak only off the record.

Over the months of Houston's long hot summer, I accumulated a stack of spiral Reporter's Notebooks filled with stories about Kent, a man who displayed a photo on his wall in chambers of himself clasping hands with President George H. W. Bush. Kent had been handed a lifetime appointment by Bush, who still lived part-time in Houston with his wife, Barbara. Many powerful and politically connected Houstonians admired Kent for his intellect and for his wit, but I found attorneys and former employees, male and female, who feared or even hated Kent. Their stories painted an increasingly detailed portrait of abuse of power.

Since I couldn't reach McBroom, I began tracking down other women with strange and shocking stories. Along the way I unearthed other troubling information about why federal judges who had begun to investigate McBroom's complaint instead seemed to be covering up Kent's misbehavior—and ordering others to stay silent. For the first time I learned about a top secret federal judicial disciplinary system that allows judges nationwide to privately review complaints against their peers. That system seemed designed to protect the reputations of federal judges rather than to provide essential information to the public about judicial rogues.

In the summer of 2007, all of my online address searches for McBroom ended at the Clear Lake house that she no longer shared with her husband and son. It appeared that her marriage had begun to crumble under the stress. Then, in late August, a new address popped up: a Houston condo where McBroom had recently reregistered an SUV. Harvey Rice and I were wearing our IDs as newspaper reporters around our necks when we knocked on the door, figuring we might have just seconds to engage with McBroom. McBroom opened the door and looked right at me. Her eyes were crystalline blue. Rice had met McBroom before—in court—but we introduced ourselves anyway.

"I can't talk," she immediately said.

I rushed to try to create a channel of communication. "If you were sexually assaulted I promise you we would not use your name without your permission, but if we do a story about your complaint, you deserve to decide whether you are named or not. Is there any way for us to stay in touch?" For professional and personal reasons, I felt strongly that sexual assault victims should have some control over their own stories—though in those days I told few people about my own experiences.

McBroom retreated into the shadows of the entryway. She seemed isolated and alone. "Please," I said. "I've already talked to others who say Kent touched or propositioned them." Then purely on impulse, I added, "I know what it's like to be sexually assaulted. And if Kent did something like that to you—he should not get away with it. Not even if he is a federal judge."

McBroom hesitated, but before shutting the door, she accepted our business cards and supplied an attorney's name. It would take years before she could finally grant an interview. But for me, this brief encounter would be the beginning of more than a decade of slowly getting to know her story.

In the 2000s, McBroom was one of the only women in the United States who was publicly raising allegations about sexual harassment and sexual misconduct by a federal judge. In 2006, an activist from New York, Tarana Burke, suggested that women should band together to combat pervasive stories of sexual abuse and assault by sharing what she called "Me Too" stories, though Burke's idea would not fully take hold until 2017. That year, other women finally began to speak out about how other powerful federal judges had committed sexual harassment and other forms of misconduct. Many men cloaked in the power of their black robes seemed to have gotten away with it.

PART I

Castes of the Courts

CHAPTER 1

An Awkward Encounter

California, 2017

Leah Litman felt eager to meet the brilliant federal judge, a man she considered "a big judicial figure." Circuit Judge Alex Kozinski arrived last for their dinner at the Canaletto, a posh Italian restaurant favored by her employer, the University of California–Irvine School of Law, as a place to take visiting dignitaries. Litman watched the sixty-six-year-old stride across the crowded room. Light from chandeliers shone on his shock of white hair as he slid onto the low-slung bench beside her. She'd met Kozinski years before—he had popped by once at the US Supreme Court during the year she spent as a law clerk for Associate Justice Anthony Kennedy. Decades earlier, Kozinski, too, had clerked for Kennedy. But Litman knew he would not remember her. Kozinski belonged to the elite cadre of judges who preside over our nation's courts.

Tonight, Kozinski and Litman, a law professor, would dine with Richard L. Hasen, one of Litman's law school colleagues and the event organizer, and Greg Stohr, a longtime legal affairs reporter for *Bloomberg News*. Tomorrow, July 10, 2017, all would participate in a panel discussion on Supreme Court cases in a popular live event televised nationwide via C-SPAN.

Kozinski ordered a Moscow Mule and insisted on the same for Litman. A few minutes later, he announced that tonight was his wedding anniversary and that he'd had sex with his wife before his hour-long trek through clogged LA suburbs to the Orange County restaurant. "You'll be glad to know it still works," Kozinski declared, reaching over to poke Litman in the ribs with one finger.[1] Litman paused to hide her surprise. The jurist's sexually charged banter continued as a waiter delivered their Moscow Mules in shining copper cups, the pasta course, and platters of fresh fish.

Kozinski was considered a celebrity even among circuit judges, those more than 170 jurists based at thirteen appellate courts nationwide who are surpassed in power only by the nine members of the Supreme Court. He'd become one of the nation's youngest federal appellate judges in history in 1985, when Litman was only an infant. Like other federal judges, he made many life-or-death decisions, but he'd also written about his experiences in articles for the *New Yorker* and *Slate*, among other publications. His eye-catching, amusing, and sometimes historic opinions made national news too. In one case, he sided with organizers of the first Gay Games. He argued in a dissent that they should have been allowed to use the name Gay Olympics, a role he later reprised by playing himself in a documentary. In another case, the hip judge ended up in the middle of a dispute between Mattel Inc. and MCA Records over a 1997 novelty song by the Danish band Aqua about life in the world of the "Barbie Girl." In his opinion, Kozinski described the case as a faceoff between freedom of "Speechzilla" and the rights of "Trademark Kong." He found in favor of free speech, after dissecting lyrics and finding them a parody rather than a rip-off. Coolly, he'd advised both parties to "chill."

As an untenured assistant professor at UC Irvine Law School, Litman wore her hair long and loose in 2017 and could easily pass for one of her own students. But at thirty-three she'd already established herself as a skilled Supreme Court commentator and constitutional law expert. That night at dinner, she artfully diverted the discussion from sex to the topic of candidates for the Supreme Court. Kennedy had recently announced plans to retire.

Perhaps, Kozinski mused, one of his own ex-clerks would soon replace Kennedy. Kozinski prided himself on being a "feeder judge"—a kingmaker who regularly referred law clerks to work at the Supreme Court. The name of one particular favorite former clerk, Brett Kavanaugh, already a federal judge on the DC Circuit Court of Appeals, had been mentioned as a contender. Kavanaugh, though, had not yet become as famous as his mentor.

Kozinski quickly returned to his riff on sex. The judge retained a thick Romanian accent more than fifty years after emigrating to America from Bucharest with his parents, Holocaust refugees who'd opened a grocery in Hollywood. He sometimes said he'd learned to speak English from a Romanian nanny and to write in English by reading *Playboy*. For years, his dad sold those magazines at the family store. He told Litman that he still kept a *Playboy* collection at work so his clerks could learn how to write well too.

Litman had been a tomboy in her school days in a Minneapolis suburb, where she competed both on swim and debate teams. She normally favored slacks, but wore a dress that night. Under the starched tablecloth, Kozinski punctuated his points about *Playboy* by sliding a hand onto her bare knee. In the background, a mélange of Italian opera and modern world music played. High above them, murals on the walls depicted the decadence and frivolity of the carnival of Venice.

As they dined, Hasen, a nationally known election law expert, could not see Kozinski repeatedly touch his colleague under the linen-covered table. But he watched as the judge pronounced his fish delicious, speared a forkful, and commanded that Litman, too, take a bite. Kozinski seemed oddly eager to share. "I remember Kozinski wanting to taste everybody's food and wanting to share his food too," Hasen later recalled.

Litman felt Kozinski touch her shoulder as he tried to feed her. In the space of an hour, the outspoken feminist and up-and-coming professor who'd previously taught as a fellow at Harvard Law and as a visiting professor at Stanford, felt herself shrinking deeper into the padded leather seat. She had clerked for two different federal judges and practiced in federal courts but had never witnessed a judicial performance anything like Kozinski's. He seemed to have masterfully reduced her to the sum of her parts: blond hair, long legs, and a youthful look. She felt like an object or a toy, perhaps one of the

Barbie Dolls in his famous Mattel–MCA Records case. Part of Kozinski's famous opinion described the doll's origins as an "adult collectors' item" made to resemble a "German street walker."

The next day, onstage at the Seventh Annual Supreme Court Term in Review in a packed performing arts center in Irvine, Litman wore pants. She smiled equally at Kozinski and other distinguished panelists. But she felt uncomfortable sitting beside him. She paused to drink deeply from a liter-sized water bottle as she spoke about the law, including how and why the Supreme Court had failed to intervene to protect the civil rights of a Mexican teenager killed when a US government official shot across the border into Ciudad Juarez. Before TV cameras, she coolly challenged Kozinski on a point of procedure. Offstage she tried to avoid him.

Litman was both a commentator and a court critic, who served as guest host for a podcast called *First Mondays* and published articles in law reviews and the popular press, including the *California Law Review* and the *New York Times*. Still, she hesitated for months to speak out about their odd dinner encounter. Nothing Kozinski did or said had caused her any lasting harm, she thought. Speaking out publicly against such a powerful jurist could ricochet and diminish her ability to fight for her own clients. Though primarily a professor, Litman handled important pro-bono cases in appellate courts, including an ongoing fight to protect the rights to work that had been granted to Dreamers, undocumented immigrants brought to the US as children. She wondered, though, how many other women had shared similar experiences with Kozinski and had also kept silent. Kozinski's dinner behavior seemed like a symptom of a bigger problem. Kozinski seemed to believe he "had enough power and implicit social capital that no one would dare to defy him," Litman later observed.

All federal circuit and district judges wield the greatest power of America's legal elites. Nominated by US presidents, vetted by the FBI, and confirmed by the Senate, they and Supreme Court justices are the only officials in our democracy who enjoy lifetime appointments. Our federal jurists no longer wear white powdered wigs, but dress in black robes and sit in ornate chairs atop elevated stages much like thrones. All rise when they enter a room, and they are addressed as "Your

Honor," a linguistic relic from the era when our colonial courts were overseen by men appointed by representatives of the English king.

Alex Kozinski, sometimes pictured wearing a broad smile and oversized tinted glasses fit for sunny Southern California, was greatly admired for his intelligence, for his well-written opinions, and for his unique perspectives as an independent-minded immigrant who was born and spent his childhood behind the Iron Curtain. Kozinski was only twelve when his family emigrated to the United States. He'd quickly absorbed the energy of his sprawling adopted hometown of Los Angeles, including its restless ambition and its hedonistic urges. As a college student at the University of California, Los Angeles, he initially attempted to follow his mother's advice to study engineering. Back in Romania, his father had been forced into a labor camp by the Nazis and his mother had been confined to a Jewish ghetto, but she'd noticed that even Nazis respected engineers, tending to spare their lives. Her son struggled with engineering classes as an undergrad. His grades rapidly improved when he later enrolled in law school. He graduated first in his class and also met and married a classmate. As a young lawyer, Kozinski clerked for Kennedy at the Ninth Circuit and for Chief Justice Warren Burger at the Supreme Court. That's when Kozinski decided he wanted to be a federal judge too. But even with such prestigious names on his resume, he faced discrimination from top firms, which in the 1970s openly refused to hire immigrants or women. He soon joined other ambitious California conservatives migrating east to Washington, DC, as part of the administration of President Ronald Reagan. And with Reagan's help, Kozinski catapulted his way into the federal judiciary.

Kozinski began his judicial career in 1982 when he was appointed chief judge of a relatively obscure DC-based court established to review legal claims against the federal government. That post was renewable—not a coveted lifetime position. Just only a scant three years later, Reagan tapped Kozinski to join the Ninth Circuit Court of Appeals based in San Francisco, now the nation's largest regional appellate court and one of the most powerful judicial bodies after the Supreme Court. Kozinski was returning home to California as a celebrity with a lifetime appointment. At thirty-five he became the youngest judge serving in any federal appellate court nationwide.

The Framers of the US Constitution deliberately granted federal judges lifetime job security to enable them to hold others accountable—even misbehaving presidents. The Founding Fathers drafted the document to guide America's newborn democracy inside a blazing hot meeting room in Philadelphia in the summer of 1787. Their debates were quite literally heated, since participants kept the windows closed to keep outsiders from overhearing. A majority became convinced that judges must have lifetime appointments to face down tyranny and to hold Congress and presidents alike accountable.

Benjamin Franklin, an eighty-one-year-old senior statesman when the Constitutional Convention met in his adopted hometown, argued that the nation also needed a peaceful way to remove presidents or federal judges. Otherwise, assassination would be the only option to dispatch an official who had "rendered himself obnoxious." The group chose impeachment, a clunky two-part system that even the British had abandoned. Presidents could be forced out of office by losing elections too. But federal judges can be removed only if members of the House of Representatives first vote to approve charges of "Treason, Bribery, or other high Crimes and Misdemeanors" and then senators hold a trial to either convict or acquit them. Over the centuries, American federal judges' tremendous independence gave them the power they needed to break up exploitative monopolies and mandate broad changes, such as the desegregation of schools and the banning of racial and sexual discrimination and harassment in the workplace.

As a Ninth Circuit judge, Kozinski became a member of an elite and mostly white male club. For two centuries, from the 1780s through the 1980s, the US judiciary was almost entirely a man's world. In 1981, only a few years before appointing Kozinski, Reagan had made good on a campaign promise and nominated a little-known Arizona judge named Sandra Day O'Connor to be the first woman on the Supreme Court—"FWOTSC," as O'Connor liked to say. Other women already served on other federal courts by then. But in 1981, Associate Justice O'Connor and all of the nation's female circuit judges (nearly all recent appointees of President Jimmy Carter) could have fit inside a twelve-passenger Volkswagen bus.

In 1988, his third year on the Ninth Circuit, Kozinski left California to attend a legal event in Baltimore. Kozinski invited along one of the few women to have served with him on the federal court of claims, Judge Christine O. C. Miller. Miller, a former federal prosecutor with a head of unruly naturally curly hair, was also married and was three years older than Kozinski. She considered Kozinski a friend and ally. But afterward, as they rode back together to Washington, DC, where she lived, he propositioned her, suggesting they stop at a motel, as Miller told a reporter for the *Washington Post* nearly three decades later. After she refused, Kozinski turned and said, "If you won't sleep with me, I want to touch you."[2] Then he reached over, grabbed her breasts, and squeezed.

Miller, a seasoned officer of the court, sat silently in shock. That night, she shared the disturbing encounter with her husband, but otherwise she kept it secret. Like other women attorneys of her generation, Miller had blazed trails in her legal career both as a federal prosecutor and as a jurist. "I never viewed my judgeship other than through the lens of how to perform my work to the highest standard. The incident with former Judge Kozinski was an aberration that I no longer want to discuss," she reflected years later in an email.[3] She never filed a formal complaint against Kozinski. As a circuit court judge, Kozinski had lifetime tenure, while her judicial appointment remained subject to regular review.

At the time of that incident, a system set up to handle misconduct complaints against federal judges was brand new. In 1980, the US Congress passed the Judicial Conduct and Disability Act in response to distrust bred by the Watergate scandal (and complaints about incompetent or crooked federal judges). Under the law, federal judges could secretly review complaints against each other and decide whether to take corrective or disciplinary action in response to any "conduct prejudicial to the effective and expeditious administration of the business of the courts." Nearly everything about the process was confidential: complaints, names of complainants, names of accused judges, those judges' responses, and any investigative reports or recommendations. Disciplinary hearings, which were rare, were always closed, and even complainants were rarely invited to attend or testify. Judges could be reprimanded, admonished, or required to take corrective action by a vote of their peers at those secret meetings. But as the decades passed, few secret disciplinary probes resulted in any public action. Many people, even attorneys and federal court employees, didn't know the system existed.

Time magazine dubbed 2017 the year of "the Silence Breakers" and, instead of its customary "Person of the Year," put a group of women on the cover. That October, Harvey Weinstein, a producer based in Hollywood, where Kozinski grew up, was outed by a string of women as a serial sexual abuser and forced from the movie studio he had cofounded following investigative reports about how he'd exposed himself to women and coerced or solicited sexual favors for decades from actresses, models, and assistants alike. Other women that year began sharing stories about sexual abuse, assault, and harassment, on the internet and among friends, using the hashtag #MeToo. Over the years Kozinski had made no attempts to hide his predilection for raunchy humor. Yet Kozinski seemed surprised when in December 2017, the *Washington Post* broke two stories in which fifteen women publicly denounced him for different forms of sexual harassment.

In the first story, Heidi Bond, an attorney and romance novelist who had worked as Kozinski's law clerk from 2006 to 2007, provided a detailed account of how Kozinski called her his "slave," kissed her, and showed her pictures of naked men and women when they were alone in chambers.[4] Bond said the year-long experience of sexual harassment affected her health and contributed to her decision to eventually leave the law. Yet for a decade she'd hesitated to speak out because of the oath she'd taken as a federal judge's clerk to keep court secrets.

The only other woman named was Emily Murphy. Murphy, a professor at the UC Hastings College of the Law in San Francisco, described an odd encounter with Kozinski at an event in 2012 held at the beginning of her year-long clerkship for one of his Ninth Circuit colleagues. In a brief conversation with her and other clerks, Kozinski had repeatedly suggested that Murphy exercise in the nude at the federal courthouse gym, Murphy said.

Kozinski's initial reaction to the story was disbelief. He declined comment to the *Post* but publicly scoffed at the allegations. He dismissed Bond as an author who wrote books featuring "torrid sex" and told a reporter for the *Los Angeles Times*, "If this is all they are able to dredge up after 35 years, I am not too worried."[5] Kozinski estimated that he'd employed more than 120 clerks and more than 400 externs over three decades, though he didn't specify how many had been women. Kozinski, the father of three, and a grandfather, said he also considered his staff to be "family" and that he never intended to make his clerks feel uncomfortable.[6] He added that he knew of no formal complaints filed by any of the women under the Judicial Conduct and Disability Act. If he'd truly offended so many people, why had none of them confronted him or filed a formal complaint?

Litman, the UC Irvine law professor, didn't know the two women named by the *Washington Post*, though they had friends in common. She felt troubled by Bond's story of how clerking for Kozinski made her feel like a "prey animal." And Murphy's experience, the brief but disturbing conversation at a circuit court event, seemed similar to behavior Kozinski had displayed at their dinner. Litman first considered anonymously contacting the *Post*. But if only two accusers gave their names, she worried there would be no broader debate about Kozinski or about sexual harassment within the federal judiciary, a world where federal judges seemed so powerful and their accusers so powerless. Litman decided to cooperate in a follow-up article on December 15 that shared stories from nine more women, including Judge Miller.

Hours before the second article was to appear, Judge Sidney R. Thomas, then chief judge of the Ninth Circuit Court of Appeals, announced the initiation of a formal misconduct investigation of allegations against Kozinski. Thomas, based in Montana, simultaneously requested that the matter be transferred to another circuit. For decades, Kozinski had been his colleague and had served as previous circuit chief.

The promised probe essentially vanished a few days later when Kozinski announced his retirement, effective immediately. As chief judge, he knew well that federal judicial misconduct probes die when judges retire or resign. By statute, the judicial misconduct review system does not apply to ex-judges. And it was a smart financial move. As a retired judge, he left behind a huge caseload and collected a pension equal to his full pay. As a result, none of the fifteen women's allegations of misbehavior spanning three decades would be formally investigated. (The complaint was dismissed in February 2018 in a judicial disciplinary order that made it clear no investigation had been conducted.)

In June 2018, members of the US Senate Judiciary Committee called a hearing to discuss what do to about sexual harassment by federal judges. Senators expressed outrage about Kozinski's behavior, and about the judiciary's seeming failure to respond. But what galled Litman, Murphy, Bond, and others who had risked their reputations and careers by speaking out about Kozinski was what happened when the same senators gathered in September to review the nomination of Kozinski's ex-clerk and friend, US Circuit Judge Kavanaugh, as associate justice of the Supreme Court.

Several senators queried Kavanaugh, then a member of the DC Circuit Court of Appeals, about his connections to Kozinski. In response to questions, Kavanaugh denied recalling any of his mentor's inappropriate behavior or dirty jokes. But as the confirmation hearings continued, a psychology professor from Palo Alto University in California named Christine Blasey Ford came forward with a complaint of her own about Kavanaugh. She alleged that at a house party held back in their teen years, Kavanaugh had trapped her in a bedroom, held her down, and tried to rape her. Suddenly, many of the same senators who'd been so critical of the courts' tolerance of sexual misconduct in June 2018 either fell silent or turned skeptical. Kavanaugh, for his part, denied involvement in the incident, which Ford described in painful detail in testimony broadcast live nationwide. Under questioning from senators, Kavanaugh further insisted that he'd never forgotten anything during episodes of binge drinking in high school, college, and law school.

Even before Kavanaugh's testimony ended, the first of what would be dozens of judicial misconduct complaints began to pour into the office of the chief judge of the DC Circuit Court of Appeals, where

Kavanaugh had been a sitting judge for a dozen years. Upon request of DC Circuit leaders, Supreme Court Chief Justice John G. Roberts Jr. transferred the review of Kavanaugh complaints to the Tenth Circuit Court of Appeals in Denver. By law, the details and authors of all eighty-three complaints were kept secret, though some of Kavanaugh's former Yale classmates and others chose to write op-eds or articles and publicly challenged his testimony as untruthful.

That judicial misconduct investigation also died and all complaints were dismissed after Kavanaugh was confirmed to the Supreme Court by a Senate majority. That's because the 1980 federal statute that created the secret system of judicial misconduct reviews has been interpreted by judges as applying only to sitting members of the courts, including all district and circuit judges nationwide. But whenever a federal judge accused of misconduct resigns or retires from those courts, judicial misconduct reviews are dropped and investigative reports are almost never revealed. Though Kavanaugh had been a circuit judge when dozens of complaints were first filed against him, judges assigned to investigate him dismissed the complaints a few weeks after Kavanaugh was confirmed to the Supreme Court by a Senate majority on October 6, 2018. Their reasoning: he was no longer a circuit judge covered by the Judicial Conduct and Disability Act. That statute excludes Supreme Court justices. Except for the threat of impeachment, Supreme Court justices, such as Kavanaugh, are essentially immune from oversight.

Thomas Jefferson, America's third president, remains the only political leader in US history to successfully push for the impeachment of a Supreme Court justice. Even when the Constitution was new, Jefferson worried that federal jurists' power rivaled that of royals he'd fought to defeat. Jefferson well remembered the imperial edicts issued by colonial judges appointed under the rule of England's King George III. Jefferson, who was away serving as ambassador to France when other Founders drafted the Constitution, considered impeachment a "bungling way" to hold anyone to account. Still, Jefferson urged congressmen to use the tool against Samuel Chase, an imperious judge known for his volcanic temper. Chase was impeached in

1804 by a majority of the House of Representatives on charges related to abuse of power, including allegations of rigging a jury and barring witnesses to favor political allies. But Chase was acquitted in a Senate trial a year later, and many historians viewed Jefferson's effort to have been a politically motivated mistake. By the time Jefferson ended his term in 1809, two federal judges had been impeached, though only one was removed from office.

More than two hundred years later, the total number of judicial impeachments stands at fifteen. In more than two centuries, only one federal judge has been impeached specifically for sexual crimes and for lying to conceal them: US District Judge Samuel Bristow Kent.

The woman who took him down was a Texan named Cathy McBroom.

CHAPTER 2

Flight

Houston and Galveston, Texas, March 2007

Cathy McBroom felt herself unraveling as she drove back to the brick house she shared with her husband, Rex, and youngest son, Caleb, in the quiet Houston suburb of Clear Lake. It was still early on Friday, March 23, 2007. She hoped to find comfort from Rex, but discovered him already asleep in his work clothes on the chestnut brown leather couch in their living room. For a while, she sat silently beside him. He didn't stir. She began to cry and to repeat her husband's name, softly and then in a staccato beat. The longer she sat there, the more her anguish and anger grew. "Wake up!" she finally screamed. Still, he slept on.

Rex was often tired on Friday nights. He worked punishing ten- to twelve-hour shifts in a chemical plant, a behemoth pressure cooker of an operation that belched out smoke and fumes and operated 24/7, often in ungodly weather. He spent many long, tense workdays responding to emergencies as a troubleshooter and often arrived home exhausted. Yet on this particular Friday, Cathy McBroom felt sure he was dozing out of a desire to avoid dealing with her crisis. She was used to managing stress as the case manager for a federal judge, but felt ready to explode.

Feeling anger surge again, McBroom abandoned efforts to wake him and strode into the master bath to wash her face. McBroom felt none of the calming effect of the cool water. She regarded the stranger in her mirror with disgust. The ravaged woman appeared distraught. Her makeup was a mess. Her eyes drifted to a red vase she'd placed on the corner of the vanity. It became a vessel for the anger she could no longer contain. She grabbed it from the counter and hurled it at the mirror. Her reflection disappeared in an explosion that sounded like a shotgun blast. Mirror shards scattered and sharp pieces of her reflected sadness now seemed to cover the cold ceramic tile, but the vase bounced. It remained uncracked and intact.

Rex McBroom finally stirred. "What's going on?"

"If you'd wake up then maybe you would know!" McBroom shouted. Then she strode across the living room, grabbed her purse, left the house, and drove away. McBroom stormed off to her friend's house and asked to stay the night, making up some excuse. But she couldn't sleep. Early the next morning, she still felt too shaken to go home.

She climbed back in her SUV and called her mother, Mary Ann Schopp. "Something terrible happened at work," McBroom said into the phone. Without thinking about it, McBroom already had begun to drive to her mother's bungalow in El Lago, a quiet neighborhood tucked behind Houston's NASA Space Center. Her visit was entirely unexpected. McBroom was supposed to be meeting her mother later that Saturday to celebrate her youngest son's thirteenth birthday. Instead, McBroom was now cancelling her part in those party plans.

"I'll need you to take over for me," McBroom told her mother, using the same businesslike tone she normally reserved for her federal court job.

"I can handle that," Schopp replied, then paused in surprise. Skipping Caleb's birthday party was totally out of synch with her daughter's supermom style. McBroom had raised three children, but Caleb, the baby, was the only one left at home. Still, Schopp knew not to ask questions. Pretty much everything that happened with her daughter's job at the federal courthouse was top secret.

Minutes later, McBroom pulled her silver Nissan Murano into the driveway. McBroom, then forty-eight, was a native Texan and nor-

mally meticulous about her appearance. She rarely appeared anywhere without her hair carefully coiffed and her makeup neatly
applied, but now she got out of the SUV looking spent and wearing borrowed jogging shorts and a wrinkled T-shirt. As she stepped
through the back door into her mother's neat kitchen, she fell silent
and fought back tears. Her mother pulled her into their usual hug
and McBroom mumbled, "I could not pretend to enjoy myself at
the birthday party." She knew (but did not say) that her insightful
youngest son, a straight-talking middle school student, would ask
questions she felt unprepared to answer. Why had she left work so
early? Why had she argued with his father and fled?

McBroom's mother fetched cups of coffee and they sat together at
the tiny wooden table. Rays of sunlight streaming in the kitchen window failed to lighten the mood. Schopp could only guess this unexpected crisis must have something to do with that white-haired giant
of a judge, the domineering man who'd styled himself as king of the
Galveston federal courthouse.

For nearly five years, McBroom had served US District Judge
Samuel Bristow Kent. Kent was part of the powerful network of
federal jurists whose lifetime appointments were guaranteed by the
Constitution. Cathy McBroom was part of a vast national court bureaucracy of people who served at the pleasure of such judges. Initially, McBroom had raved about her "dream job," which provided
the financial stability she'd craved and a federal salary of more than
$70,000 plus benefits. Later there had been trouble with the judge,
though McBroom had explained to her mother that she, like all federal court employees, was bound by an oath to respect court confidentiality. She and other employees were subject to a strict code
of conduct and generally never discussed the inner workings of the
court or any judge's behind-the-scenes behavior.

Whatever Kent had done, it had been bad, Schopp knew. Her eldest child had always been a steady, strong woman on whom Schopp
herself had leaned when her first marriage fell apart and she'd divorced McBroom's father. But this morning all of her daughter's self-
confidence and control appeared cracked, if not shattered.

McBroom kept repeating in a monotone that she couldn't discuss
anything.

"If you can't talk about it, you've got to get it out," Schopp insisted. "Go use the computer in my studio. . . . Type down every little incident you can remember."

Schopp wasn't sure she should leave her anguished daughter behind, but birthday duty called. She drove off to fetch her grandson and ferried a carload of gangly adolescents with floppy hair and feet too big for the rest of their growing bodies to Clear Lake's AMF Alpha Lanes, the bowling alley where the usual cake, Cokes, and souvenir ten-pin awaited. She invented excuses when her grandson asked about his missing mom.

Alone in the snug yellow-brick house, McBroom felt marginally safer surrounded by the comfortable clutter of her mother and stepfather's blended lives, their cobbled-together furniture, aging housecats, and many memories of family gatherings and home-cooked meals. This was not McBroom's childhood home, but it was a familiar place—her mother had purchased it more than twenty years before with Don, her mother's second husband. McBroom had grown up in the industrialized Houston suburb of Channelview, where she had learned from her own dad, a tough chemical plant worker, to fight for herself as a girl, even when that meant using her fists to quiet a bully or walking away from the boyfriend who punched a hole in her parents' garage wall. Today, though, she felt none of that strength.

McBroom shut herself up in the front bedroom that served as a combination office and a studio for her mother's oil painting. Colorful canvases filled with hand-painted roses and chrysanthemums surrounded McBroom as she stared into the void of the computer screen, digging deep inside to find words. Beside her in frames and on the wall of the hallway just outside the small room were images from other stages of her life. McBroom as a chubby toddler with her hair pulled back in a ponytail; McBroom smiling in a crowded gathering at her grandmother's ninetieth birthday; formal portraits of the two children, Evelyn, and Casey, whom she'd had after marrying her childhood sweetheart; and a party picture of McBroom in a glittery black dress and holding hands with her second husband, Rex, the father of her son Caleb, whose birthday party she was missing.

Mostly she'd been a good mother. Her children knew she had their backs. And she'd often acted as the fixer for her parents and her younger brother, too, providing the glue that held the family together or, when that proved impossible, providing comfort when things fell apart. Along the way, she'd built a solid career as an experienced assistant in the cutthroat legal profession in lawyers' offices and later attained an important post in the federal district court clerk's office, workplaces that in the 1990s and 2000s remained largely male-dominated worlds tinged with sexism. In her forties, she'd begun to run marathons and completed five races in one memorable year. She normally buzzed with energy. But she'd never faced anything as difficult as this self-appointed task.

McBroom had decided to denounce a powerful federal judge. And she would do this alone. She knew her written words, once shared, would make an enemy of a jurist who'd earned a national reputation among law professors as a bully, and who had repeatedly proved himself capable of humiliating, harassing, and harming the careers of anyone who crossed him. This man had both an extraordinarily domineering personality and the formidable power of the robe he wore.

McBroom had never known any woman personally who had taken on a federal jurist for sexual misconduct except what she'd read and seen about Anita Hill. Back in 1991, McBroom and many other American women had been outraged and inspired as they watched the University of Oklahoma law professor testify before an all-male US Senate Judicial Committee about how Clarence Thomas, then a federal judge and US Supreme Court nominee, had sexually harassed her in his years as her boss in two different federal government jobs. Hill had worked for Thomas both in the Office of Civil Rights at the US Department of Education and again when he became chair of the US Equal Employment Opportunity Commission, the federal agency that supposedly specializes in helping people who struggle with on-the-job harassment and discrimination. The experience hadn't turned out so well for Hill, McBroom knew. Thomas had won a seat on the Supreme Court anyway. Hill had been branded as a liar by conservative commentators and ridiculed for testifying about how Thomas asked her about pubic hair on a Coke can and described scenes in porn films featuring large-breasted women having sex with men and animals.

McBroom still felt physically sick when she recalled what had happened to her that Friday inside Kent's wood-paneled chambers—a formal yet intimate space that smelled of the judge's illicit cigar breaks, his collection of law books, and his bulldogs. She feared that her decision to flee meant that he would seek revenge and ruin her career.

In 1999, McBroom had been a forty-year-old mother of three when she finally felt she'd gained enough experience and connections as a longtime legal secretary to compete for a coveted opening in the federal courts. She bested one hundred applicants to win the post of assistant clerk for US District Judge Nancy Atlas, who was one of a handful of female judges in the Southern District of Texas. The world McBroom entered was controlled by federal judges, a group that remained more male-dominated than the rest of the legal field. Nationwide, the percentage of women enrolling in law schools had slowly risen from about 35 percent of new law students in 1980 and reached 49 percent by 2000, according to American Bar Association law school enrollment data, and yet partnerships in law firms and posts in the judiciary remained dominated by men. Two of nine members of the Supreme Court were women—Associate Justices Sandra Day O'Connor and Ruth Bader Ginsburg—but across all the federal courts, women held only 16 percent of district court judgeships and 17 percent in the circuit courts in 2001, annual ABA "Women in the Profession" statistics showed.[1]

McBroom had always been interested in the law, though she'd never felt that law school was an option for someone like her, a blue-collar worker's child from Channelview. Instead, she made her career in the vast federal court bureaucracy. She soon learned that the courts could be both a rigid and quirky workplace full of ceremony, rules, and demands dictated by eclectic and sometimes eccentric federal judges. McBroom's first boss, Judge Atlas, a native New Yorker, had a tough and competitive side. Atlas, who kept her East Coast accent and wore her jet-black hair cut in a bob, was a decade older than McBroom. Atlas was, and still is, a trailblazer. She had earned degrees from Tufts and New York University and, as a new lawyer, had clerked for a federal judge from 1974 to 1976 in an era when few male judges hired women as clerks. She'd also worked as a federal prosecutor prior to becoming one of the first female partners at a Houston law firm. She was a new US District judge in 1999, nominated only four years before by President Bill Clinton.

McBroom had never lived outside Texas and had never finished college, yet she felt unintimidated and respected by Atlas, another ambitious working mom. Atlas could be stern and demanding but didn't swear or require female employees to wear high heels or fetch coffee as some male judges in Houston did. McBroom enjoyed working as a judicial assistant, though that job required an intense focus on deadlines and mind-numbing details and offered little independence.

The empire of the nation's courts is divided into ninety-four districts whose appeals are overseen by judges in the nation's twelve regional circuit courts. (There's also another circuit court known as the federal court of appeals.) In the 1990s, a group called the National Commission on Judicial Discipline and Removal held hearings on sexual harassment by federal judges and urged courts nationwide to tackle the issues. Eight of the twelve regional circuit courts established task forces to explore underrepresentation of women among jurists, gender bias, and sexual harassment. In 1993, Lynn Hecht Schafran, an attorney expert who advised the task forces, testified to the commission about federal courts that had tolerated sexual misbehavior, including judges who systematically traumatized female clerks through serial sexual harassment. Schafran also told of a federal court judge in New York who fired a court reporter after his wife learned of their affair. That court reporter alleged in a lawsuit (later settled) that the judge got drunk in a bar and physically attacked her, tearing open her blouse. The jurist, John T. Elfvin, of the Western District of New York, was investigated but not disciplined after a misconduct probe found that his drinking had not affected his performance in court and that he had "sought medical advice on whether his behavior may have been influenced by the synergistic effect of a prescription drug medication and alcohol." (Elfvin remained on the bench until 2007.)

The bias task force in the Ninth Circuit Court of Appeals, based in San Francisco, was the first to publish its final report in July 1993.

The report urged further audits of gender bias, policy reforms, and other strong actions to counter what it considered widespread sexual harassment in the federal courts. Meanwhile, a vocal group of judges from the DC Circuit Court of Appeals, including Clarence Thomas, protested that proposed reforms went too far. In 1995, Congress defunded the task forces after several senators declared that the project was "ill-conceived," "deeply flawed," and "divisive" during the Senate's debates on the budget. At the time the program was defunded, some circuits had never bothered to form a task force at all, including the enormous Fifth Circuit Court of Appeals, which oversees policy for federal courts in Mississippi, Louisiana, and Texas.[2]

In 2002, McBroom decided to compete for a promotion that would allow her to be closer to court power centers. She sought the challenging—and elite—position as a judge's case manager. "Case managers—they were where the action was," she later said. "They got to attend court hearings and were responsible for bringing the other agencies together. They were what I considered to be the hub." She began working as a relief case manager, helping out different judges when their own case managers were away. She felt excited when she spotted the announcement for an unexpected opening as case manager for US District Judge Kent, whose Galveston Island court was closer to her own home. She'd never met Kent and heard he could be outspoken and mercurial, but quickly applied for the job. Simultaneously training for a series of marathons, McBroom pursued the position with all of the energy she devoted to an important race. She ignored the fact that others in Houston considered Galveston's federal courthouse a backwater.

The tremendous caseloads of the Southern District of Texas, one of the nation's busiest districts, fills up several far-flung courthouses from Houston to the Mexico border. The squat, blazing-white Houston courthouse—nicknamed the Sugar Cube—was a busy hub with more than a dozen district judges, while Kent was the lone district judge on the island. In any district court, a federal judge's case manager acts as master of ceremonies, serving justice in an important behind-the-scenes role. McBroom, outgoing and gregarious, enjoyed networking and organizing and believed this job would make her career.

Houston and Galveston are only an hour's drive apart on the Gulf Freeway but represent different worlds. The island city is older. Founded by pirates, its Strand Historic District resembles a miniature version of New Orleans's French Quarter. Prior to damage caused by the 1900 hurricane, which remains one of the deadliest in US history, Galveston had been Texas's most important port city and its natives were proud of being BOI: born on the island.

McBroom met Kent for the first time in a brief interview in his office. She was struck, as most people were, by his height. At around six feet four inches, Kent stood nearly a foot taller than she. A native Coloradoan, Kent had played basketball after moving to Houston's Spring Branch neighborhood. He invited McBroom to sit inside his chambers, a masculine enclave with plush carpets and shelves lined with legal books. Even seated, he impressed her as intense and immense. During the interview she noticed how his gaze strayed from her face to the rest of her body, muscular from regular training runs and workouts. She ignored it. McBroom had years of experience ignoring unwanted on-the-job attention in the male-dominated legal profession.

McBroom kept things light, punctuating her answers to Kent's many questions with a ready smile. Her voice had a veneer of formality from time spent in courtrooms, but she spoke with a Southeast Texas lilt, a mixture of charm and sass. He disarmed her with his own mix of thoughtful questions and humorous quips. She felt comfortable and smiled and laughed as she spoke with Judge Kent that first time. Alongside framed photos and formal furniture she'd seen in other judges' offices, Kent displayed a figurine of Alfred E. Neuman, the *Mad* magazine avatar, and the ubiquitous joke gift Big Mouth Billy Bass, a plastic plaque with an animated fish trophy that turned its head and sang "Don't worry, be happy" at the press of a button. His sense of humor—and his roving eye—at first seemed harmless, typical of the kinds of behavior she'd seen before. She got the job, on a trial basis.

From the day McBroom started, she felt convinced she'd love this new job. For the first time in her life she had a private office—a room with a view of the narrow island that jutted out into the sparkling Gulf of Mexico. When Kent wanted to, he could turn on a mesmerizing charm and wit. McBroom soon warmed to him. He could be thoughtful about allowing employees to take time off to spend with children and even let one woman bring her baby to work in an emergency, gestures McBroom, a longtime working mom, found endearing. At times, Kent could be laugh-out-loud funny, though his jokes could be crude and often skewered some lawyer or lackey.

Kent was a war history buff and somehow had obtained funding to restore his 1937 US District courtroom to its original glory. He thoroughly inhabited and dominated that space as the most powerful judge in residence. But he also had a rebellious and playful side. On the back of the bench, where spectators could not see, he kept a bumper sticker with a line from a favorite country song by Texas crooner Robert Earl Keen. It read: "The Road Goes on Forever and the Party Never Ends."

In her forties, McBroom still saw herself as a "pleaser" and a "fixer"—the roles she'd always played in her family as an eldest child. She maintained the strong bonds she'd built with childhood friends and family, and as a working woman, she used the same skills to succeed with lawyers and judges, powerful bosses who could be ill-tempered, feel entitled to take liberties, or just push people around. Even in Houston, she had heard stories about Kent's arrogance, his domineering ways, and his love of salty jokes but felt sure she could deal with him.

After her first few weeks, Kent visited McBroom's office, two floors down from his own, to express his approval of what a great job she was doing. He smiled. "It's wonderful to be down here in Galveston, isn't it?" he said. Then he requested a hug. At the time McBroom figured Kent was just being welcoming—making her feel "part of the team." She appreciated his warmth, and only later did she start to suspect that Kent had delivered the hug as a test to "see how comfortable I was with that physical contact," as a way to groom her to accept more.

By 2007, Cathy McBroom had worked for Kent for nearly five years, long enough to learn about how Kent administered doses of charm, humor, and abuse to control and cultivate an extremely loyal and fearful following among employees. She knew Kent had established a strong hold over Donna Wilkerson, his judicial secretary. Wilkerson, like McBroom, was often subjected to the judge's whims, as were a cast of young ambitious clerks: handpicked recent law school graduates whose names and faces changed each year. Like every federal judge nationwide, Kent had extremely close contact and tight control over the members of his chambers staff, a team composed of the judge's secretary and a small group of hand-picked attorneys, called clerks, who shared a suite of connected offices. They and other federal court employees swore oaths to observe elaborate codes of ethical conduct. The Code of Conduct for Judicial Employees still requires them to promise never (even after leaving their jobs) to disclose "any confidential information received in the course of official duties except as required in the performance of such duties." But in March 2019, that code was amended to make it clear that the restriction "does not prevent, nor should it discourage, an employee or former employee from reporting or disclosing misconduct, including sexual or other forms of harassment by a judge, supervisor or other person."[3] Prior to that change, some employees were left to wonder if they had the freedom to speak even if a federal judge harassed them or broke the law.

Superficially, Wilkerson and McBroom seemed similar. Both were fashionable, ambitious, smart, and physically fit working moms in their forties who'd grown up in Texas towns on the edges of the bustling Houston metro area. Even after Wilkerson had worked for Kent for six years and McBroom for five, they were not friends. Kent deliberately fueled animosity between them. The big judge flirted with and regularly sexually harassed each woman, though he played more mind games with Wilkerson, repeatedly telling her that McBroom was jealous and coveted her job.

The truth was that McBroom didn't envy Wilkerson. She wondered, in fact, how Wilkerson was able to survive as a member of Kent's judicial staff. Both she and Wilkerson carried out Kent's direct orders, yet McBroom was better able to keep her distance from Kent. McBroom worked closely with Kent. But McBroom also belonged to the larger federal court clerk's bureaucracy and reported separately to supervisors in the Galveston and Houston offices, who oversee the courts' administrative support and record-keeping services throughout the vast Southern District of Texas. Whenever possible, McBroom conferred with Kent by phone, but Wilkerson worked in Kent's chambers, an enclave similar to a private suite complete with its own kitchen and bathroom. Often, the two were alone there for hours.

Though neither McBroom nor Wilkerson felt free to speak, the truth was that both felt vulnerable and muzzled, both bound as federal court employees to adhere to strict codes of conduct and swear oaths to maintain the court's dignity and its confidentiality. Indoctrinated into that world, they carefully heeded Kent's edicts about never sharing his personal or court business with outsiders or colleagues. They knew Kent could dismiss them for virtually any reason. Based on their training and treatment, each avoided discussing the judge's increasingly abusive behavior with each other or with their husbands.

Despite the courthouse code of silence, over the years McBroom heard gossip about Kent's behavior with Wilkerson from more senior court employees. Both McBroom's supervisor and Felicia Williams, her predecessor as Kent's case manager, told McBroom they worried about Wilkerson because they'd caught glimpses of Kent in the act of fondling or kissing his secretary. Even Kent's daily rituals with Wilkerson in their compound seemed oddly controlling. All of the court staff knew, for example, that Wilkerson was the only one Kent trusted to tidy his office and make sure all eight lamps were illuminated each morning and extinguished each afternoon. Wilkerson, everyone knew, had been asked to memorize the locations of all items on Kent's desk so they could be precisely replaced after cleaning. And Wilkerson was entrusted with refilling his "Lion King" mug with coffee whenever King Kent wanted it.

McBroom, in contrast, worked mostly with Kent in his public courtroom, arranging gatherings for trials, hearings, and mediations. In closed mediation sessions, Kent sometimes berated attorneys, especially those he considered sloppy or who balked at settling cases he considered a waste of time. McBroom could handle Kent's flashes of anger but worried about his other habits. Several federal employees had seen Kent hug McBroom or heard him loudly suggest that she wear a thong as a costume for a Halloween office party. She had told very few people about how Kent had cornered and physically attacked her inside the courthouse exercise room in her first six months of work, though that turned out to be only a prelude to the behavior that would ultimately force her to flee.

McBroom wondered how Wilkerson managed to avoid Kent's roaming hands and oversized demands in close quarters, but for years, McBroom never dared question Wilkerson, who always seemed both uncomfortable and distant. Further tension built after Wilkerson walked into Kent's chambers one day in early 2007 to announce the imminent arrival of Kent's wife and saw Kent and McBroom breaking apart from what must have looked like an intimate embrace. McBroom felt mortified by the judge's secretary witnessing another of Kent's unwanted "hugs." She immediately fled to the elevators and retreated to her own office.

Minutes later, Kent called McBroom. He joked about what had happened, saying, "Holy shit, Cathy, I expected Mother Teresa to walk in next!" Then Kent informed McBroom that his secretary was upset and feared McBroom was "after her job." He suggested McBroom phone Wilkerson to smooth things over.

McBroom felt confounded by the judge's request. Kent seemed to be speaking in some kind of code. Why would Wilkerson be upset— rather than the judge's wife? And why should McBroom be forced to explain Kent's improper behavior? Though she felt exceedingly uncomfortable, McBroom decided to make the call. The Galveston staff was small and she didn't need enemies. After settling back in, McBroom dialed Wilkerson's direct line and invited her to lunch.

Together, McBroom and Wilkerson drove to a café and began a conversation that both remember as upsetting and awkward. It was one of those sunny but blissfully cool afternoons that visit the island in late winter, so they chose one of the restaurants that line the Galveston Seawall. A mammoth concrete walkway that stretches for ten miles along the Gulf of Mexico, the seawall helps protect the island's more densely populated eastern half from the fury of coastal storms. The first such barrier was erected after more than six thousand people died in the 1900 hurricane, leaving vast piles of wreckage and corpses. Both Wilkerson and McBroom, as lifelong coastal Texans, knew they were sitting atop a thin strip of shifting sand. Later, the

two women would disagree on which café they chose. Yet each recalled clearly what they discussed—and what they left unsaid.

"Number one, it's not what you think and it's not what it looked
like," McBroom told Wilkerson. "He's been messing with me and
he's harassing me all the time, and furthermore, I do not want your
job." McBroom hesitated and then confided that for years she'd been
pawed by Kent and actively avoided being alone with him, especially
after his long drinking lunches with lawyer friends. She confided that
she'd be afraid to spend as much time alone with Kent as Wilkerson did.

Wilkerson stared at McBroom. From the very first day on the job,
Kent had touched her too. Until that moment, Wilkerson had believed she "was the only one."

"He's doing the same thing to me," Wilkerson finally admitted.
"But what can we do?"

Both women felt tears form as they gazed out a window at the
Gulf of Mexico's deceptively gentle wintry waters. For Galveston
Islanders the Gulf of Mexico always holds the promise of another
storm. The recent passage of Hurricane Rita had delivered a glancing
blow; the next year, Hurricane Ike would pummel the island again.

Wilkerson told McBroom she believed there was "really no one
they could tell, nothing they could do and no one they could trust
to help."

Neither felt ready to risk her career by formally complaining about
a federal judge. Neither shared graphic details of how far Kent's assaults had gone. Before they parted, they made a pact that would
prove impossible for McBroom to keep: If one decided to come forward, she'd let the other know in advance. They split the check and
drove back to the courthouse together. That hour of exchanged confidences, however, did nothing to bring them closer. Without ever discussing it again, each woman still considered herself Kent's primary
victim and wondered whether the other had been acting as his agent
or accomplice.

In chambers, Kent kept feeding Wilkerson his version of the relationship with McBroom. He painted McBroom as an ambitious
office rival capable of deception to advance her career. He repeatedly told Wilkerson that McBroom was both "jealous of her" and

"wanted him." Wilkerson began "to believe it," she later recalled. "Or at least wonder if it was true. Our relationship was strained. He pitted her against me."

McBroom had hoped to build a bridge with Wilkerson after the confidences they shared. She watched instead as Wilkerson grew frostier toward her and closer to Kent. Wilkerson seemed to assume the role of his confidante, spokeswoman, and ally. By March 2007, Wilkerson had morphed into a sidekick whom McBroom absolutely believed she could not trust. McBroom found little respite from rising office tension even at home, where she and her husband increasingly fought over whether she should quit.

Rex McBroom served as safety and security manager inside a huge refinery complex east of Houston. In his job, he helped prevent accidents and protect thousands of employees from fumes, fires, and other on-the-job dangers as they blended up petroleum products inside towering metal structures topped by flares and smokestacks. He knew that his wife had been propositioned, attacked, and groped by the judge—but she refused to quit her job. Tending to demonstrate love in actions rather than words, he never understood her decision to continue working for Kent, despite the judge's sexually charged comments, nasty moods, and physical advances. Adept at analyzing and minimizing workplace risks, Rex McBroom viewed Kent as a dangerous predator. He wanted his wife to get away.

Cathy McBroom thought Rex failed to grasp how hard she had fought to create a career inside the highly competitive federal courts with only a high school diploma. He didn't seem to understand how proud she felt to be a court case manager. McBroom hated the idea of abandoning her government position, by far the best job she'd ever had. Feeling vulnerable and stressed out at work, McBroom considered the possibility of a separation to diminish anxiety and pressure at home.

At work, McBroom coped by pushing herself harder and by focusing on long lists of tasks she had to complete each week to coordinate hearings and negotiations in Kent's court, which was full of fascinating maritime accident cases involving shipping interests all along the Gulf of Mexico and beyond. Her job brought her into contact with a revolving cast of intriguing characters, though she tried to avoid one-on-one encounters with Kent. Naturally outgoing, she developed a professional shell that enabled her to maintain a formal yet friendly tone with Kent and to hold herself apart without seeming hostile. Despite her efforts, tensions built and McBroom began butting heads with Wilkerson and with Marianne Gore, the deputy in charge who was her boss in the Galveston clerk's office. McBroom considered both women to be Kent's allies—and also his victims.

McBroom had tried to tell Gore about her troubles with Kent. But that seemed to have backfired. McBroom came to believe that Gore saw her as far too outspoken—a troublemaker. Their biggest conflict involved McBroom's handling of a court exhibit filed in a quirky case that had briefly attracted international publicity.

The case involved an enterprising Galveston tavern owner named Rex "Wrecks" Bell, who dreamed up his own microbrew and dubbed it "Star Bock beer" as a way to attract more customers to his bar in the Strand Historic District, a sort of mini French Quarter. An eccentric local musician, Bell sold his creation straight from the keg at his Old Acoustic Café, a music venue only open on weekends, though he planned to market his brew off-island too. In 2004, he applied for a trademark in order to use the name elsewhere.

Bell's dimly lit tavern sat only blocks from where Starbucks, the Seattle-based corporate giant, had planted one of its chain coffee shops, transforming the interior of another historic brick building into a Pacific Northwest café clone with its signature light fixtures, autumn color scheme, and cookie-cutter décor. In contrast, Bell's place had a homegrown and funky feel. He hung up ornaments and changed them with the seasons and papered the walls with flyers featuring musician friends, including big Texas names like Fort Worth folksinger Townes Van Zandt and Samuel John "Lightnin'" Hopkins, a legendary blues singer-songwriter. Bell still wore his hair in a ponytail, though it was white now, and still clambered atop the small stage with a bass guitar in hand to play and sing music he composed himself.

Despite Bell's down-home approach, Starbucks's corporate attorneys opposed his efforts to seek the rights to market his beer as Star

Bock and filed a countersuit in Kent's court that challenged the name as an infringement of as many as sixty-one similar trademarked names. Starbucks had already developed its own coffee-based liquor and didn't want to share the potentially lucrative market with the brew of an aging island hippie.

"I'm not trying to attack big business. I'm just a small-time bar owner trying to make a Bock," argued Bell, in one of many amusing updates he posted about the dispute on his bar blog. Bell's business boomed as his case attracted network TV coverage, including a call from *The Tonight Show with Jay Leno*. Journalists covering the case went wild with puns, describing islanders as getting "steamed" over what the *Houston Press* called the "Beer Brawl," and the *Houston Business Journal* dubbed the "Brewhaha."

The case offered exactly the kind of notoriety—and national publicity—that Kent seemed to crave. Ultimately, Kent delivered a decision that awarded something to each side in Galveston's tempest in a coffeepot. Bell agreed to several changes: adding a blue star and the words "Born in Galveston" to his beer label. Then, in August 2005, Kent ruled that Bell could market his brew either at his own bar or another "local facility," but could not distribute his wares further without violating Starbucks's rights. For nearly two years after the last call in that legal dispute, an unusual souvenir lingered in the clerk's office vault: a single bottle of coffee liquor that Starbucks's lawyers had supplied as an exhibit. The attorneys had used the unopened bottle to illustrate Starbucks's competing plans for coffee-related alcohol products.

Gore instructed McBroom to contact Starbucks's attorneys and ask them to substitute a photograph, since the clerk's office didn't provide long-term storage for breakable or bulky items.

As ordered, McBroom made the telephone call, and a lawyer promptly sent the photo and told McBroom to discard the bottle. She had done so but forgot to get a signed receipt to formalize the exchange. After the lawyers agreed to its disposal, McBroom had taken the liquor home to try. The drink had been overly sweet and unmemorable. She'd forgotten all about the bottle when, two years later, Gore discovered there was no receipt inside the case file.

Gore was furious. She immediately called McBroom and threatened to fire her for the error, which she called a serious breach of court protocol.

McBroom apologized. She contacted the same attorneys again, belatedly obtained the receipt, and updated the record, just as Gore demanded. No one besides Gore complained or even noticed the missing receipt. The coffee case was closed. Still, to avoid further issues, McBroom figured she should inform Kent, who summoned her for a face-to-face meeting.

In a federal court clerk's office, few things are more sacred than records.

McBroom told Kent she recognized she'd made a mistake by failing to immediately document the destruction of the original exhibit and apologized yet again.

Kent said he personally considered the paperwork error relatively minor, but added that Gore was angry and seemed to be looking for a reason to fire McBroom. To smooth things over, Kent magnanimously offered to add his own formal memorandum to the file, McBroom later recalled.

McBroom thanked Kent, figuring the episode would finally end with his help. Instead, on Friday, March 23, 2007, she received a reprimand anyway. It was the first formal discipline of McBroom's eight-year federal career and she felt its sting. She responded immediately when Kent summoned her again to discuss it. As McBroom left the elevator on the sixth floor, a courthouse security officer quietly called out a warning as she passed the outpost on her way to chambers. "Be careful," the guard said, without explanation. Kent, it turned out, had just returned from a long lunch with lawyer friends.

Over the years, McBroom had become increasingly adept at avoiding solo visits to Kent's chambers—his lair. That Friday, though, she felt unconcerned about Kent, who had recently been behaving himself, and was too flustered to heed the warning. She feared she'd lose her job over a filing mistake related to—of all things—a bottle of booze. McBroom passed a desk normally occupied by Wilkerson, who was away that Friday afternoon.

Inside his office, Kent waited for McBroom; he had his bulldog, General Henry Knox. with him. Kent had named that dog for one of his favorite Revolutionary War heroes: Henry Knox, who, at age twenty-five, abandoned his Boston bookbindery and ran off to help lead the revolt against the British, later giving orders to fire cannons on the front lines.

McBroom loved dogs, but General made her nervous. He could be a nasty beast when crossed. Her high heels sank into plush blue carpet as she strode across the formal room, its walls laden with plaques and photographs, to where Kent waited behind an oversized wooden desk. She carried along a stack of court filings, including documents related to the reprimand she expected to discuss.

Kent's room reeked of cigar smoke. As he rose to meet McBroom, he projected a physical and mental presence that dominated his enclave even more intensely than it dominated his larger courtroom, where even veteran trial attorneys and deputy marshals sometimes cowered before Kent. Kent was only a few years older than McBroom, but she felt dwarfed by his size and his power. As she got closer, she noticed his breath still smelled of the liquor consumed at lunch. His blue eyes blazed and his booming voice seemed to bounce off the walls.

Kent said he'd read the reprimand and pronounced it "heavy-handed." The punishment felt unfair and out of proportion, he agreed, given the magnitude of McBroom's error. He reminded McBroom that it could have been worse: If it weren't for his help she might have been fired. Then he opened his arms and demanded a hug.

McBroom refused. "Just because I'm down doesn't mean you can take advantage of me," she said, allowing a sharp edge to her voice she normally avoided with King Kent.

"Look, I've done you a big favor," Kent said, still smiling. "The least you can do is give me a hug."

McBroom felt both extremely upset and genuinely grateful. She hoped this time Kent would behave himself. So she reluctantly approached.

Then Kent grabbed McBroom in an embrace and refused to let go, sending papers flying. General barked as she struggled, causing Kent to grip her even more tightly. He hoisted up her shirt with one hand. With the other he pushed aside her bra and pressed his lips on her naked breast. Kent released McBroom briefly when he noticed

General stepping on scattered files. But as McBroom bent to retrieve them and leave, he grabbed her again, shoving her head toward his crotch and ordering her to "suck me off."

McBroom kept struggling but made no progress against Kent, who kept her locked in his grasp. He grabbed one flailing hand, pushed her palm against his groin and held it there. McBroom thought she felt an erection and recoiled, though Kent, in his efforts to discredit her, would later claim he suffered from impotence and erectile dysfunction. She had begun yelling loudly for help, when she heard a quiet tap on the chamber door. No visitor dared enter, yet that knock served to remind Kent of potential witnesses waiting just outside. He released McBroom and they broke apart.

Despite her anguish and horror, McBroom crouched again to retrieve the scattered paperwork. The message emphasized in that disturbing personnel matter still echoed in her head. Nothing in the clerk's office is more sacred than records.

Kent watched her rearrange her clothes and the documents and then remarked as she left: "You know, Cathy, I keep you around because you are a great case manager. . . . That doesn't change the fact that I want to spend about six hours licking your clit."

CHAPTER 3

Kings of the Courts

Galveston, Texas, 1990–2002

In 1990, US president George H. W. Bush nominated Samuel Bristow Kent, then an ambitious attorney with a near-perfect memory, to the US District Court in Galveston at only forty-one. A likeable, larger-than-life Texas lawyer, Kent earned a unanimous vote of support from the Senate. No warning signs or red flags turned up in the FBI background check required of all federal court nominees, though if anyone had asked women who worked at his Galveston law firm, Kent might have been pegged as a sexist. He once joked at a public event that the only mistake he ever made as a lawyer was never "banging the secretary." In 1990, both the federal courts and the US Senate remained very much a man's world. Only two members of the Senate were women. Sexual harassment was not yet on the agenda of the all-white and all-male Senate Judiciary Committee, the same group that Anita Hill would address a year later in her testimony about humiliating verbal abuse she suffered under her former boss, Clarence Thomas.

As a US district judge, Kent became part of a powerful fraternity of active and senior district and circuit judges nationwide, all with lifetime appointments under Article III of the US Constitution. But on Galveston Island, Kent was the only federal judge bearing the rank of district judge, after his predecessor died in 1998. On Kent's watch, the island's coastal court took on more importance, dominating the nation's vast maritime docket. Annually, he handled hundreds of cases involving injuries and deaths suffered by mariners, roustabouts, ferrymen, and others laboring offshore or at sea, whose cases are governed by a federal law known as the Jones Act. Litigation under the Jones Act could be lucrative for attorneys working on commission who managed to win big settlements (or jury verdicts) for their clients. Those cases would become even more important for injured workers and their attorneys after Texas tort reform capped damage awards for similar civil cases filed in state courts at $250,000.

National press attention focused for the first time on novice US District Judge Kent when a massive airline antitrust price war landed in his backwater district court in July 1993. The high-profile case pitted Continental Airlines and Northwest Airlines against American Airlines in a court battle in which nearly everyone who ever traveled by plane had a stake. The two allied airlines sought $1 billion in damages, claiming a new fare structure engineered by American was predatory pricing intended to destroy Northwest and establish an illegal monopoly that would ultimately hurt consumers by cutting competition in the nation's skies.

Northwest Airlines hired a Houston lawyer considered the biggest swaggering star in the freewheeling US trial lawyer world—Joe Jamail. The son of a Lebanese grocery store owner, Jamail was already legendary. He had won a jury verdict and damages of $10.53 billion in 1985 for his client, Pennzoil, against Texaco, an amount that remained the largest civil verdict ever upheld on appeal in American history.

The battle between the airlines played out inside the gray Galveston federal courthouse, which rises like a proud castle on Twenty-Fifth Street on the edge of the Strand, the island's historic Victorian heart. From the first day, every wooden bench in Kent's courtroom was jammed with spectators for what promised to be an intense and dramatic jury trial. In the back, reporters from wire services, as well as Texas and national newspapers, stood shoulder to shoulder sweating as the great Jamail, then fifty-eight, took the floor. The ancient air-conditioning system in the courthouse basement sputtered and failed to keep out the sweltering summer heat. Everyone expected a real show from Jamail, whose riveting intelligence came packaged in an expensive power suit.

Instead of letting Jamail command the stage, Samuel Bristow Kent, an unknown rookie judge much younger than the litigating legend, repeatedly interrupted him. It seemed like every time Jamail tried to make a point with the jury, Kent would butt in. From the bench, Kent kept issuing reminders about rules and decorum in his booming bass voice. Kent seemed to use all of his considerable physical force to deliver remarks aimed at cutting down Jamail and other fancy attorneys from high-powered firms, quoting rules of evidence from memory and fixing the players with riveting stares. He enforced time limits on attorneys' remarks and cut the number of pages they could file in briefs. He required overheated lawyers to wear their suit jackets and kept the curtains open on the courtroom's wall of windows so that the sun shone directly in their faces.

Jamail had been known as the "King of Torts" since his record-setting Pennzoil win, but Kent wanted everyone to know he was king in this courthouse. In the end, Jamail lost his case. The jury took just three hours to return a verdict that favored his client's rival, American. And Sam Kent became known to legal observers and local and national reporters alike as a brash brainiac who managed complex cases with seemingly little effort and brooked no interference from anyone, not even the nation's wealthiest practicing litigator.

Kent later retold friends over dinners and drinks about how he'd privately called the great Jamail afterward to explain that his judicial role in the well-publicized loss was "nothing personal." Kent usually ended the anecdote by chuckling that Jamail had been unforgiving. "Fuck you, fat man," Jamail supposedly told Kent in the version the judge's buddies repeated and laughed about.

With or without a national audience, Kent reigned as king over Galveston's courthouse. No one was allowed to forget it. He sometimes made absurd declarations such as "I'm the emperor of Galveston" or "I am the government" or "It's good to be king." Friends figured that Kent, as an amateur historian, intended these remarks in a self-mocking way: he sometimes joked about feeling like the man who wore a horned hat aboard a Viking ship in what he called his "island dominion." But his employees and minions saw cold truth in the jests. Galveston, as the county seat, was well stocked with city and county officials and state judges, yet Kent in his federal courthouse was considered the most powerful man in local legal circles. His word literally was law. Kent abhorred any tardiness or disrespect or sloppiness in court, though he disregarded rules he personally considered inconvenient. He smoked cigars wherever he liked, declaring that the courthouse's smoking zone followed him wherever he roamed. (His habits didn't change after the building became "smoke-free.") He sometimes dispatched law clerks or deputy US marshals, sworn law enforcement officers, to fetch burgers or run errands. And he let others clean up after his bulldogs when he brought his pets to work.

Several people told variations of a story about how, one day in the early 2000s, Kent strode into the post office, which occupies the first floor of the courthouse, puffing a stogie and pulling along a bulldog on a leash. There was a long line, and when a postal customer, irritated by the fumes, challenged Kent and reminded him of the building's smoking ban, Kent exploded, reportedly saying, "I'm the judge here! I can do whatever I want." And then he retreated upstairs to his chambers and raged.

Many attorneys who practiced in the federal courts nationwide joked about a disease called "robe-itis" that seemed to afflict Article III judges who wore black robes. Also known as "black robe disease," it was so common that a band of attorneys who called themselves the Bar and Grill Singers wrote new lyrics to the tune of "Happy Together" that they performed in three-part harmony. The first verse is:

Imagine me as God. I do.
I think about it day and night.
It feels so right.
To be a federal district judge and know that I'm
Appointed forever.[1]

In the 1990s and 2000s, a new generation of legal bloggers and journalists began to circulate stories on the web about judicial bullies who repeatedly mocked, insulted, or threatened litigants or lawyers. Those stories aired courthouse dirty laundry in the wider world. In Spokane, Washington, US District Judge Alan McDonald was caught passing notes with crude and race-based comments to a staffer during hearings; a reporter had fished the papers out of the trash. In one note, McDonald mocked a Black bank official who appeared in court by writing, "Ah is impotent." Meanwhile, in Tennessee, District Judge Jon McCalla was accused of abusing attorneys verbally and, in one case, physically after he grabbed one by the lapels. And in Fort Worth, Texas, a diverse group of attorneys filed a complaint claiming that District Judge John H. McBryde punished lawyers who displeased him by means of excessive fines, court-ordered remedial reading classes, and jail. In McBryde's case, the Fifth Circuit Judicial Council hired psychiatrists to observe his courtroom behavior and later heard testimony from twenty prosecutors and defense attorneys in a closed disciplinary hearing. In an interview afterward, one witness called McBryde "an equal opportunity tyrant."[2] Federal judges intervened in all three cases and took unusual disciplinary action. In the aftermath, McCalla cooperated with the other judges' instructions and was considered rehabilitated. But court critics faulted judicial leaders for taking too long or doing too little to address seemingly egregious abuses of power in cases involving McBryde, McDonald, and other jurists inflicted with the condition known as "robe-itis."

During his judicial career, Kent had received national attention for writing humorous opinions that ridiculed or punished attorneys. One of Kent's most widely circulated opinions belittled two lawyers for arguments Kent compared to scribbling school kids. "Both attorneys have obviously entered into a secret pact—complete with hats, handshakes and cryptic words—to draft their pleadings entirely in crayon on the back sides of gravy-stained paper place mats in the hope that the Court would be so charmed by their child-like efforts that their utter dearth of legal authorities in their briefing would go unnoticed," Kent wrote. The opinion received both praise and publicity from lawyers and commentators who found him funny. In

2007, David Lat, a former federal prosecutor and nationally known commentator, posted about Kent in his blog *Above the Law*. So did criminal defense attorney Scott Greenfield on his blog *Simple Justice*. They and others both shared and praised excerpts from two of Kent's comical and critical opinions. In one post, Greenfield described Kent as "my new hero."[3]

But in the far-off halls of Northwestern University's Pritzker School of Law, Kent's written words attracted less flattering attention from a professor named Steven Lubet. As it happened, Lubet was conducting a scientific analysis of insulting words used by federal judges in a database of published legal opinions. He combed court documents with computers for terms such as *asinine, preposterous, ridiculous, ludicrous,* and *absurd.* In Lubet's tallies, Kent repeatedly came out number one for the use of insulting language. In a law re-view article called "Bullying from the Bench," Lubet wrote that Kent had used the word "asinine" at least thirteen times, while all thou-sand other US judges combined had used it only twenty-three times in the same period. Lubet lambasted Kent, writing, "By belittling the lawyers who appear before him, Judge Kent has used his authority to humiliate people who—in the courtroom environment—are com-paratively powerless. There's a name for that sort of behavior and it isn't adjudication. It's bullying. It smacks of nothing so much as the biggest boy on the playground picking on the smaller kids who are unable to fight back."[4]

Stories that began to circulate about Kent's imperial attitude sur-prised many who'd supported his bid for the bench. Kent had been popular when he first took over the island's lone district court. He'd been seen as a smart guy, a back-slapping maritime attorney who represented insurance companies and large corporations but was respectful toward opponents and serious about the law. Royston, Rayzor, a law firm founded in 1892, when Galveston was the state's wealthiest city, had long dominated maritime cases in the federal court. Kent claimed to have tried more cases in the Galveston Divi-sion of the Southern District than "any [other] living attorney."

True, some female colleagues had been offended by Kent's ma-cho talk and off-color jokes, but many eclectic members of the lo-cal bar backed his judicial nomination. Kent positioned himself as heir apparent both by courting the previous district judge and by sucking up to US Senator Phil Gramm; senators have a major say in judicial appointments. No locals wanted an outsider to get the Galveston bench. Islanders took a dim view of Houstonians, who were said to arrive with a five-dollar bill and a dirty shirt and never change either. Though born in Denver and raised in a Houston suburb, Kent had been accepted by the island's close-knit Galveston natives when he joined Royston, Rayzor. He and his wife had bought a two-story brick home in the Denver Court neighborhood and raised two daughters on the island.

As judge, Kent established a rocket pace and high standards for his docket. In and out of court, he used cutting remarks, his piercing stare, and his physical size to display displeasure at any signs of tardiness or ineptitude. He later complained in a letter sent to a reporter at the *Houston Chronicle* that legal standards had declined to the point that "virtually nothing is expected from practitioners." Kent proclaimed he intended to raise the bar.

In the first years of his reign, Kent was viewed as a benevolent though demanding monarch. His efficient style and tough settlement strategies soon attracted maritime injury and death cases from all along the Gulf Coast. Somehow cases from as far away as Louisiana and Florida made their way to his court. Some observers considered that to be a sign of corruption. Critics argued that Kent's favorites, a handful of attorneys that some called gatekeepers, were actively diverting cases to Galveston that rightly should have been filed elsewhere. Some maneuvering unquestionably occurred, but it appeared perfectly legal. Most cases had some Texas tie to justify the island venue.

Though Kent had defended corporations as an attorney, as a judge he sometimes openly sympathized with accident victims. In 1994, he presided over the case of a seventeen-year-old named Charity Freeland, who had suffered burns over most of her body in a horrific car crash. Kent, who had daughters of his own, took a personal interest in Freeland. The Houston teen had lost all of the fingers of her right hand. At the time of her trial, she had no hair, which stubbornly refused to regrow over her reddened and scarred scalp. She testified eloquently about her suffering. After seven surgeries and an entire year of wearing a pressure mask, she had continued to endure the emotional pain of seeing other kids recoil at the sight of her burns. With Kent applying pressure to the defendant, Freeland eventually won a substantial settlement above the cost of her treatments, according to court documents and Kent's recollections of the case in his letter. She used part of the money to found a small charity to help other burned children. Her life deeply touched his. More than a decade later, her case would remain his favorite.

Lawyers who represented injured workers and the families of workers who had died of injuries preferred Kent's fast-track style of pushing settlements, since many of their clients were beset with creditors trying to get payment for unpaid hospital or funeral bills. Some company lawyers also preferred Kent's methods. Arthur Schechter, a politically connected maritime attorney who served as ambassador to the Bahamas from 1998 to 2001, later described Kent as one of the most efficient federal jurists around. "He is smart and focused," Schechter said. "I never knew him to favor any lawyer on one side or the other."[5]

There was no question Kent knew the law. He rarely seemed to need to crack the legal tomes decorating his office to refresh his memory. Kent's rocket docket was fueled by an unusually aggressive settlement style, which often involved Kent ushering parties into chambers and loudly lecturing one side or the other about what to do or else risk incurring his wrath. Lawyers noticed, and discussed among themselves, that Kent processed so many cases that his annual statistics made other judges look slow or lazy by comparison. Kent liked to say that his was "one of the largest individual civil dockets in the country."

But on and off the bench, Kent's ego appeared to grow along with his sense of power. He demanded Secret Service–style treatment from the US Marshals Service such as providing rides to and from the airport in Houston, fetching dry cleaning, and performing demeaning personal favors. Once, when stuck on the tarmac in an airplane, Kent used his cell phone to order a deputy marshal to contact air traffic control and demand an explanation for the delay. Kent's law clerks, other court employees, and anyone who visited his court regularly learned to do whatever the judge asked without asking whether the judge's oddball requests fell outside court policies. Employees traded stories about how he'd arranged unwelcome transfers—considered banishments—for more than one veteran federal employee who dared to cross him. Increasingly, Kent's outrageous behavior and remarks targeted women.

Kent's salary as a federal judge was generous but didn't match the big earnings of his civil attorney friends. He came to expect lawyers to treat him to long lunches and drinks at exclusive island venues, like the Galveston Yacht Club and the members-only Pelican Club. The Pelican Club was technically part of the historic Gaido's, a Seawall tourist attraction known for its souvenir shop and for a restaurant that had masterfully served up Gulf seafood for ninety years. But the club had its own private entrance behind the restaurant, marked by a pair of brown pelicans carved out of driftwood, that led to an exclusive members-only dining room. Kent often turned up on Fridays wearing jeans, an oversized cowboy hat, and boots. His entourage included friendly lawyers who practiced in his court, as well as his young law clerks, a group of junior attorneys that usually included at least one attractive young woman. Kent favored a table on the left side of the maître d' stand from which he could oversee the entire club. After eating, Kent liked to linger over drinks, usually glasses of wine or an occasional whiskey. And as he drank, Kent tended to wave his long arms and broadcast courtroom anecdotes, Civil War trivia, and crude sexual innuendos in his brassy baritone. One day he eyeballed the chest of one clerk, a young attorney and bride-to-be, and loudly commented that she'd probably have to custom-order her wedding gown given the size of her "rack." One long-time maître d' recalled how another of Kent's particularly crude jokes prompted other patrons to request their bills. "What do you get when you bury a naked woman head first in the sand?" Kent asked, waiting a beat before bellowing out the response. "Clam dip." Several distraught diners rose to leave even as Kent continued to guffaw.

Federal judges don't have bosses. But back in 1939, Congress passed a statute that reorganized the federal court administration and created judicial councils, groups in each circuit assigned to set policy so that the work of the courts could be "effectively and expeditiously transacted." Over the years, each council developed myriad rules on how to handle complaints involving judges' misconduct or disability. In 1980, Congress passed a new law, the Judicial Conduct and Disability Act, which formalized the secret disciplinary system and gave chief circuit judges responsibility for overseeing those reviews and acting as gatekeepers for complaints. Judicial councils still retained responsibility for voting on any formal disciplinary actions. Mostly they worked behind the scenes. By the early 2000s, federal courts were receiving an average of 700 complaints each year. Nearly all complaints were dismissed. But from 2001 to 2003, judges quietly resolved 29 out of 2,115 complaints with some kind of corrective action—mostly behind-the-scenes.

In the early 2000s, Collins T. Fitzpatrick, circuit executive for the Chicago-based Seventh Circuit Court of Appeals, canvassed chief judges nationwide about the secret disciplinary system for an informative article that demystified the process and recommended reforms. Fitzpatrick, who was directly involved as a staff member in assisting the chief judge with misconduct reviews in his own circuit, heard about cases of "robe-itis" and of do-nothing judges, as well as issues involving alcoholism and drug addiction. He also heard about judges who were either overly "friendly" or were sexual harassers. "Sometimes a judge who is merely friendly is misperceived as flirting or sexually harassing someone," Fitzpatrick wrote.[6] "If no one informs the judge of this perception, the conduct deemed offensive will continue." Fitzpatrick wrote that he believed that it was imperative that problems involving actual sexual, racial, or other forms of bias or harassment be "ended by a change in the judge's behavior or by removal." Rare complaints involving criminal issues of integrity should be "directly and expeditiously referred to prosecutors," he added. Fitzpatrick, a court insider himself, knew most people were reluctant to report misbehaving judges. He also called for more hotlines, for lawyers' advisory committees, and for anonymous surveys of attorneys to improve troubleshooting. Few federal circuit courts adopted those practices.

During Kent's first few years on the bench, his predecessor, Hugh Gibson, retained an office into his late seventies and still heard cases as a senior judge, despite worsening health. From 1995 to 1998, a promising young lawyer served as Gibson's briefing clerk. The clerk often talked to Kent, who considered himself a mentor. On her last day of work, she stopped at Kent's chambers to say goodbye. The attorney, like others in Galveston that summer, knew the judge's beloved first wife, Mary Ann, had recently been diagnosed with brain cancer. Still, her mood going into his chambers alone had been upbeat. Her fiancé was graduating from medical school and they were about to begin their life together. A few minutes later, she fled in visible distress.

The young lawyer was still shaking when she approached a deputy US marshal. She told him that Kent had grabbed her, pushed her into a corner, and forced his tongue into her mouth. The federal officer immediately informed her that she could file a complaint. She declined, telling him she feared tainting her whole legal career by confronting a US district judge.

Minutes later, Kent approached the same federal officer. That young clerk of Gibson's had stopped by and tried to kiss him! Kent said. In retirement, more than a decade later, the veteran deputy marshal still felt disgusted when he repeated Kent's cover story, which he considered a blatant and self-serving lie. No complaint was filed and the incident went unrecorded at that time, though years later current and former court employers told investigators and a journalist about the incident.

At that time, Kent was attracting sympathy even from people who disliked him. His wife, Mary Ann, had been diagnosed with what Kent later described as "an enormous brain tumor" in 1996 and had been told that her situation was hopeless. Cancer had stalked the big judge earlier in his life. Kent's father, a painter, died of cancer when Kent was a teenager, leaving his mother to raise him and four siblings alone. Kent had known Mary Ann twice as long as he had known his own father. Mary Ann, a year older than Kent, was his high school basketball coach's daughter. He courted her for years before she agreed to marry him. Outspoken and intelligent, Mary Ann Kent had earned an education degree, but always supported Kent's career. She really never pursued her own, though at various times she taught art and music and became an accomplished photographer, potter, guitarist, and writer. From 1996 to 2001, Kent continued to handle a huge caseload, though he frequently altered his schedule as his wife underwent five years of surgery and experimental treatments that he hoped would save her life. Kent drove her regularly to and from Houston's massive cancer treatment complex, MD Anderson. "I found the entire experience to be extremely devastating. I gained about 60 pounds, drank too much in the evenings and cried a lot," Kent later said.[7] During his wife's long illness, Kent increasingly railed at attorneys in his court.

In a January 2000 hearing, Kent lashed out at Mark W. Stevens, a dapper Harvard law school grad who'd formerly been Kent's rival for the island federal bench. Stevens came to Kent's court that day to argue on behalf of a woman who claimed she'd been wrongfully fired by a local foundation after telling her boss she'd received Pap smear results that indicated abnormal cells. After being fired, the woman learned that she did not have cancer, the lawsuit said. Stevens argued that his client had suffered wrongful discrimination, losing both her job and income, because of her boss's desire to avoid medical expenses. Stevens hoped his client would receive a fair hearing from a judge who islanders knew was dealing with his own wife's expensive cancer treatments.

Kent attacked the claim as fake and threatened "thermonuclear" sanctions. "I think this is the most personally insulting allegation to have ever been brought before this court given the personal circumstances of this court and I am not going to take this lightly," Kent said.

Stevens, who himself has suffered from clinical depression, saw the outburst as a sign of both abuse of power and possible mental illness in Kent. Stevens decided to send a formal complaint privately to judicial leaders, following procedure outlined by the 1980 law that allows anyone to confidentially report either judicial misconduct or disability. Stevens felt sorry for Kent but didn't think his client—or anyone else—should be forced to appear before a judge who seemed mentally unbalanced. In a formal complaint that Stevens sent to the chief judge on January 20, 2000, Stevens claimed that Kent, who "operates under obvious stress at the courthouse and at home," had repeatedly and improperly unleashed his anger on attorneys and litigants. . . . Verbally or in his privileged published opinions, he has systematically abused many of the ablest and most respected lawyers on this Island."

Many federal judicial misconduct complaints are dismissed as "frivolous." Even when action is taken, it's usually in a confidential process that chief judges say is effective in deterring further misconduct and protects the dignity of the court. But complainants often have no idea whether anything happened. The only response Stevens recalls receiving to his complaint was a form letter suggesting that some type of administrative action had been taken.

Kent later recused himself from all of Stevens's cases. In the process he made Stevens's formerly confidential complaint part of the public record, which exposed Stevens as a whistleblower. Stevens believed at least one Houston judge subsequently retaliated against him. Other lawyers who have filed high-profile complaints against judges or who were compelled to testify in federal judicial disciplinary matters have also complained that they'd been retaliated against by accused jurists or their allies.

Whether or not a behind-the-scenes discussion with the chief judge had any impact, Kent later said he realized that his anger had gotten out of control during his wife's long illness. He sought professional counseling and advice from a trusted pastor. Still, he struggled. As the health of his wife steadily declined throughout 2000, Kent remained on the bench but began drinking more heavily. He spent some nights guzzling wine in the ill-lit den of the two-story brick house, where the couple had raised their daughters together. Some nights, Kent held a gun to his head and contemplated suicide. He rarely left Mary Ann alone with a caregiver, though in June 2000, he decided to attend the Fifth Circuit's weekend judicial conference in an upscale hotel on the Riverwalk in San Antonio; it was the annual ceremonial roundup of the circuit's judges and their spouses or other invitees.

Kent did not get to enjoy the party. He rushed out early after his wife's doctors called to inform him that she was dying. On June 21, 2000, Mary Ann Kent died at fifty-two—a day before Kent's fifty-first birthday. The long-expected death of his "beloved wife" after a "long, courageous battle with brain cancer," as her obituary said, unleashed a reckless and self-destructive side that Kent had previously tried harder to suppress. "I was a mess," he later said.

Kent took a road trip several months after his wife's death to the vacation home of a Galveston lawyer friend in Colorado, where Kent met a single working mom named Sarah. Kent seemed instantly smitten. By the time Kent attended the Fifth Circuit's next judicial conference in New Orleans, he had courted and married her. In February 2001, Kent's best friend, the attorney Richard Melancon, who had supported him during Mary Ann's long illness, served as best man at Kent's second marriage ceremony. He also hosted a reception with a string quartet at his sprawling mansion in the Houston suburb of Friendswood. Melancon hired one of the island's top caterers and provided seafood, wine, and champagne for the couple and a sizable crowd of guests, including federal courthouse employees and local attorneys.

Judges who failed to accurately report travel and other gifts or who ruled on cases that presented blatant conflicts of interest were another common theme in federal judicial misconduct complaints. It concerned Kent's critics that a circle of attorney favorites such as Melancon enjoyed seemingly unfettered access to the judge. The year of the reception, Melancon's firm was handling dozens of cases in Kent's court. Sometime in 2000 or 2001, someone apparently questioned the appearance of favoritism and possible conflicts of interest, though no formal federal misconduct complaint was ever disclosed.

Even if a complaint of misconduct is confirmed with hard evidence, a chief district or chief circuit judge cannot dock the pay of a fellow judge with a lifetime appointment. The most common behind-the-scenes actions include recommending counseling or another form of corrective action, which could include an apology or medical treatment. A chief judge also can quietly transfer away some or all of a judge's caseload. In July 2001, an unusual and unexpected order to transfer all eighty-five cases handled by Melancon's firm out of Kent's court was signed by George Kazen, of Laredo, the chief judge for the Southern District of Texas from 1996 to 2003. The only public reason provided was that the transfers were "in the interest of the improved administration of justice," but a *Houston Chronicle* story pointed out that questions had been raised about the unusually close friendship between Melancon and Kent.[8]

Felicia Williams, a tough but sweet woman who was a US Coast Guard reservist, worked as Kent's case manager back then. She heard Kent fume about negative publicity. A savvy senior court employee, Williams long employed her instincts and her sense of humor to stay in Kent's good graces. "You had to know how to play the game—do what he wanted and butter him up," she recalled years later. In 2002, she was undergoing treatment for hepatitis C. She often felt exhausted and irritable from the after-effects of the grueling treatment regimen, and felt compelled to hide the symptoms from Kent. "I was throwing up in the trash can," she said. "I took very few days off—and tried to stay in his good graces." Williams was getting close to federal retirement age and needed her job and medical insurance. Kent's court was much closer to her home in Texas City than Houston, where she had previously worked for prosecutors in the US Attorney's Office. Still, she found his mood swings and erratic behavior increasingly hard to tolerate.

After his long drinking lunches, Kent would return and act overly affectionate, trying to give Williams and other female staff lingering hugs. She tried to avoid them. She didn't laugh when her husband, Mike, was treated for prostate cancer and Kent smiled and offered to "service her." She suspected he'd gotten away with worse behavior with others. She'd heard that he'd attacked and French-kissed a law clerk. She knew a paralegal who made excuses to never visit his office. And Williams believed that Kent had groped his secretary too.

In court, Williams sometimes felt forced to cover for Kent when he arrived hours late or appeared visibly tipsy after long lunches. She'd survived so long because she worked hard, and could sometimes make Kent laugh. On Friday September 13, 2002, Kent went out for a long lunch with his secretary, Donna Wilkerson. The two dined on crab cakes and other delicacies and failed to arrive in time for a 1 p.m. sentencing hearing. Williams found herself stuck in the front of the courtroom for forty-five minutes, stalling and attempting to placate a dozen people, including federal prosecutors, defense attorneys, and at least one defendant waiting in shackles to hear his fate. It's not unusual for a federal judge to arrive a few minutes late, but Kent pushed the limits. Williams pondered what to do. She feared this time Kent wouldn't show up at all or would arrive inebriated. Then, to her relief, Kent walked in wearing his black robe and offering no explanation or excuse.

He behaved normally. The sentencing was routine. Predictably Kent gave the prisoner the same punishment he had dispensed earlier that day to codefendants involved in the same crime. Afterward, Williams felt so relieved that when the courtroom emptied, she dared to offer her own joke: "Don't worry—we could have done it without you."

Kent said nothing. Instead, he went to his office, made a few calls, and arranged that same afternoon for Williams to be involuntarily transferred to Houston. The following Monday, Williams reported to work, but Kent, the man she'd served for years and referred to only as "Judge," completely ignored her. He never spoke to her again. Williams finally learned from the deputy clerk in charge, Marianne Gore, that she'd been terminated. She never got any explanation from Kent. Williams was forced to accept a demotion, a pay cut, and a commute of more than sixty minutes each way. It was hell for Williams, whom Kent knew was suffering through treatment for a potentially life-threatening illness. She'd become gaunt and had lost so much of her curly hair that she'd begun to wear a wig. Learning a new job put a further strain on her health.

Kent told those who asked about her disappearance that Williams "just wasn't any fun anymore."

CHAPTER 4

Chambers and Secrets

Pasadena, California, 2006–2007

Heidi Bond graduated from the University of Michigan Law School summa cum laude in 2006, and landed a position prized by many elite young lawyers: a clerkship with Alex Kozinski, a widely respected and unconventional federal judge on the prestigious Ninth Circuit Court of Appeals. She had heard of Kozinski's appreciation for the unusual and had won the post partly by demonstrating a quirky skill: "I had a line on my résumé at the time that said I could fold a stegosaurus out of a single piece of paper," Bond recalled. She received a rapid reply from one of Kozinski's clerks, who said the judge "doubted this was possible." So Bond promptly mailed back two folded stegosauruses, one of which, when unfolded, displayed her excellent final law school grades. She got an interview and an offer one week later.

A clerkship with Judge Alex Kozinski made for an eye-catching line on any résumé, and the bespectacled jurist with the wide smile and sharp wit served as what law professors called a "feeder": his top clerks often landed positions with the Supreme Court, usually with Justices Kennedy or Sandra Day O'Connor. Bond was the only woman chosen for a clerkship with Kozinski that year.

A dark-haired dreamer, as a girl Bond had wanted to be a novel-ist, burying herself in books such as J. R. R. Tolkien's stories about Middle-earth and the works of Robin McKinley, whose fantasies had a decidedly feminine twist. She grew up in Riverside, California, where she and her six siblings played practical jokes on each other in a somewhat rough and tumble environment. By age ten Bond had finished her first novella, "To Bring Back the Buffalo," about ten thousand words written in longhand, but she soon gave up the idea of becoming an author as impractical. In elementary school she was often the only nonwhite student in "gifted and talented" classes and was sometimes teased by kids who singled her out as the proud daughter of a father of mixed European origins and a Chinese Amer-ican mother. Bond, who was shy as a child, decided early to ignore bullies, noticing that any response only gave them more ammunition. It took several years before she unraveled the racism behind insulting rhymes and gestures she'd first encountered on the schoolyard.

Bond's world opened up in her twenties to include challenging studies on both coasts: a double major in math and chemistry at Florida State University and later graduate school at the University of California–Berkeley, where she studied theoretical statistical me-chanics. As the sixth of seven ambitious siblings, Bond had to figure out how to pay her own way through college. She worked and took out $100,000 in student loans. She had already zigged from math to chemistry and then zagged to statistics, and her career plans took another detour when an advisor at Berkeley told her to focus her research on "something she couldn't stop thinking about." At the time, Bond was obsessed with the law—a copyright case before the Supreme Court—and so to her advisor's surprise, she enrolled in law school at Michigan. Her ability to pivot and excel was a strength, but years later Bond also recognized that trait as a symptom of an illness. She sometimes suffered bouts of depression so intense that it was "much, much easier for me to change things around and do something completely different." That's because part of her brain was constantly telling her, "Ho hum, all your achievements thus far are actually meaningless."

As a new University of Michigan Law School graduate, Bond knew that the opportunity to clerk with Kozinski could make her legal career and that working for a judge considered one of the profession's leading wordsmiths would improve her writing too. Bond still loved to write, though at that time her goal was to be a law professor.

The world of the federal courts that Bond entered in May 2006 was—and remains—highly stratified, with judges at the top of the heap and clerks and other federal employees far below. Law clerks, all hand-picked by the judges for whom they will work, enjoy symbiotic relationships with those jurists. Part of the ritualistic federal court culture and the close clerk-judge relationship involves keeping secrets, both to protect the dignity of the judiciary and to safeguard the confidentiality of the process. When Bond arrived in Kozinski's chambers, a suite of offices where her own space was located closest to his, she took the required oath to uphold the Code of Conduct for Judicial Employees. She also received a copy of the thick *Handbook for Law Clerks to Federal Judges*, which spelled out more rules. In part, the handbook said: "The relationship between judge and law clerk is essentially a confidential one. A law clerk should abstain from public comment about a pending or impending proceeding in the court in which the law clerk serves. A law clerk should never disclose to any person any confidential information received in the course of the law clerk's duties."[1] Because Bond was starting in May, earlier than her counterparts, she received no formal orientation but knew that judicial positions like hers were "at will" appointments that could be "terminated with or without cause by the Court," according to the clerkship handbook. At the time, the handbook did not make it clear that clerks had a right to seek confidential assistance or to file formal complaints if they were sexually harassed or abused by judges. Just after Bond finished reciting the oath and signed a form to affirm her acceptance, Kozinski grabbed her arm.

"It's too late now," he said. "She can't escape any longer. She's my slave."[2]

Bond tried to make light of his declaration, suggesting the term "indentured servant" might be more appropriate for the one-year stint.

"No, I meant slave," he insisted, smiling.

Bond was startled by the term. *What the fuck?* she thought. She felt shocked. Years later, when Bond looked back on that moment, she was offended for other reasons: she knew there was "absolutely no comparison" between actual slavery and her federal clerkship, which paid reasonably well and opened up many other opportunities. But as a young lawyer, she could not escape the powerful suggestion Kozinski had planted in her mind. For the next year she would be his slave and follow his orders.

As a law student Bond had been part of an outspoken new wave of legal bloggers who in the late 2000s were spicing up national discourse by posting insightful commentary and excerpts from oddball or revelatory opinions. Bond called her blog the *Letters of Marque*. She published entries regularly from 2002 to 2005, during all three years of law school, and gained a following by exploring "eclectic subjects from obscure case law to predictions about how the Harry Potter series might end," a fan later wrote.[3] Bond continued to read constantly as a law student and young lawyer, consuming as many as a thousand books a year, including romance and fantasy novels. She produced one of her most popular blog entries after staying up most of the night reading the newly released book 6 of the Harry Potter series and at around 3 a.m. posted her theory that Harry himself was a Horcrux. She thereby became one of the first in the world to accurately predict that the popular fictional hero's destruction would ultimately be necessary to eliminate all pieces of the fractured soul hidden inside magical objects called Horcruxes by his nemesis, Voldemort. Bond felt proud that for a while her blog ranked number one in searches for that obscure term, "Horcrux."

When Bond began her clerkship in May 2006, Kozinski had served on the Ninth Circuit for more than twenty years. Bond had wanted to work for him because of his reputation as one of the court's top legal minds and finest writers. But as a law clerk, Bond was told to stop blogging on any subject and avoid speaking or writing about her experiences. So she took down her blog from the internet. Later, she felt that Kozinski erased most of the self-worth and enthusiasm she'd built up as a budding attorney.

By the 2000s, university admission policies and antidiscrimination laws had vastly improved. It was no longer legal for colleges to exclude women as students or for law firms to exclude them as partners. Female graduates had begun to outnumber men in some law schools. And through years of legal battles, the protections of Title VII of the Civil Rights Act had been extended to prohibit sexual harassment in most workplaces, though the federal courts remained exempt from those workplace laws.

The ranks of law clerks remained shockingly white and mostly male, though complete statistics on the diversity in the federal courts are hard to find. In 1998, Tony Mauro, then national court reporter for *USA Today*, tracked down all 394 Supreme Court clerks who'd been hired by the nine members of the high court under Chief Justice William Rehnquist. Mauro's investigation revealed that men had been hired for 75 percent of all of these most elite clerkships, though the two women justices had hired far more female clerks than had the male jurists. Four justices—Rehnquist, Kennedy, Antonin Scalia, and David Souter—had never hired any Black law attorney as clerk. Scalia never hired any clerks of color. No justice had ever hired a clerk who self-identified as Native American. "Even though more than 40% of law school graduates now are women and nearly 20% are minorities, they largely have been bypassed for the most prestigious work a young lawyer could have," Mauro wrote. "As a result, law clerks' powerful dual jobs of screening cases and drafting opinions—which often have dramatic effect on race and gender relations, among many other issues—remain mostly in the hands of white men."[4] In response, court leaders claimed it wasn't their fault: not enough women or candidates of color in the late 1990s were applying from elite law schools such as Harvard or Yale or were being recommended by a dozen feeder judges, such as Kozinski. The diversity numbers were so low that if the federal courts had been a private employer subject to Title VII of the 1964 Civil Rights Act, the Supreme Court justices could have been sued for discrimination in the hiring of their clerks "based on the statistics alone," Stetson University law professor Mark Brown told Mauro in 1998.

Though Mauro's story generated controversy and lively debate, the deeper issues of gender bias and sexual harassment remained largely unaddressed. When Mauro updated his research in 2018, he found little improvement: "Since 2005, 85% of all Supreme Court law clerks have been white. The percentage of African-Americans and Hispanics has increased at a glacial pace. Women comprise a third of the clerks instead of a fourth, even though more than half of law students now are female."[5] What had changed, Mauro was discouraged to discover, was that Supreme Court Justices were even less willing than they had been in the 1990s to publicly discuss those disparities or to use their power to try to pressure law school deans or feeder judges, like Kozinski, to send more diverse candidates.

As a federal judge, Kozinski was very familiar with sexual harassment cases that he and other judges ruled on under Title VII. Generally, the law, which applies to most private workplaces and most other federal government agencies, prohibits both a classic quid pro quo in which a supervisor requests sex from an employee in exchange for a job or a favor as well as situations in which an employee suffers from "a hostile workplace," one that features forms of harassment that might involve several players.

In 1991, Kozinski joined a panel assigned to review an early sexual harassment case involving a complaint from a female employee of the Internal Revenue Service. The legal dispute began after Kerry Ellison met another employee, Sterling Gray, in training. Gray pestered her for lunch dates and, after she refused, wrote to her. The first note began "I cried over you last night and I'm totally drained today." Ellison reported Gray and requested help, but Gray persisted: "I know that you are worth knowing with or without sex. . . . Don't you think it odd that two people who have never even talked together, alone, are striking off such intense sparks?" Ellison reported the behavior and requested action. The IRS temporarily separated them via a temporary transfer but later allowed Gray to return to the same workplace. So Ellison filed suit in a case that became known as *Kerry Ellison v. Nicolas F. Brady, Secretary of the Treasury.*

As part of an all-male panel, Kozinski sided with another male colleague in a 2–1 decision that found that Ellison—or any woman— might find certain behavior, such as aggressive flirtatious letters, more threatening than a man. The 1991 opinion adopted what was then called a "reasonable woman standard" (later renamed the "reasonable worker" standard) for defining workplace harassment. Later, Kozinski elaborated on his views in the foreword he wrote for a manual, *Sexual Harassment in Employment Law*, by advocating restraint on both sides. Men "must be aware of the boundaries of propriety and learn to stay well within them. Women must be vigilant of their rights, but must also have some forgiveness for human foibles: misplaced humor, misunderstanding, or just plain stupidity."[6] But the otherwise brilliant jurist seemed unaware how his own behavior and work habits made some women colleagues and court employees feel uncomfortable.

Kozinski was more outspoken than his counterparts. Most elite circuit judges, like their more powerful colleagues on the Supreme Court, tend to be both reclusive and workaholic. They work in secluded enclaves inside often palatial regional courthouses. They rarely oversee trials and instead dedicate most of their time to deciding diverse types of appeals of district court rulings, often deciding cases in panels of three. Circuit judges often closet themselves away with staff in chambers, those suites of interconnected offices.

Even more than in other workplaces characterized by huge imbalances in authority, law clerks and other court employees may feel unable to protest if a powerful federal judge sexually harasses them or commits another kind of misconduct. Clerkships "can place young women in a particularly vulnerable position—the job, by its nature, requires young clerks to work in close and secluded quarters with judges who have the power to make or break their careers," wrote Catherine Crump, an assistant clinical professor of law at Berkeley Law, in a 2017 commentary for the *Washington Post*.[7] "The current system encourages women to put up with bad behavior or forgo certain opportunities rather than insist on fair and equitable treatment," she observed.

Joanna Grossman, now a law professor at Southern Methodist University in Dallas, first met Kozinski in the 1990s when she clerked for a different Ninth Circuit judge. Grossman, now a specialist in sexual harrassment and related legal issues, later recalled that the thing Kozinski most seemed to notice about the new wave of female lawyers arriving in his court in the 1990s was their breasts. Grossman later observed that Kozinski's disrespect for women already was "legendary" during her clerkship with Circuit Judge William A. Norris from 1994 to 1995. At one point during her clerkship,

Kozinski sent out a memo to all judges suggesting that "a rule prohibiting female attorneys from wearing push-up bras would be more
effective than the [circuit's] Gender Bias Task Force," Grossman recalled in a tweet.[8]

The Ninth Circuit bias task force spent more than two years in
the 1990s studying gender issues and inequality. Its July 1993 final
report concluded that 60 percent of the women attorneys practicing
in the circuit had been subjected to "unwanted sexual advances or
other forms of sexual harassment by colleagues, opposing counsel,
clients, judges or other court personnel."[9] Among other recommendations, the group called for a prohibition of gender bias and sexual
harassment to be included in the federal judicial canons or codes of
ethics, but progress on those proposals later fizzled.

In the aftermath, the famously sexualized behavior of some federal judges, like Kozinski's, altered little. Kozinski has said that he
treated his male and female clerks alike. He expected all of his clerks
to work sixteen-hour days, to draft as many as twenty versions of
opinions, and to listen to the same dirty jokes and the same kinds of
suggestive or insulting remarks. Kozinski never hid his interest in sex
and his love of off-color jokes. In 1996, he wrote an essay for *Slate*
that described getting a male clerk to land invitations for the two of
them to attend a lingerie party at the Malibu beach house of an unidentified millionaire. Kozinski's article described how they'd seen a
bondage peep show, a body painter, a man clad in only a codpiece
(a "clip-on cup"), and a woman wearing dominatrix regalia bearing
handcuffs and a "coiled whip." In conclusion, Kozinski described the
experience as "different and wonderful in many ways, and breath-
takingly expensive. But decadent? Not really."[10]

Dahlia Lithwick, a witty and whip-smart graduate of Yale Law
School, met Kozinski during her 1996 orientation as a Ninth Circuit
law clerk in San Francisco, where he ogled her at a reception for so
long that it made her feel "quite small and very dirty."[11] Lithwick
was clerking that year for Proctor Ralph Hug, whose chambers were
in Reno, Nevada, but she frequently traveled with him for cases. On
another visit to California, Lithwick spoke to Kozinski accidentally
by phone when she called his chambers to reach one of his clerks, a
college friend who was working late. "The judge asked where I was.

I said I was in my hotel room. Then he said: What are you wearing?" Lithwick knew Kozinski had a raunchy sense of humor, but his comment shocked her.[12]

Lithwick mentioned the suggestive remark to Hug, who served as chief circuit judge from 1996 to 2000. As chief judge, Hug spent some of his time handling formal and informal complaints about his peers, though Lithwick knew nothing about the federal judicial misconduct complaint process. Hug never discussed confidential reviews of misconduct matters with Lithwick in her time as clerk, she recalled in an interview years later. Hug also did not tell her that she could pursue a formal or informal complaint against Kozinski. "I was so protective of my judge that I didn't want to distress him or ask him to take a bullet for me," she said. "I think I told him about the remark. I didn't expect him to resolve it. I didn't have any reason to believe anything to be done. There was always a sense I had at the Ninth [Circuit] that everybody knew this about Kozinski and that he was outside of whatever formal policy or procedure there was." For two decades after her clerkship, Lithwick, who became a nationally known legal commentator, kept meeting up with Kozinski periodically at legal events, where she caught other glimpses of what she saw as his strange hypersexualized world. But she hesitated to write about them. She still felt bound by the relationships between law clerks and judges, which were built on a tradition of worshipful silence. That didn't change until 2017, after other women began to speak out.

In 2003, when Katherine Ku, a Stanford Law graduate, came to clerk for Kozinski, she anticipated an "arduous apprenticeship with this brilliant jurist and writer."[13] She was flabbergasted to learn how controlling the judge could be. More even than other jurists, Kozinski required 24/7 availability from clerks—sometimes calling or sending emails in the middle of the night—and emphasized the need for absolute secrecy and loyalty. During Ku's clerkship, he sought to be given right of approval on the location of her apartment and complained when she chose salad for lunch instead of whatever he was eating. Worse, Ku said Kozinski frequently made sexist remarks and fostered what she later called a "persistently sexualized" work environment.

One day, Kozinski invited Ku into his office to view a photograph on his computer. The image of a naked man had nothing to do with any case. After that, Ku tried to keep to her own small office in chambers and limit further one-on-one contact with the judge during her clerkship in 2003–04. Ku's career continued to prosper after her difficult year with Kozinski. She went on to clerk for Associate Justice Ruth Bader Ginsburg in 2004–05 and later to practice corporate and securities law at prominent LA firms.

Bond didn't know about Ku's experience before her own clerkship began in May 2006. But she knew another former clerk from Michigan Law who had described Kozinski as a tough boss who went through an insane number of drafts but had a lot of fun with his clerks. She'd also read Kozinski's *Yale Law Journal* article, "Confessions of a Bad Apple," in which he described sharing a lifelong connection with his clerks. Kozinski had written that "by accepting a judge's clerkship offer, a young lawyer becomes part of the judge's extended family, a disciple, an ally, quite possibly a friend."[14] The only really negative thing Bond heard was that Kozinski supposedly had pulled a woman's hair in chambers. Her friend the ex-clerk also told her the judge played around and teased people.

Bond later remembered thinking: *I'm from a big family, and I was like, okay, I can handle teasing.* Bond had a healthy sense of humor fostered by practical jokes she and her siblings played on each other growing up. Bond was tiny when she'd been pranked for the first time by a sibling who told her that chocolate milk, which her mother offered as a treat, was "dirty" as a ruse to get her share. Her mother took part in the pranks, too, sometimes supplying bogus excuse notes to school, like one that read "Please excuse Heidi's absence yesterday. She was sick (of school)." And another that read "Heidi was sick yesterday. Sincerely, my mother."[15] Given her upbringing, she figured she could handle Kozinski's jibes.

Soon after Bond began her clerkship, another Kozinski clerk suggested that in order to prepare for whatever the judge might say or do, she should review a raunchy documentary called *The Aristocrats*. Bond watched the 2005 film in chambers, gradually feeling more freaked out as one hundred different comedians told increasingly obscene variations on an old joke about a group of performers auditioning for a show—each comic trying to outdo the other with more elaborate and disgusting details about the nature of their act. Versions of the joke included over-the-top accounts of bestiality, incest, group sex, vomiting, and defecation. Only the punch line stayed the same: "And what do you call your act?" "The Aristocrats." Many people considered the film a classic raunchy comedy. But after watching it Bond felt "a little shell-shocked." She wondered: *What have I gotten myself into?*

At first Bond was the only woman of three clerks tapped to work for Kozinski. A fourth man joined their group about six months later. (Kozinski anticipated needing more help since in December 2007 he would become chief circuit judge.) Of the four clerks, only Bond had studied science in graduate school. She had conducted research on networks called "computer clusters" back in her UC Berkeley days and along the way she'd also worked as a tech in a computer shop. Kozinski dubbed her his "computer clerk" and would rely on her for computer-related issues.

Bond felt more comfortable with Kozinski's humor and trash talk when he did it around her male counterparts: then she could pretend to be one of the boys. But she felt repelled by his sexually charged banter when they were alone. Once Kozinski showed Bond a typewritten page of what he called his "knock chart," a list of girls he and his friends had "banged in college." Another time, Kozinski told Bond he hated the 2000s' emphasis on STDs because "nobody wanted just to fuck anymore." At least three times during her clerkship, the judge initiated awkward private reviews of nude photos on his computer.

One afternoon Bond was sitting inside her own small office when the phone on her desk beeped twice. It was a signal. Two beeps meant drop everything and come right away. She walked into Kozinski's office next door, passing his long brag wall of "grip and grin" photos of himself with dignitaries and his favorite movie posters. Kozinski's chambers were inside the lovely Pasadena circuit courthouse, formerly a historic resort hotel built along the banks of the Arroyo Seco. But during her clerkship, Bond often felt down, and when she entered his office, her eyes tended to fix on its view of the Colorado Street Bridge. She knew that historic structure, towering 150 feet over the arroyo, is better known by Angelinos as the Suicide Bridge in memory of hundreds of people who have leapt to their deaths into the mostly dry riverbed below. Sometimes court employees would see jumpers and summon 911 for help. On that afternoon, the sounds of cars crossing the bridge seemed particularly loud.

As Bond approached Kozinski's desk, he was already staring at a set of photos on his computer screen. "I don't think your co-clerks would be interested in this," he said.

His first question was technical. Did Bond think the photo had been digitally altered ("Photoshopped")?[16] Bond glanced at the screen and immediately felt uncomfortable. The photo depicted a party of men and women who looked like college students. Some were fully clothed and others inexplicably nude. The domain name associated with the files included his last name, Kozinski.com. He often showed his clerks files and photos he kept on that private server based in his home. She did as the judge directed, scanning for signs of whether images had been altered. In a portion of the photo depicting a nude couple on a couch, she spotted blurred details and indications that parts of the images and backgrounds did not quite match.

"Yes," she told him. It had been altered for sure.

Kozinski sometimes asked his clerks to review material for cases. And he sometimes reviewed pornography submitted as evidence in obscenity matters. Reviewing porn could be part of regular court business, especially in Los Angeles, home to the lucrative American adult film industry. But the party pics he asked her to examine didn't have anything to do with a case. Nor did his next question.

"Does this kind of thing turn you on?" Kozinski asked.

"No," she said. She maintained her composure, but inside, a fight or flight response had been triggered. She later described feeling temporarily "paralyzed."

"Why not?" Kozinski asked.

"It doesn't look like they're having fun," she said, expressionless.

"It doesn't do anything for me either," he said. "People just send me these things. I don't know why but I like to keep them as a curiosity. I don't understand why people find this sort of thing arousing,"

Kozinski retained his Romanian accent but had long ago discarded the caution he'd been forced to adopt in publicly expressing opinions after a joke he'd told as a boy got his father into trouble with his Communist employers. Someone had uploaded to YouTube an old episode of *The Dating Game* during which Kozinski, by then an eighteen-year-old living in LA, charmed a woman by calling her the "flower of my heart." Kozinski, aka Bachelor No. 2, then delivered a lingering kiss that knocked the floppy hat off the female contestant's head. (Later she stood him up, Kozinski told friends). As a judge, Kozinski continued to bestow hugs and kisses on male and female clerks and other employees, sometimes loudly declaring his "love." He repeatedly told Bond he "loved" her. He asked her to tell him that she loved him back and requested kisses too. Perhaps Kozinski considered those exchanges to be signs of affection. Yet similar patterns of controlling behavior, sexual remarks, and physical contact initiated by employers toward employees were also sometimes presented in federal court cases as evidence of a hostile workplace in sexual harassment cases.

Clerks who worked for Kozinski had little time to relax inside the lovely Pasadena circuit courthouse, a palatial building in an upscale neighborhood that was surrounded by flowering formal gardens. Many judges' clerks worked longer than the standard eight-hour day. But Kozinski was proud of his reputation as a taskmaster. He liked to say his clerks got far more than a year's worth of experience in their time with him. His clerks' workdays stretched to sixteen or seventeen hours. Their only real breaks came when Kozinski drove off at around 6 p.m. to eat dinner at home. They were expected to return when he did and work until about 1:30 a.m.

Bond enjoyed reading romance novels over dinner breaks to release stress. Then one evening Kozinski caught her with a book and seemed furious. He told her that reading romance novels was an addiction, a form of "porn" for women, and ordered her to stop wasting time.

"But it's on my dinner break," she protested.

"I control what you read, what you write, when you eat," he said. "You don't sleep if I say so. You don't *shit* unless I say so. Do you understand?"

Secretly, Bond kept reading romances. She still read voraciously, as she had since girlhood. But she began writing romances too that year, in what she considered a private act of defiance.

Though other federal judges required long hours for clerks, or worked late, the hours Kozinski routinely required of his team were considered extreme even in that workaholic environment, other former Ninth Circuit clerks say. Even after she finally got home at night, Bond had trouble sleeping. She kept dreaming that her office phone was beeping and wondering what else Kozinski might require of his "slave." She struggled with depression and considered quitting early but worried how she'd repay all those student loans if she received a negative review. At Kozinski's urging, she interviewed and received an offer in October 2006 to clerk at the Supreme Court with Sandra Day O'Connor, who had retired but still hired clerks for 2007 to 2008, since she continued to wrap up court business as a senior justice. Bond knew that after accepting the honor of clerking for the nation's first woman justice, there was no way she could ever leave Kozinski's service early. She would somehow have to survive until her clerkship with him ended in May 2007.

In her final days on the job, Kozinski asked Bond whether she'd like to join an email joke group he ran for friends he called the Easy Rider Gag List. Easy Rider was Kozinski's snowboarding handle, and he gave list members their own monikers. Members were regularly sent jokes, photos, and videos, many of them sexually explicit, that Kozinski and other members considered funny. To gauge Bond's interest he sent several samples from his private collection—including this joke quiz that he'd already kept around for ten years:

> **Forwarded message**
> **Date:** Wed, 22 Oct 1997 01:00:27 -0700 (PDT)
> **From:** The Easy Rider
> **To:** Easy Rider Gag List
> **Subject:** Rogue Male (P&T)
>
> **From:** The Big Ukrainian
>
> Are You an Unreconstructed, Right-on, Rogue Male or a Delivery Boy of the New Male Order? Are You a Man or a Louse? Find Out Below.

1. A woman whispers "Do me now, big boy . . ." in your ear. She
   is obviously:
   a) Short sighted.
   b) Attempting to overcome a lack of self-esteem through
      meaningless sexual gratification.
   c) Begging for it.
   d) A recording.

2. In the company of feminists, coitus should be referred to as:
   a) Sex.
   b) Fucking.
   c) Enclosure.
   d) The pigskin bus pulling into tuna town.[17]

From the emailer's nickname, Bond figured the quiz had been forwarded by one of Kozinski's former clerks, though more than one had Eastern European roots. Bond wasn't interested in the gag list but told Kozinski she would join anyway. As clerk, she had learned that her life was better if she pretended to appreciate the judge's jokes and made him laugh. A judge's chambers could be an echo chamber. Federal judges were often surrounded there by junior employees who felt compelled to laugh at a judge's jokes whether they found them funny or not.

Inside, Bond felt constantly anxious as Kozinski's clerk—like a "prey animal," she later said. She dreaded any one-on-one encounters. She couldn't sleep and began to overeat. By the time her clerkship ended in late May 2007, she'd gained nearly forty pounds.

As soon as Bond finished her clerkship, she climbed into her 1993 Toyota Paseo and headed east. She drove more than two hundred miles across the mountains and Mojave Desert until she reached the town of Primm, just across the Nevada state line, all to avoid spending another night in the same state with Kozinski. She checked into the Buffalo Bill Hotel, a gaudy place with a pool shaped like a buffalo, clanging slot machines, and a roller coaster. Instead of lingering, Bond rose early and kept her Paseo pointed east, racking up two speeding tickets on her way to Chicago, where her boyfriend was waiting. As she crossed an empty stretch of Utah on I-70, the small Toyota's speedometer hit 104 mph.

Both before and during Heidi Bond's year as Kozinski's clerk, a Los Angeles–based attorney named Cyrus Sanai had a series of run-ins with Kozinski after Sanai wrote a piece in September 2005 for the San Francisco *Recorder* that criticized the Ninth Circuit judge's extensive use of unpublished opinions. Kozinski, in an unusual move for a federal judge, publicly replied to the criticism in a September 23, 2005, article entitled "Kozinski Strikes Back."[18] In support of his arguments, he included a link to a court document stored at the URL www.alexkozinski.com. Subsequently, in October 2005, Sanai filed a judicial misconduct complaint alleging that Kozinski was improperly keeping federal documents on a private server and also had misused the server to share case-related information with the public via the link to a document embedded in Kozinski's article. More than a year later, in December 2006, Chief Judge Mary Schroeder of the Ninth Circuit dismissed Sanai's 2005 misconduct complaint, saying she had found no evidence that the link or Kozinski's personal website existed. It turned out that Kozinski had taken his website offline sometime in 2006, Sanai noticed. But at that time, Sanai had no idea that Kozinski also had stored any nude pictures on that same web server.

In December 2007, Sanai was surfing the web again when he rediscovered that Kozinski's personal web domain had reappeared. Examining it he stumbled onto a publicly accessible folder full of sexually explicit images, videos, and dirty jokes. To Sanai, some images looked as though they'd been downloaded from porn websites. But it seemed like a waste of time to Sanai to file another formal misconduct complaint against Kozinski, given that Kozinski had recently replaced Schroeder as chief circuit judge and thus was now in charge of reviewing those complaints. In 2008, Sanai began to hear that Kozinski was distributing samples of his joke archive to lawyers and to other judges via email. Sanai downloaded several samples of the archive and tipped off several reporters.

On June 11, 2008, Scott Glover of the *Los Angeles Times* reported that Kozinski maintained a large, publicly accessible collection of sexually explicit material, including a photo that showed two half-naked women on all fours wearing body paint that made them look like dairy cows, and a naked man cavorting with an erect donkey.[19] The timing of the article was particularly awkward for Kozinski: Kozinski was then assigned to preside over a criminal obscenity trial in a Los Angeles district court, where Ira Isaacs, a self-described shock porn king known for films that featured bestiality and that mixed excrement with sex acts, had been charged with violating obscenity laws. Isaacs had at that time gained a cult following for distributing a Brazilian porn video considered so disgusting that it had become popular as a dare: viewers were challenged to watch an online excerpt without vomiting. Kozinski, now known as a collector of what the *Los Angeles Times* described as "sexually explicit material," quickly announced that he would recuse himself from *USA. v. Ira Isaacs.*

Kozinski, as chief circuit judge, then used his authority to initiate a misconduct complaint against himself based on the *Los Angeles Times* article. He then requested that the chief judge of another circuit be assigned to handle the review to avoid any conflict of interest. The Third Circuit Court of Appeals took up the matter beginning in the fall of 2008.

Chief Judge Anthony J. Scirica of the Third Circuit Court of Appeals formed a formal investigatory committee in the fall of 2008. When the probe began, Heidi Bond was finishing up her year as a clerk at the Supreme Court. Though O'Connor was retired, Bond kept busy wrapping up O'Connor's court business and gained more experience by simultaneously working for Kennedy. Bond read newspaper articles on the internet about the complaint about Kozinski's porn collection and his private website. She also saw articles about the judicial misconduct probe. But none of the members of the judicial investigatory committee or the lawyers they hired to help ever contacted her. She did, however, receive a call from Kozinski's office, inquiring whether she would testify in his defense if that ever became necessary. Ultimately, she was never asked to do so.

Scirica's probe lasted about nine months. Other than Kozinski himself, it wasn't clear how many witnesses were interviewed by the committee or by the law firms it hired to investigate, though Mecham and Sanai were asked to provide sworn statements. After conducting a closed hearing, the Philadelphia-based Third Circuit judicial council voted to admonish Kozinski and to accept his formal apology for failing to better secure the contents of his private server to keep it from being accessed by members of the public. In an order issued on June 5, 2009, Scirica summarized the findings. The disciplinary order said that Kozinski had "explained and admitted his error; apologized for it, recognizing its impact on the judiciary; and committed to changing his conduct to avoid any recurrence of the error." Only a few sentences of Kozinski's lengthy response to the complaints were ever disclosed to the public: "I have caused embarrassment to the federal judiciary. I put myself in a position where my private conduct became the subject of public controversy. While this was painful for me personally, my greatest regret is that I was identified as a federal judge, indeed, as a Chief Judge of the nation's largest federal circuit." But in the opinion of Scirica and the rest of the council, that was enough. "The judge's acknowledgment of responsibility combined with the corrective actions he has already completed or has committed to pursue . . . properly remedy the problems raised by the complaint," Scirica wrote.

In the aftermath, some court critics praised Kozinski for having proactively initiated a complaint against himself and for having referred it to another circuit. The *Wall Street Journal*'s July 2, 2009, headline on the matter read "A Pleased Kozinski Cleared of Wrongdoing."

But in a 2018 letter to Scirica and another judge, Sanai described the investigation as a whitewash. "Judge Scirica's Committee interviewed no witnesses; it refused to talk to me, and refused to talk to Judge Kozinski's staff, clerks in the Pasadena Courthouse, or anyone else who was primed and ready to reveal what Judge Kozinski was doing. At the hearing, the only percipient witness that Judge Scirica wanted to hear from was Judge Kozinski. Thus, in a judicial misconduct proceeding brought by Alex Kozinski against Alex Kozinski, the sole witness for the prosecution and defense was Alex Kozinski. Not surprisingly, Alex Kozinski was largely vindicated."[20]

Later, in a 2019 federal civil lawsuit, Sanai claimed that the investigation only opened the door for US Circuit Judge Stephen Reinhardt and for other Ninth Circuit judges to later retaliate against him for having filed misconduct complaints.[21] (In a response to the lawsuit, Kozinski and other current and former court officials have defended their actions as justified.) In interviews, Sanai separately posed questions about why during the Third Circuit's investigation, no officials appear to have asked whether Kozinski had improperly shown nude photos or other samples of his so-called joke collection to law clerks like Heidi Bond.

After finishing her Supreme Court clerkship, Bond applied for a job teaching at Kozinski's alma mater, UCLA Law, and was invited for a site visit. But she declined after realizing that she never again wanted to work in the same city as Kozinski. Instead, she kept writing romance novels and later accepted a professorship at Seattle University School of Law. On the side, she began to publish books under the nom de plume Courtney Milan. In her first novels, which had titles like *Proof by Seduction* and *Trial by Desire*, Bond created complex historical romances powered by plots that reflected her inner struggles. Her heroines harbored secrets and faced conflicts with powerful people from higher castes. In her stories, strong women eventually spoke out, overcame obstacles, enjoyed hot sex, and found love—or, as she would say, "Women won, again and again." Bond later reflected that, as an author, she was grappling with her own secrets through fiction: "In book after book, I wrote the happy ending I couldn't quite reach myself."

Writing as Milan, Bond hit the *New York Times* bestseller list in 2011 and decided to stop teaching and to write full-time. Her improbable girlhood dream came true: she became an author. But Bond hesitated to write one word about Kozinski for a decade after her clerkship ended. She still felt compelled by her oath of confidentiality never even to speak of what had occurred. She never considered the idea of filing a judicial misconduct complaint—that option did not seem open to her as a clerk. "It didn't occur to me that anyone would care or listen."

The same year that Bond sped away from her clerkship in her Toyota Paseo, Cathy McBroom was reaching her breaking point at the federal courthouse in Galveston.

CHAPTER 5

The Reluctant Whistleblower

Channelview, Galveston, and Houston, Texas, 1960s–2003

Cathy Carnew McBroom grew up in the 1960s in Channelview, a town on the industrial fringes of Houston, as the eldest child of working parents who managed to keep their household together—though barely—through her childhood. Cathy had the same blue eyes and broad smile as her mother, but her character had been shaped by her father, a handsome and funny man who did shift work at a chemical plant. He often slept during the days, so he expected his daughter to be absolutely silent and respectful at home. But elsewhere, he expected his eldest child to be outspoken, self-sufficient, and independent. If she faltered, he would tease her until she laughed or else sternly prod her. "He wanted me to be tough from the very beginning. If he saw me crying, he told me to suck it up—Stop it! Stop it right now!" she later remembered.

Her girlhood provided her with tools she tapped when she was thrust into the unwelcome role of a whistleblower. She told her folks when a bully circulated a nasty note about her at school and was encouraged to confront the girl on her own. When a drunken friend's father asked her to play the piano and groped her on the bench beside him, she kept quiet and put him on her list of people to avoid. And she stuck up for her younger brother too.

By her teen years in the rebellious 1970s, Cathy knew her mind and often engaged her parents in debates. When they refused to let her attend senior prom as a freshman, she lost the argument, but never forgot the fight. She had plenty of fun in high school as a member of the drill team, who dated football players, and ran around with her best friend, Charlene Clark. Her parents forced her to take typing, though she rejected the idea of becoming a secretary like her mother and dreamed of college and a career. But she was a sucker for romance and accepted when her childhood sweetheart, Mac Baldwin, proposed marriage in 1978 only two years after her graduation from high school. She became a mother at twenty, ending college early and buying a house in her hometown. She watched her parents' marriage fail in 1981, the year she gave them their first grandchild, Amanda Evelyn. "There was a miserable back and forth," she remembers. Her dad began seeing another woman; her mom responded by drinking heavily. Cathy ended up holding her newborn daughter many nights in one hand and the phone in the other when one or another parent called, screaming. Eventually, both parents calmed down and remarried new spouses. By that time Cathy had cemented her role as the family fixer.

She loved her first husband, yet their marriage failed to mesh with her dreams. Cathy soon gave birth to a son, named Casey, and found herself watching two kids alone while her husband worked or went out to play softball, drink, hunt, or fish. She got divorced in 1990 soon after landing her first job as a legal secretary—taking her mother's career path after all. She'd always been interested in the law, but attending law school never seemed possible for a working-class mom from a blue-collar company town.

For years, she drove her kids around in her aging red Honda, which was losing its paint when a mutual friend fixed her up with sandy-haired Rex McBroom. She was outgoing and extroverted. He was quiet and introverted. Still, they clicked. Rex talked her into marriage in 1991. He quickly stepped in as a stepfather for her two kids, and they later had a son together. Caleb was still small when she decided to move beyond secretarial and paralegal work for law firms. In 1999, she launched a new career in the Houston federal courts, at the square building nicknamed the Sugar Cube. McBroom soon learned that each court in the Sugar Cube had a distinctive culture shaped by the whims and wishes of each federal judge.

Federal judges across the United States were generally powerful and intelligent but appointed by very different (and often rival) US presidents. Their job security put circuit and district judges at the very top of the federal court caste system, followed by US magistrates and US bankruptcy court judges, who lacked lifetime appointments. Each judge picked a case manager and a secretary. Each also had several law clerks, often recent law school graduates who work shorter stints. In a sense, then, each judge was king or queen of a court populated with a tightly controlled circle of followers.

Many district judge's chambers in Houston in the 1990s and 2000s were steeped in machismo. One judge, a bachelor, took his entire staff on an annual cruise that some dubbed "the Love Boat," after the eponymous 1970s TV sitcom that churned out syrupy cruise ship romances. Another judge sometimes referred to his female staff, female prosecutors, and FBI agents alike as "girls," an enduring habit that eventually earned him a public scolding in a footnote in a ruling written by a judge on the Fifth Circuit Court of Appeals. Yet another bachelor on the bench sometimes asked female staff to help arrange dates with attractive women he spied in his courtroom.

Both the Congress and the judiciary were exempt from Title VII of the Civil Rights Act, the law that banned gender and racial discrimination and later was interpreted by the courts as prohibiting sexual harassment in nearly all other workplaces nationwide. But under pressure, Congress decades later passed another statute, the Congressional Accountability Act of 1995, to extend protections against discrimination and harassment to its own employees. Senator Chuck Grassley, among others, urged federal court leaders to support a law to guarantee the same rights to its employees.

Federal court leaders rejected the argument. In a meeting in 1996, members of the powerful Judicial Conference of the United States, the national policy-making body of judges, declared that their group was already committed to voluntarily providing protections to court employees. They argued that submitting to employment laws under Title VII that interfered in any way with judges' hiring and firing decisions would infringe on the judges' "fundamental need for judicial independence." Later, individual district and circuit courts each adopted voluntary Equal Employment Opportunity plans, which generally gave chief judges broad discretion in how to apply rules. In 1998, the Southern District of Texas adopted its first Equal Employment Opportunity Plan; updated in August 2002, it called for furnishing a workplace "free of sexual harassment." McBroom and other clerk's office employees attended trainings, but most judges did not. McBroom never realized that all federal judges were basically excluded from employment laws on gender bias and sexual harassment. The concept was confusing, especially since federal judges regularly interpreted those laws in their rulings.

Late in 2002, McBroom received an offer to become Judge Kent's case manager in Galveston. Before accepting, McBroom decided to seek out Felicia Williams, Kent's former case manager. McBroom knew Williams had been transferred back to Houston from Galveston only a few months before, though the two women had never previously spoken. McBroom had heard other employees gossip about Williams's quick exit from Galveston and wondered whether she should be concerned. She asked Williams to meet for coffee in the Houston courthouse cafeteria.

The cafeteria is wedged into a fluorescent-lit L-shaped enclave on the austere ground floor. The space lacked the grandeur of well-appointed chambers and stately courtrooms of the upper floors, but its Cajun fare and burgers were surprisingly good. It was one of the few places in the courthouse where high-powered lawyers, janitors, clerks, secretaries, and sometimes judges informally mixed. The two women chose a quiet spot among the windowless room's square metal tables.

"You worked for Judge Kent for almost ten years," McBroom began. "What happened?"

"I loved my job," Williams said, not answering the question. "He's like all judges—demanding and expects total loyalty."

McBroom waited for Williams to say more. She wondered if Williams had been ill or even had cancer. Williams was obviously wearing a wig, she looked exhausted, and her answers seemed disjointed.

Finally, Williams went on. "And like other avid fishermen, Kent sometimes stretches the truth. . . . Just remember, when he says a fish is this big," she said, holding her palms as far apart as they would go, "it's probably really this big." She grinned and brought her hands so close together they could have barely held a minnow.

McBroom saw the other woman's tired face come to life with the unexpected joke and issued one of her signature belly laughs. "Anything else I should know?" she said. Both women were now smiling. They instantly liked one another.

"Kent and his secretary, Donna, are really tight," Williams confided, crossing her index and third fingers suggestively. "Don't tell Donna anything that you don't want Kent to know immediately."

McBroom had watched a lot of skilled attorneys operate over the years and she'd saved her most important question for last: "If you could, would you go back?"

Another long pause. "If I had the opportunity, yes."

McBroom seized on that last answer. She felt a surge of enthusiasm. If Williams would return, how bad could Kent be?

Williams walked away from their conversation feeling unsettled. She had always been an athlete, and excelled in aqua aerobics, but she'd been ill after undergoing treatment for hepatitis. She had wanted to warn McBroom but could not risk saying anything that might jeopardize her federal paycheck or health benefits. Kent had already exiled her from Galveston, and he had plenty of Houston allies. Williams applied, but no other judge ever offered her a job as case manager. She knew he could make her life much worse if he suspected she'd been disloyal. Out-of-pocket medical bills for her own illness and her husband's recent cancer treatment had eaten up their savings. In light of these realities, Williams had provided only a hint of what it was like to work for Kent. She'd left out Kent's full body hugs, his graphic comments, his long drinking lunches, and his pawing of women employees. Williams figured McBroom, an attractive athletic woman with oversized blue eyes and shiny black hair, would soon learn. Williams feared that McBroom was certain to attract unwanted attention from the man Williams always referred to as "Judge."

In her early days on the job, McBroom refused to be put off by warnings that came from her female supervisor, Marianne Gore, who was younger than McBroom but had seniority in the clerk's office pecking order. Gore cautioned McBroom not to share in the judge's jokes. "Kent seems friendly and he's funny, but he's got a volatile temper and he can let you go in a heartbeat," McBroom remembers Gore telling her. McBroom thought Gore seemed grumpy. Gore didn't seem to appreciate her sense of humor or share her philosophy that of course work must be done well, but you could still have a little fun.

In that first year, Cathy McBroom prospered. She loved meeting people and finding diplomatic ways to convey Kent's commands to a diverse group of powerful attorneys, mostly members of the offbeat maritime bar. Like any new employee, McBroom made rookie mistakes. One time she forgot to remind Kent of a hearing and the judge showed up in flip-flops and shorts. He quickly hid his beachwear under his robe, strode into court, and later laughed about it. Another time she failed to inform the US Marshals Service to bring prisoners from the Houston lockup to attend a Galveston sentencing, thereby leaving other parties assembled and waiting in court for defendants who never arrived. McBroom realized her error just in time and apologized in embarrassment to the entire group. To her surprise, Kent was forgiving, telling her to ease up and relax. In the beginning anyway, McBroom enjoyed the judge's favor. She knew keeping her job depended on that.

McBroom quickly came to know members of Kent's inner circle. Kent had a large group of lawyer friends who practiced in his island court. McBroom had heard how Kent had been embarrassed back in 2001 over the well-publicized transfer of dozens of cases involving his close friend, Richard Melancon. He now seemed closer to other lawyers, including Tony Buzbee, one of Kent's former law clerks who also had worked with Melancon.

A burly ex-Marine who kept his curly hair cropped short, Buzbee remained friendly with Kent, one of his earliest mentors, for more than a decade after his clerkship. Buzbee, who was raised on a farm near Atlanta, Texas, population 5,500, never completely lost his East Texas twang or his tough military demeanor. He'd earned his law degree in May 1997 as a returning Persian Gulf War veteran at the University of Houston law school before becoming Kent's law clerk. But by 2003, only six years out of law school, Buzbee already had become a high-rolling trial attorney. In the 2000s and beyond, his oversized image sometimes appeared on billboards lining the highway bridge that connected Galveston to the mainland. Over time, Buzbee kept winning big cases and accumulating "toys." He bought yachts (one was dubbed the *Más Grande*), a tank, a jet, and a mansion in Houston's elite River Oaks. He moved his legal headquarters to a flashy penthouse inside the tallest skyscraper in Houston, though he long remained a member of Kent's island inner circle. But Kent and Buzbee, despite their long connection, sometimes butted heads. Even as a clerk, Buzbee had never really kowtowed to Kent the way others did.

Many federal court clerks establish lifelong connections with judges and often feel intensely loyal and grateful to their mentors. As his clerk, Buzbee had admired Kent, whom he saw as a brilliant legal mind. Early on, Buzbee had benefitted from Kent's help. But over the years, their relationship became increasingly dysfunctional. Like other former law clerks, Buzbee admits he had a hard time ever saying no to his former boss, the federal judge. When he opened his first law office in Galveston, Buzbee included a replica of a historic bar, fully stocked with liquor that he offered to clients and used for after-hours parties to which he often invited Kent. Later, Kent began showing up on random afternoons unannounced to demand drinks and hit on female staff members. The visits became so tiresome that Buzbee later said he began to instruct employees to leave whenever the big judge stopped by. Once Kent met Buzbee at a yacht the attorney kept docked at a pier in downtown Galveston and, after cocktails, insisted on going for a cruise. Buzbee objected—he didn't know how to sail and didn't trust the judge to do so. Kent insisted, steering them out onto the Gulf of Mexico before admitting he had no idea how to return. They ended up having to call for a tow, Buzbee said. Buzbee was watching Kent spin out of control but didn't know what to do about it.

One Friday in April 2003, after a long lunch with Buzbee, Kent abruptly ordered McBroom to call a New Orleans law firm and cancel a trial scheduled to begin that Monday concerning a shipping company employee who'd been injured in an offshore accident. Often, such injury cases ended in a settlement, but this time the man's employer had refused to negotiate and claimed the worker, Buzbee's client, had invented his injuries. Buzbee later denied he used his lunch with Kent to privately request a delay in the pending case, which would have been inappropriate "ex parte" communications. Buzbee said Kent sometimes arbitrarily rescheduled hearings or trials whenever the judge just didn't feel like working.

Whatever Kent's reasons, on that Friday afternoon McBroom knew that canceling a scheduled trial via cell phone late on Friday afternoon was a bizarre move guaranteed to anger the out-of-town attorneys, who had already left New Orleans to meet with their corporate client in Texas prior to the trial. She finally reached one of the shipping company's lawyers, James Cobb, a colorful Big Easy attorney who'd had prior dealings with Kent. Cobb told her that he knew of lawyers who had been fined thousands of dollars for arriving only minutes late to Kent's courtroom. He wasn't going to risk not showing up for a trial that still appeared on the official federal court calendar.

McBroom was forced to report to Kent that her efforts had been unsuccessful.

Early on Monday, April 7, 2003, Cobb, another lawyer, and their client arrived at the courthouse wearing suits and carrying briefcases loaded with paperwork for the trial. They were stopped immediately by a security officer, who told them they could not take the elevator up to Kent's courtroom or even visit the clerk's office, a government facility normally open to all visitors during regular business hours. Cobb fumed at treatment he considered outrageous: King Kent appeared to have closed down portions of a public courthouse just because he felt like it.

It wasn't the first or last time Kent made odd decisions after a long Friday lunch. In fact, on Friday afternoons when Kent rolled into the courthouse over-loud and seemingly impaired after eating out with friends, in-the-know courthouse and security staff sometimes sounded an unofficial alert.

But as of August 2003, Cathy McBroom had not yet learned to monitor those subtle warning signs. She went to check her mailbox on the sixth floor one afternoon when the elevator doors eased open and Kent staggered out. Kent stopped and loudly asked McBroom to show him "that new workout room," a few pieces of inexpensive weight training equipment that had been set up in a vacant area by the fitness-conscious court security officers. McBroom, still a dedicated marathon runner, sometimes used the weights and padded benches in that room but found the request bizarre. Kent's only workout regime appeared to be lifting a pen or a glass of wine. Still, she'd gotten used to following his orders without question. The no-frills room was empty when they arrived. "Well, here it is," McBroom said.

"Yes, indeed," Kent mumbled. The judge towered over McBroom and had gained weight. He was about twice her size. He looked around, apparently to assure himself that they were alone, and then grabbed her, forcibly attempting to stick his tongue down her throat when she opened her mouth to protest. He kept her pinioned with one arm, then quickly used his free hand to pull up her blouse. She twisted and squirmed as he stuck his huge hands inside her bra, hoisting it high and exposing both breasts. She caught her breath in shock and tried to pull away.

Even in her panic, McBroom feared offending the judge, whom she knew could fire her on the spot. She could not fight him off. Her only weapons were words. "No Judge, this is inappropriate," McBroom said, at first maintaining her courteous case manager tone even as she struggled.

Kent kept his hands roving over her bare breasts and the rest of her body, so she threatened to alert security. "I'm going to scream if you don't leave me alone," she managed to say. Several guards were based at the sixth-floor command center, only about ten feet from the room's entrance.

"Do you think I care?" Kent replied. "Do you think I care if anyone hears? They're afraid of me."

His confidence only increased her panic. "Please, Judge," she begged. Her voice broke. *How could he do this? How could he do this with the court security officers listening? And why didn't anyone come help? They had to be hearing this!*

McBroom's pleas, now mixed with sobs, rose to a pitch that finally appeared to penetrate Kent's stupor. He turned and then abruptly left, leaving her disheveled and alone. She sat down on an exercise bench and wept. A few minutes later, McBroom managed to rearrange her bra and shirt and catch her breath. She walked outside to the command center but found it empty. The officers normally stationed there had abandoned the post. McBroom knew their main job was to protect the judge. Still, she felt angry and betrayed. "They heard what was going on and they didn't want any part of it," she later said.

McBroom rode the elevator back down to the clerk's office. She intended to immediately report the incident to her boss, Marianne Gore, the deputy-in-charge of the clerk's office employees in Galveston, though Kent dispensed most of the orders. McBroom, whose eyes were still reddened by tears, found Gore and requested an immediate meeting.

The woman pulled McBroom inside her private office and shut the door.

"The judge just attacked me," McBroom began, still trying to calm herself with deep breaths. "I showed him the exercise room and some pretty awful things went on up there."

Gore asked if she wanted to make a complaint, heaving an audible sigh. "He's the judge—he's got the lifetime appointment," Gore said. Filing a complaint could put McBroom's job at risk, she suggested. For the first time McBroom was told that federal judges such as Kent were not covered under Title VII of the Civil Rights Act or under other labor laws that, for decades, had given other federal employees a well-defined process on how to report sexual harassment complaints or even file civil lawsuits.

McBroom felt upset and exasperated. She'd never run into a judge like Kent, but every federal judge, she knew, was powerful. All of them had big egos and answered to no one. She didn't know whether it would be wise to formally object if that action was more likely to affect her career than his.

Gore quickly supplied an alternative. They could just talk about the incident off the record and then act as if "the conversation never happened," McBroom later recalled.

On the basis of her own experiences, Gore predicted that Kent would apologize. She said the judge had kissed her, too—once. The supervisor added that she sometimes worried about what might be happening to the judge's secretary, Donna, who daily worked side by side with Kent in an office adjoining his chambers.

Embarrassed and upset, McBroom agreed to try to put the incident behind her.

She left the meeting determined to protect her career—and to avoid any situation that could lead to another unpleasant encounter. At that time McBroom knew nothing about any federal judicial misconduct complaint process, and Gore didn't mention it.

With the attack still fresh in her mind, McBroom found a quiet spot and used her cell phone to call her husband. McBroom's friends considered Rex a stereotypically strong-and-silent type. In his job, Rex sometimes dealt with sexual harassment complaints, and he'd previously expressed concerns about the atmosphere Kent had established. Rex McBroom had seen others cower before Kent even in social settings. He immediately voiced a strong opinion about what she should do now: quit.

McBroom balked. She protested that she should not be forced to forfeit her career in the federal courts because of the indecent behavior of some man—even if he was a federal judge. She assured Rex she could find ways to avoid being alone with Kent. "It doesn't have to happen again," she insisted.

Her husband was unhappy. He told her he hated the idea that he couldn't protect his own wife at her job. It was just the first of many arguments the couple would have about Kent.

The next morning at dawn McBroom set off to meet her running club for their regular Saturday morning workout in the waterfront town of Kemah. It was late August, the hottest month of the year in Texas's humid coastal hothouse. But a gentle breeze was blowing and the temperature had not yet climbed to the day's high of ninety-one degrees. Even on a run, McBroom knew she would not escape reminders of the previous afternoon's attack. One of the people she'd agreed to meet was a court security officer, a man she'd invited to join the group just a few days before. She'd deliberately decided to go ahead with their running plans that Saturday, even though she figured he had been one of the officers who had abandoned her and his post.

As the group gathered to warm up, McBroom decided against an immediate confrontation. Instead, she greeted him with her usual wide smile and waited for an opportunity to speak privately. Her chance came as the runners spread out after their warm-up laps. He was taller than she, a physically fit former police officer, but he shortened his stride to match her pace. She ran slowly—finishing a marathon was always her goal, not marking the fastest time.

As they ran side by side and others faded back or raced ahead, she began by sharing advice she'd gotten from Rex: her husband wanted her to quit her job, she said, and she wondered whether Rex was right.

At first the security officer stayed quiet and looked down at the laces of his tennis shoes. He still had not said much by the time the two completed the first phase of their run by climbing and crossing "the Hill," an arching bridge on busy State Highway 146 that linked the resort village of Kemah to the grittier fishing town of Seabrook. The bridge, which rises seventy-three feet above the Clear Creek Channel, was pretty much the only "hill" that local runners could use to train in the Galveston Bay area, an otherwise flat coastal plain. That day's plan involved running two or three laps over the bridge and then looping back down and around. McBroom enjoyed running the Hill, even though each time her thighs and calves burned.

Both stopped speaking and started breathing harder as they climbed the 4.5 percent grade for the second time, and then headed back toward their cars, parked on the Kemah side of the bridge. Normally, McBroom enjoyed the view from the top of the bridge. She considered the breeze and coastal scenery as a reward whenever she summited the bridge. But on this August Saturday, she barely noticed the parade of vessels traveling the busy waterway where muddy Clear Lake meets the shallow Galveston Bay beyond. Instead, the incident in the exercise room replayed on a mental loop. It had been shockingly violent and too close to attempted rape to dismiss. Her companion's silence seemed to confirm his knowledge.

She tried again to get him to talk as they increased their pace on the final downhill, still side by side. She used the same general language she'd used the day before with her female supervisor. Kent had attacked her in the exercise room and some pretty awful things went on.

Finally, he admitted he'd overheard the struggle.

Adrenaline shot through her that had nothing to do with heat or exertion. The attack had been sexual and frightening, she said. Only the fact that she was breathing deeply in time with her pace helped keep her emotions in check. She was not going to cry.

The security officer brushed her off, suggesting she should confide instead in her female supervisor. He did not want to know details, he said, according to McBroom's recollection of their conversation that day.

"You knew what was going on and you just left me there," McBroom said, her voice sharpened by anger. They were breaking taboos by discussing the judge. Kent always made it clear that his business stayed inside the courthouse. Both she and the security officer knew that "you were expected to do your job and not comment about what you saw," McBroom later said.

The security officer insisted that his primary responsibility was protecting Kent. And he admitted that he felt vulnerable as a court contract worker. Like many other federal court employees in Galveston and beyond, he felt he couldn't risk angering a judge. Court security guards weren't even part of the federal court bureaucracy. McBroom could seek a transfer inside the clerk's office bureaucracy; he and other guards in Galveston were contractors with even less job security.

He was focused on his own survival, McBroom realized. He didn't really care what happened to her. In the hierarchy of the federal courthouse, both lacked power. McBroom had already worked for Kent long enough by then to have heard how other employees with far more years of experience and authority had been exiled by Kent, including Williams, her predecessor. McBroom could understand the guard's fear, but she lost faith in him as a friend.

McBroom returned to work that Monday. Just as her female supervisor predicted, Kent soon summoned her to chambers. She remembers his apology as perfunctory: "I'm really sorry. I hope I didn't make you too uncomfortable. Believe me, it has nothing to do with your job." Kent didn't have to repeat what he'd told her before: he expected her to keep his secrets.

Afterward, McBroom pretended she'd been unaffected and hoped the incident would be a "one-time blip." As she'd promised her husband, she found ways to avoid being alone with Kent. She worked as often as possible in her own office on the fourth floor, two floors below his, and communicated with Kent mostly by phone. On the days that he enjoyed long drinking lunches with buddies, she deliberately ignored his summons. McBroom knew that if she quit her job suddenly, as her husband urged her to do, Kent would provide no reference and would effectively end her career in the federal courts. Beyond that, she feared that he could use his considerable clout to blackball her and ruin her reputation so that she'd never be able to get a job with any law firm in Texas, the state she never planned to leave.

McBroom had seen firsthand how Kent could use his power to punish attorneys with more status, education, wealth, and independence than she had. In late 2002, McBroom had watched Kent publicly humiliate an attorney, Valorie Wells Davenport, who had angered him by requesting delays in two cases after she'd suffered a brain injury. Kent refused to grant Davenport any extra time, accused her of exaggerating her injuries, and dismissed both of her clients' cases, writing an order that described Davenport as incompetent and "mentally ill." In 2003, Davenport lapsed into a ten-day coma that doctors attributed to toxic shock. Davenport recovered. (She continued to practice law until she died in 2014 at the age of fifty-eight.) But her life changed as a result of the coma and damage to her career caused by Kent's public comments, and in an interview, she blamed these outcomes in part on Kent.

Kent had not again attempted to sexually assault McBroom after that ugly afternoon in the exercise room in March 2003, but for the next four years kept up a steady barrage of disgusting jokes and suggestive sexual comments. A couple of times he had also come down to her office and cornered her there for unwelcome "hugs." One office episode had frightened her, though it did not escalate to the level of the 2003 attack. When Kent knew he'd crossed the line, he apologized. And she pretended to believe him. Kent had spells of good behavior: sometimes he stopped drinking and moderated his remarks for months. The respites gave McBroom time to rebuild her self-confidence and to convince herself she could "control" King Kent. Unfortunately, she was wrong.

PART II
The Secret System

CHAPTER 6

The Complaint

Galveston and Houston, Texas, 2007

On Friday, March 23, 2007, when Kent attacked again, McBroom fled his chambers, jumped into the elevator and rode down to the probation department to hide inside a friend's office. Soon her cell phone began to buzz. The federal judge kept calling, but McBroom refused to answer. A carpooler, McBroom was temporarily stranded without her car. So she stayed hidden the rest of the afternoon, avoiding Kent's summons and coworkers' questions. Finally, a colleague broke away to take her home.

McBroom rode quietly during the achingly familiar commute along the Gulf Freeway, a buzzing interstate highway that begins in sleepy Galveston, slices through the heart of Houston, and continues north to Dallas. She stared out the passenger's side window of the SUV at the causeway, marsh grasses, smokestacks, and strip malls that flashed past every day. All of that familiar scenery seemed altered. Inside her, something felt broken. The weekend ahead—and her own future—contracted like a black hole. Her job, her career, and her self-confidence all seemed gone. McBroom began to cry and soon was sobbing so hard she could barely speak.

Her commuting partner didn't ask questions. As a longtime federal employee, she knew the courthouse code of silence as well as McBroom did.

Around 3 p.m., McBroom's cell phone rang. Her best friend, Charlene Clark, was making her daily check-in. Charlene Clark and Cathy McBroom had been inseparable since their girlhood days in Channelview, where they first met at a Girl Scout meeting and later belonged to the same drill team. Clark had been there for McBroom when her parents' marriage failed, and later when McBroom's first marriage failed too. Long ago, Clark had moved away to work in San Antonio, first as an insurance executive and later as a schoolteacher. Despite the distance of more than two hundred miles, the pair remained as close as sisters. For a full decade, Clark regularly phoned to deliver after-school updates. This time as she began babbling about the latest classroom antics, McBroom remained quiet. Clark quickly realized her attentive friend wasn't listening at all.

"What's the matter?" Clark asked.

"We're going to have to find me a different job," McBroom said, speaking over the muffled roar of high-speed highway traffic.

To Clark that background noise sounded wrong. At 3 p.m., she knew that McBroom should still have been at the office—not heading home. She immediately guessed something must have happened with Kent. Clark was one of the few people who knew Kent had made offensive remarks and, at least once, had pinned McBroom in an unwanted embrace in her office. But even Clark didn't know McBroom had suffered two violent sexual attacks at Kent's hands.

McBroom already had called Rex from the courthouse. She still felt spent from the strain of describing Kent's sexual aggression to him. She knew her husband loved her, yet he had expressed no surprise or shock. She felt stung by what she perceived as an "I-told-you-so" attitude. To her best friend, McBroom confirmed in a matter-of-fact monotone that something had happened. She could not discuss it.

Clark reacted to the cold comment with rising panic. "What can we do?" Clark asked. Her thoughts raced. She instinctively knew her friend was in real trouble. Without meaning to, Clark reverted to teacher mode in response to the emergency. She pivoted and lectured

McBroom. "We've got to do something!" Clark said. "You're never going back there! If I were there, I would shake you. You are never going back!"

McBroom listened silently until Clark said, "Maybe we should call the police."

Then the tide of emotions that she'd held back came flooding out. "The police will do nothing!" McBroom hissed. McBroom felt as though she might literally explode. So she took a deep breath and told Clark she intended to keep a planned engagement to meet another girlfriend for dinner at a Mexican restaurant, as a way to end that Friday with some semblance of normalcy. After that she'd go home to face Rex. And tomorrow, she'd decide what else to do.

Still in teacher mode, Clark made McBroom promise to create one last formal document about Judge Kent—a memo that described all of his attacks. "Just get it down! Get it all down on paper and we will figure it out. We will figure out something."

Clark knew even then that she would be part of her friend's fight, though she had no idea how much McBroom would suffer in the grueling lopsided struggle.

A few hours later, Clark called a mutual friend, a nerdier Channelview high school buddy who had been their class valedictorian and now ran a prosperous law practice in San Antonio. Mark Lindow was in the midst of celebrating his fiftieth birthday but broke away from the dinner party to talk. He immediately offered his assistance. As an attorney who regularly practiced in the federal courts, he told Clark that McBroom would need all the help she could get if she planned to take on a federal judge.

McBroom got through dinner with girlfriends by making small talk and by consuming a margarita in an oversized goblet with fresh limes and salt on the rim. It was still early when she drove home, but Rex had already fallen asleep. By the time she managed to rouse him, they ended up having a fight—and she left again to spend the night with one of the friends from dinner, making up some excuse.

The next morning, McBroom rose early to go to her mother's house. As both her mother and Clark suggested, she decided to "get it all down." Then she was going to take some other kind of action. But what?

For years, McBroom had kept dark secrets about Kent locked inside mental compartments along with other troubling incidents from
her girlhood and early adult life. She respected courthouse confidentiality but was starting to crack. She retreated to her mother's tiny office
and stayed there typing into a computer document all day Saturday
and Sunday. She knew she risked both public humiliation and retaliation by daring to denounce a judge. But pouring out her dark memories
felt good. Raw pain and ugliness seeped through the formal language
she used. Her first rough notes screamed with humiliation and anger.
Part of her anguish sprang from the knowledge that all of her carefully
chosen words would eventually force an ugly confrontation.

Years of practice as a legal assistant kicked in, and a request for
an immediate transfer slowly took shape from her emotional raw
notes. She used her own words and language suggested by Lindow,
whom she had contacted that weekend. The final letter, dated March
26, 2007, and directed toward her supervisor, Marianne Gore, was
crafted in educated and legalistic terms, but it branded a federal
judge as a criminal, a repeat attempted rapist. She hated the idea
that others—certainly Gore and other supervisors at the clerk's office
for the Southern District of Texas, and likely Kent and other federal
judges—would see what she'd felt forced to write. She worried that
colleagues and even her own friends and family might hear rumors
and judge her rather than Kent. Whatever the cost, she knew now she
had to escape. "Working in this dangerous and hostile environment
is no longer acceptable for me, as I fear for my personal safety," she
wrote in her request for an emergency transfer. "I hope this entire
ordeal can end with my transfer as requested. . . . Also, please let
me know if there are other administrative steps or formal grievance
procedures that I must follow. As you can imagine, under no circumstances will I allow myself to be alone with Judge Kent."

After several revisions, McBroom printed out her letter late Sunday and read it one last time. Then she handed a copy to her mother,
who'd been waiting two days for some sort of explanation.

Horror surged inside Mary Ann Schopp as she read her daughter's words. "You have to call the police," she said.

"No!" McBroom answered. McBroom recalled how Kent bragged
of talking his way out of tickets. He used retired Galveston police-

men as security officers, and they had looked the other way when she'd desperately needed their help. No one would dare to arrest a federal judge. "Judge Kent has the local cops in his pocket," she told her mother.

She'd decided to act, even though she figured Kent would deny everything. And if she failed, she knew he could use his power to ruin her. On Monday, McBroom rose early to make the familiar trip to Galveston. Instead of her regular commuting partner, McBroom and her mother made the journey in her Nissan Murano along the billboard-lined Gulf Freeway and then across the causeway to Galveston Island, not noticing the glittering water of the bay, the gulls, or the sailboats far below the arching bridge. McBroom remained focused on her mission: Lindow had instructed her to hand-deliver the letter that she'd spent all weekend writing and to take her mother along as a witness.

McBroom parked in her usual spot outside the courthouse. Then she and her mother walked inside the towering gray edifice, where a pair of carved eagles, symbols of freedom, watch over those who enter. McBroom had dressed in work clothes and had applied makeup with her usual care. Guards at the security checkpoint greeted her as if it were any ordinary Monday. She and her mother presented their purses for inspection and passed through the metal detector. Then they made their way up to Marianne Gore's small office.

Gore smiled at McBroom and expressed surprise and pleasure at seeing McBroom's mother, whom she'd previously met at work-related parties at McBroom's own home. If Gore had heard the rumors of how McBroom had fled crying from Kent's chambers, she showed no sign of it.

"This isn't a social call," McBroom said, not smiling back. "I want you to have this." The letter, still in its sealed envelope, passed from McBroom's hand to Gore's. As soon as the transfer was complete, McBroom and her mother turned and left. McBroom wasn't sure she'd ever return to the building.

Within minutes, her explosive words had been carried to the judge's personal secretary, Donna Wilkerson. Wilkerson quickly called Kent on his cell phone and reached him in his car. He was already on his way to the courthouse. At his insistence, she read the letter aloud to him. Wilkerson could hear her own voice, echoing on the judge's speaker phone as she read. She was no shrinking southern belle but found the descriptions in McBroom's letter about attacks carried out by Kent to be both graphic and embarrassing. She was upset that Mc-Broom had broken their pact and provided no advance warning.

Kent listened in his car until Wilkerson finished reading. Then he bellowed out a response. "That fucking bitch . . . It was all consensual between us." No one would believe McBroom, Kent assured Wilkerson. It would be just one woman's absurd accusation against the word of a federal judge.

At that point, Wilkerson had no doubt that Kent would prevail. In all the stories he'd told her, Samuel Bristow Kent always appeared larger than life. He'd been the hero; the brilliant judge whose decisions were always right or the man who, in more personal stories, often felt wronged. No one would believe anyone who denounced Kent, she thought. No one could touch him.

As this battle began, Wilkerson stayed at the side of her judge.

McBroom quickly received the emergency transfer to Houston she'd requested. But she was just getting used to her new job in May 2007 when she was summoned to the office of a powerful judge she had never met: US District Judge Hayden Head Jr., chief judge of the Southern District of Texas. Head was normally based in the coastal city of Corpus Christi but was making one of his periodic visits to Houston when he requested a private meeting.

McBroom felt nervous about talking to Head alone. She assumed he wanted to discuss Kent, a topic she'd been avoiding. She knew colleagues gossiped anyway about her sudden reappearance in a low-profile position in Houston after nearly five years away as the Galveston district judge's case manager. Her new job, the only opening available on short notice, involved entry-level paper pushing, but had the advantage of being a full hour's drive away from Kent's island courthouse. Despite the distance, McBroom continued to battle anxiety, sleeplessness, and nightmares.

Head had a reputation even among other judges for being tough and hardheaded. But Head seemed to be making an effort to appear friendly as he ushered McBroom into a spare office he used in Houston, which held few of the trappings common in other judicial chambers. Then in his early sixties, with thick steel-gray hair, Head peered at McBroom with what seemed like genuine compassion. He quickly dispensed with formalities and gently queried McBroom about her unusual emergency transfer request.

McBroom told Head she'd been wondering about whether to file a complaint with the Equal Opportunity Employment Commission. She was dismayed when Head confirmed that Title VII of the Civil Rights Act didn't apply to the judicial branch. Gore, her supervisor in Galveston, had told McBroom the same thing back in 2003, after Kent's first attack. But McBroom had always hoped that Gore was wrong. How could judges be exempt from laws that banned sexual harassment in the workplace, one of the legal issues they regularly interpreted and enforced through court rulings?

"I just wanted to let you know that there is another avenue," Head told her. "You can file a complaint of judicial misconduct." Head explained that anyone could use a federal statute that was far more obscure than Title VII to file a complaint against a federal judge and have a fair opportunity to be heard. All complaints were secret, he said, but other judges who secretly reviewed would know if she filed one. And so would Kent.

McBroom sat in silence. She felt floored. From what Head was telling her, the law creating a process to report federal judicial misconduct had existed since 1980—nearly twenty years before she'd become an employee of the federal government. Yet McBroom could recall no mention of that law or the complaint procedure in any of the court employee training sessions she'd attended. Gore had not described the process even when McBroom went to her for help in 2003. By 2007, information about misconduct complaints had been added to the Fifth Circuit Court of Appeals website, but McBroom had never seen it.

In fact, a lot of people, including prominent members of Congress, thought that the complaint system for federal judges was broken. In March 2004, a Wisconsin representative named James Sensenbrenner, an independent-minded Republican and long-time court critic, went personally to the hallowed halls of the federal judiciary to complain directly to Chief Justice William Rehnquist about federal judges' lack of accountability. For years, by tradition, chief justices annually invited members of Congress to address the Judicial Conference of the United States—a national policy-making body composed of about thirty federal judges from district and circuit courts nationwide and headed by the Supreme Court chief justice. The gatherings tended to be budget-focused and businesslike under Rehnquist. The balding Wisconsin native was well-known among colleagues for his ability to create consensus and his dislike of long meetings. Congressmen who addressed the gathering, often leaders of key committees, were expected to provide brief updates on pertinent issues like lagging judicial salaries, the huge backlog in federal cases, or the seemingly endless delays in filling court vacancies. Instead, Sensenbrenner shocked the gathering by blasting judicial leaders with a barrage of criticism.

An independent thinker and multimillionaire, Sensenbrenner was then the chairman of the House Judiciary Committee. Over the years, he had taken the role of house manager (essentially a prosecutor) in the judicial impeachment both of US District Judge Walter Nixon in the 1980s and of President Bill Clinton in 1990s. And he was, in a way, part of the federal judicial family too—his father-in-law had served as a US district judge. Sensenbrenner began his speech diplomatically enough by reflecting on our nation's proud history and the strength of the US Constitution. He wanted the judges to know that he respected both the power and the independence of the judiciary. "As we all know, the Founders of our Republic drafted a blueprint for self-government that has endured for well over two centuries because it delineated a balanced relationship among the legislative, executive and judicial branches," he said, according to a copy of the 2004 statement released by his congressional office. "The tripartite system engrafted into our Constitution has served as a model charter of government for nations around the world; and is the proud birthright of every American. . . . While sometimes rivalrous, relations among the branches have been free of the destructive impulses that have proven ruinous to other nations."

Then Sensenbrenner launched into a detailed critique of what he saw as acts of deliberate misconduct by some federal judges, who he claimed had abused their guaranteed lifetime appointments to defy laws. He had personally filed complaints against two different federal judges. One, Sensenbrenner alleged, had lied under oath in his testimony to Congress about having broken federal sentencing guidelines. The other, Sensenbrenner claimed, had illegally leaked confidential government documents to an Associated Press reporter. And yet neither of his complaints had ever been properly addressed or investigated under the system in which other federal judges were supposed to both review and act on them, he said. Sensenbrenner thought that the secret review system had allowed chief judges in some cases to ignore or whitewash serious misconduct. "Article III judges have been given lifetime tenure precisely to be better able to withstand such criticism, not to be immune from it!" he said. He was disappointed not just in one or two cases but in the entire 1980 Judicial Conduct and Disability Act, the statute that had given federal judges the power to oversee complaints about their peers.

Chief Justice Rehnquist, characteristically, said little in response. The famously taciturn chief justice was known to cut debates short even in complex court cases. But he later reacted in a dramatic way to what he called "some recent criticism about the way in which the Judicial Conduct and Disability Act of 1980 is being implemented." Rehnquist tapped the popular, bike-riding Associate US Supreme Court Associate Justice Stephen Breyer from Boston to chair a comprehensive study of the system.

Breyer had the advantage of having worked for years as a staff attorney for the Senate Judiciary Committee, where he had worked well with senators from both parties. The group, formally known as the Judicial Conduct and Disability Act Study Committee, was quickly nicknamed the Breyer Committee. The group was composed of judicial insiders: Breyer and four other judges from both district and circuit courts and the chief justice's own administrative assistant. The committee had no funding of its own, but received help from the staff of the Federal Judicial Center, a government agency that handles research and education for the judicial branch. Breyer chaired the committee, which spent the next two years studying disciplinary statistics, reviewing a sample of cases, and privately interviewing chief judges about their role in the secret system.

Sensenbrenner was getting impatient. For decades prior to the approval of the Judicial Conduct and Disability Act, the staff and members of the House Judiciary Committee had shouldered much of the responsibility for reviewing and responding to complaints about federal judges. He saw the judiciary's twenty-five years of efforts to investigate and discipline its own members as having a "mixed record." Tired of waiting for a report from the Breyer Committee, he began in 2005 to push for the appointment of an inspector general for the courts. Senator Chuck Grassley, considered a powerful advocate for whistleblowers, also separately pushed for an IG for the federal courts. Many political science professors and federal judges responded to the proposal with outrage. Some saw the congressional efforts as an attack on judicial independence, prompting even Associate Justice Ruth Bader Ginsburg to react with alarm. In a speech to a gathering of the American Bar Association, she called the proposal "a really scary idea" that "sounds to me very much like [how] the Soviet Union was" under Stalin.

By 2006, Sensenbrenner also was angry about reports that the Ninth Circuit chief judge, Mary Schroeder, and its judicial council had repeatedly failed to investigate a formal complaint or take any action against a senior district judge, Manuel Real, based in the Central District of California. Some of the nation's most respected jurists have used their judicial independence to pen courageous and historic landmark decisions, such as desegregating the nation's schools, outlawing capital punishment for juveniles, and protecting cherished constitutional rights. Real was such a judge. An octogenarian with decades on the bench in Los Angeles, Real was a former federal prosecutor who, as judge, had desegregated the elite Pasadena school system by ordering busing back in the 1970s.

But Real also had a serious case of "robe-itis." Critics saw him as a crusader who often bent or broke federal law and court rules to attack people he disliked or to help people whom he favored, believing himself immune to any consequences. Though Real was considered kind and compassionate off the bench, a 2003 misconduct complaint alleged that he had morphed into a judicial monster in one case by repeatedly abusing his power to assist a probationer who was also an attractive young divorcée. The complaint described how Real had defied federal court rules to take over a bankruptcy matter involving Deborah M. Canter (who was on probation in an unrelated case) and then made rulings that financially benefited Canter. Federal court records showed that Real systematically refused to rule on any motions in the case filed by the other side, legal representatives of her ex-husband's family trust that owned a luxury condo. Real's actions allowed Canter to live rent-free in the condo for three years. Yet Schroeder, chief judge from 2000 to 2007, and her colleagues seemed reluctant even to investigate Real, a former chief district judge who served in the US Naval Reserves during World War II. Instead, Schroeder sought to quietly resolve the matter behind the scenes.

Then one particularly powerful Ninth Circuit judge, Alex Kozinski, spoke out to criticize the process. In an unusually long published dissent issued in September 2005, Kozinski lambasted his colleagues' delays both in investigating and acting on the misconduct complaint against Real, one of his longtime judicial colleagues and a fellow resident of the exclusive LA suburb of Rancho Palos Verdes. "I believe the judge who is the subject of the complaint in this case has committed serious misconduct by abusing his judicial powers," Kozinski wrote in a thirty-nine-page dissenting opinion that read more like a position paper. He seemed to be sending a warning to Schroeder and other jurists that failure to take action against Real could have broader consequences. The opinion said: "Disciplining our colleagues is a delicate and uncomfortable task, not merely because those accused of misconduct are often men and women we know and admire. It is also uncomfortable because we tend to empathize with the accused, whose conduct might not be all that different from what we have done—or been tempted to do—in a moment of weakness or thoughtlessness."

Soon after Kozinski's dissent was issued, Schroeder reopened the Real matter, and formed a special investigatory committee. In a closed meeting, the Ninth Circuit judicial council subsequently voted to reprimand Real on November 16, 2006, more than three years after the complaint had been filed. But even then the reprimand was kept secret. It became public only after Henry Weinstein, an attorney and enterprising *Los Angeles Times* reporter, managed to obtain a copy for a front-page story published on December 23, 2006.[1] Separately, Sensenbrenner had convened a hearing that same year in an attempt to impeach Real that was ultimately unsuccessful. Real would never be forced to relinquish his bench. When he died in 2019, at the age of ninety-five, Real was the nation's longest-serving active federal judge.

Meanwhile, in September 2006, the Breyer Committee issued its long-awaited report on the federal judicial misconduct complaint system. The committee, which lacked any special funding, said it had been unable to review all two thousand complaints filed between 2001 and 2005. Instead, members examined a sample of all the complaints and then reviewed seventeen matters that it considered "high-profile" in greater detail. The report concluded that although the system worked "properly" for the "vast bulk" of routine misconduct matters, five out of the seventeen high-profile complaints were "problematic," including the handling of the complaint against Real and the two complaints filed against federal judges by Sensenbrenner. The error rate in those seventeen heavily publicized complaints of close to 30 percent (five out of seventeen) was "far too high," the report said. The committee also issued broader criticisms of the secret system. Generally, too few people knew the process existed and the rules were inconsistent from one circuit to another. Standardized rules should be developed, the report said.

The Breyer Committee report and its recommendations had national impact. For the first time court leaders in all federal court circuits began to post information about the complaint process on circuit websites. Some chief judges, such as Kozinski, also began to post orders they wrote in response to complaints, though those orders almost never contained the names either of judges or of complainants. The Judicial Conference of the United States moved to adopt standardized Rules for Judicial Conduct and Disability Proceedings in 2008. Previously, each circuit had made up its own rules (though there were model "illustrative" rules).

But other recommendations were ignored. Neither Congress nor the courts clarified the responsibilities of chief judges, all of whom handled limited reviews and investigations quite differently. Some chief judges revealed a lot in rare disciplinary orders and others, almost nothing. No changes were made in the law to require additional disclosure of judges' misconduct, even when rare disciplinary action is taken. The 188-page report said nothing about the thorny issue of sexual harassment, nor why it typically went unreported, though Breyer was certainly aware of that issue. He had been a DC circuit judge when its bias task force was active in the 1990s.

But problems persisted. Too often, as the law professor and author Lara Bazelon later wrote, judges misused the secret misconduct complaint process by "sweeping the embarrassing allegations under the rug, issuing cryptic dismissal orders or responding with sanctions that are inadequate or ill-justified."[2] In an analysis of problematic cases like Real's, Bazelon identified several systemic issues. Generally, the secret system gave more rights to judges than to the complainants: it discouraged disciplinary action and allowed chief judges to ignore conflicts of interest. Judges "have a tendency to let their accused colleagues off the hook out of favoritism, undue sympathy and a desire to protect the reputation of their circuit."[3] For all those reasons, complainants such as Cathy McBroom, were unlikely to prevail.

A formal man who retained a military bearing, Head gave McBroom an overview of the judicial misconduct complaint process in their May 2007 meeting. Head knew the system well. As chief district judge, he served as a member of the national body overseeing court policy, the Judicial Conference of the United States. Part of Head's role as chief judge involved dealing informally with personnel problems involving judges concerning matters that did not rise to the level of generating a formal misconduct complaint. Although Head didn't mention it to McBroom, he'd heard complaints about Kent before, albeit not of a sexual nature. One Galveston attorney had formally complained about Kent's demeanor. Others had groused about how he ignored potential conflicts of interest. In 2001, the previous chief district judge, George Kazen, had ordered the transfer of eighty-five cases away from Kent's court, the decision that publicly embarrassed Kent. Many believed the order came in response to criticism or a behind-the-scenes complaint that Kent too often ruled on cases involving a law firm run by his closest friend, Richard Melancon.

A sense of honor and of the duty to protect others ran particularly strong in Head's family. He was a fourth-generation Texan, the son and grandson of prominent lawyers and the great-grandson of one of the state's earliest frontier-era judges. Head was a US Navy veteran, and his dad, Hayden Head Sr., had been a fighter pilot in World War II. Head lost his father, who was also an attorney, when the ex-fighter pilot crashed his Cessna in 1988 on the family ranch. A ranch foreman arrived at the burning cockpit in time, but Head Sr. had urged the foreman to rescue his wife first, and ultimately, she was the only survivor.

In their meeting, Head told McBroom that he was making no recommendation about whether she should pursue a formal complaint. In fact, he warned that the process, though confidential, would subject her to additional scrutiny from both judges and other court officials, especially if there was a formal investigation. Her complaint itself would be kept secret under the 1980 federal law, but Kent would immediately be told and could respond privately and defend himself. Head had his own sizable ego, which was not surprising for a chief district judge with a presidential appointment. Even other judges described Head as tough and hardheaded, yet McBroom thought Head seemed kind and patient as he explained what seemed like a bizarre and complex process.

There was, Head added, no guarantee that any judicial misconduct complaint would formally be investigated. Very few complaints ever got that far. If her complaint was investigated and taken seriously, then an even larger group of court officials and judges would get involved—the entire judicial council of the Fifth Circuit, Head told McBroom. He didn't tell her that statistics produced by the federal courts showed that the odds of any judicial disciplinary action taking place were incredibly low. Year after year, 97 to 98 percent of the complaints filed against federal judges nationwide were dismissed without any kind of formal investigation.

After learning about this potentially explosive option, McBroom thanked Head and left his office. Instead of returning directly to work, she ducked out an emergency exit door to take refuge in an empty public stairwell. She'd begun to visit that gray limbo between floors whenever she needed privacy. The thick walls of the Sugar

Cube blocked cell phone signals in many halls and offices. But Mc-Broom had discovered that her signal remained strong in certain stairwells, which were among the few spots she could speak without risk of being overheard. She used her cell phone to reach Lindow, the attorney she knew from high school.

Lindow, who practiced in federal courts, responded quickly—and negatively. He warned McBroom that filing a formal judicial misconduct complaint was a risky move that might have no effect on Kent and might only anger other judges. Head might have ulterior motives and be using her. Even though the process was confidential, Lindow believed that news about her complaint would inevitably leak to the press and that Kent would vigorously defend himself. McBroom later recalled him telling her, "Somebody is wanting you to pull the trigger on this guy. You have absolutely everything to lose and nothing to gain. Your name is going to be plastered all over the papers. It's going to be horrible and he's going to win."

McBroom listened to his advice, her emotions fluctuating between anger and fear. She returned to her desk, avoiding colleagues' gazes. Once again she felt exposed to courthouse speculation and was overcome by anxiety. The afternoon seemed endless. That night McBroom spent hours awake, pondering her options. She felt irritated, though, whenever she replayed her old friend's advice to forget filing a judicial misconduct complaint. She conjured up a vision of Lindow as he'd spoken to her, likely relaxing with his feet up on a desk, and being attended by his own attractive secretary.

A few days later, she called Head in Corpus Christi with a final question: "Do you think if I file this complaint any other judge would ever hire me as a case manager?"

Head responded without hesitation. "I think an honest judge would."

Ultimately, McBroom felt compelled to act. She figured she "would have a very small voice in the system. But I felt I would never be happy with myself if I didn't do it." She filed her complaint on May 21, 2007. In a three-page letter, McBroom briefly described how Kent had assaulted her in the federal courthouse in both 2003 and in 2007, focusing on the worst of a series of incidents. She also described how she'd previously shared details of the 2003 attack with a female supervisor but had received no support. In many ways, the complaint was a continuation of her emergency transfer request: Mc-Broom again claimed that she believed Kent had targeted other court employees as well. She reported that she'd learned through conversations that her supervisor, Gore, and the judge's secretary, Wilkerson, had been forcibly kissed and manhandled.

McBroom knew that both women would be angry and likely would deny the allegations, but she felt compelled to explain that Kent's misbehavior already had affected others. "Judge Kent has engaged in conduct that is *prejudicial to the effective and expeditious administration of the business of the courts*," McBroom wrote in her May 2007 complaint, quoting directly from the 1980 federal judicial misconduct law. "His position requires him to preside over cases involving sexual discrimination and harassment and he is guilty of engaging in that very behavior himself. His use of alcohol exacerbates the problem. I am convinced that I am not the only person that has been a victim."

McBroom knew that her experience had already taken a serious toll on herself and on her family, and she felt ready to accept whatever consequences came from filing a complaint. Her complaint said: "I want the Fifth Circuit, Judge Kent and the members of the Judicial Council to know that inappropriate behavior such as this can destroy a person's dignity and sense of self-worth. Because I personally felt that remaining silent was like granting permission, I decided to come forward with the truth."

The decision of whether to investigate McBroom's complaint would not be made by Head. As a chief district judge, he could offer advice and act informally, but federal law dictated that the chief circuit judge would decide whether to investigate any formal complaint. Consequently, McBroom's complaint went directly to Edith Jones, chief judge of the Fifth Circuit Court of Appeals, the second largest regional appellate court in the country both in terms of the number of judges and size of the population served. Jones was a formidable ultraconservative figure known in Houston and far beyond for her sharp mind and equally sharp tongue. Jones had been a trailblazer as a woman jurist, though she repeatedly had been rejected as a nominee for the US Supreme Court as being *too* conservative. She was despised by some feminists for having ruled against women plaintiffs in both reproductive rights and sexual discrimination cases.

With Jones alone deciding whether to formally investigate a complaint that boiled down to a he-said-she-said case, it seemed unlikely that McBroom could ever prevail.

CHAPTER 7

Her Honor

Houston, 2006–2007

In 2006, Edith Hollan Jones became chief judge of the Fifth Circuit Court of Appeals and thus the overseer of an enormous circuit based at a leafy 1900s historic square in New Orleans. Jones was a thirty-five-year-old mother of two when she was nominated to the bench by President Ronald Reagan in 1985. She'd become a judicial celebrity in twenty-one years as one of the most outspoken women conservative federal judges. Though millennials have never given her a nickname like "Notorious RBG," aka the late Associate Justice Ruth Bader Ginsburg, Jones has earned her own group of followers among young conservatives. On and off the bench, Jones has a colorful and confrontational style. In her abundant YouTube lectures and law school appearances, Jones often wears a tight smile and a single strand of pearls as she rails against the "administrative state," abortion rights, and what she calls the government's "gradual and silent encroachment" into Americans' personal lives. She also has a well-documented dislike of inserting judicial powers into matters involving gender or sex.

As chief judge, Jones became a kind of queen. She oversaw important hearings and set rules and finalized the budget on top of all her other duties. In addition, she managed all reviews of complaints of misconduct filed against other federal judges in her turf, which included Texas, Louisiana, and Mississippi. In a far from public fashion, Jones and other chief judges in twelve circuit courthouses from coast to coast quietly vetted complaints on top of carrying large caseloads. It was a time-consuming and thankless task for which they received no additional training or funds. The entire process depends heavily on powerful chief judges, like Jones, who act as gatekeepers for complaints in all of the federal circuits.

For decades, Professor Arthur D. Hellman, of the University of Pittsburgh Law School, one of the leading experts in that disciplinary system, has called for clarifying rules about the responsibility of chief judges, and for amending the law to require more transparency in the process, especially in high-profile cases. Chief judges wield huge control over the secret system. They can use their powers to initiate a complaint themselves—or to completely ignore even an egregious public abuse of power. They alone, assisted by small circuit staffs, decide whether to conduct "limited reviews" of some of the most serious complaints filed by others. Chief judges also decide when to form an investigatory committee. And chief judges later decide what to disclose in the public orders they write in response to misconduct complaints—at least, those orders are supposed to be public. In reality, however, copies of most of the hundreds of orders that Jones and other chiefs have written each year in response to judicial misconduct complaints remain hidden away in obscure archives in circuit courthouses in New Orleans, San Francisco, Chicago, Philadelphia, and Washington, DC. Though some circuits post more recent disciplinary orders on court websites, the orders are not indexed and are often difficult to decipher. Hellman is one of the few experts who has spent years collecting obscure orders stashed in court archives nationwide in his own efforts to demystify and describe the secretive process, though disciplinary orders regarding complaints can often be reviewed by making a special request to the circuit or administrative court staff.

Many years' worth of orders signed by Jones and other chief judges are warehoused at the main Fifth Circuit courthouse in New Orleans. (Many more disciplinary orders from circuits nationwide are stored in the Washington, DC, Administrative Office of the US

Courts.) Nationwide, most complaints relate to allegations made by prisoners or disgruntled litigants, court disciplinary statistics show. Some complainants submitted bizarre rants, according to an on-site review of dozens of orders that were issued during Jones's seven-year tenure as chief. One man claimed a federal judge had seized his homes, "sold them and pocketed the money," and then had ordered that he find "$100,000 more in CASH, take it to a friend of the Judge's and they would make everything go away."[1] This complaint seemed to reflect the litigant's distorted interpretation of a normal bankruptcy proceeding.

Jones, like all federal chief circuit judges, was personally responsible for reviewing every complaint—even those she found outlandish. It was up to chief judges and their busy staffs to decide whether facts presented in any complaint added up. A few regular complainants contributed so many repetitive rants that Jones wrote "WARN" in capital letters to instruct her staff to warn such complaint writers to cease wasting her time or else risk sanctions. Jones had the power to conduct a "limited inquiry." Even legitimate issues raised in complaints could often be settled by reviewing paperwork or through quiet conversations. But chief judges were generally required to form an investigatory committee to examine allegations involving judicial misconduct when the facts were considered "reasonably in dispute." Even if she formed an investigatory committee, though, Jones was not obligated to divulge any findings to the public. The options for action were limited but included recommending that the offending judge undergo counseling, make apologies, or take a leave of absence or other corrective action. In very rare cases an investigatory committee formed by a chief judge might recommend that the circuit judicial council vote to issue a formal admonishment or even a reprimand.

Few complaints came from attorneys or federal court employees— men and women with a front-row seat on courthouse misconduct. But in Jones's first year as chief, at least three lawyers complained about judges who had allegedly acted unethically or abused their power, according to information included in her dismissal orders. One attorney argued that he had been unjustly disbarred from Texas federal courts, as "one of the many targets" of a particular jurist's "personal hatred." Another claimed that a judge had angrily rejected a recusal request and improperly presided over a case involving the wife of the judge's close friend. A third alleged that a powerful jurist had displayed erratic, abusive, and bizarre behavior—one day entering the courtroom singing and dancing to Johnny Cash and another day deliberately insulting a litigant's wife as well as threatening to expel a lawyer who dared to roll his eyes. For Jones, none of that behavior qualified as judicial misconduct, least of all the judge belting out Cash classics. "The court's dignity does not appear to have been unduly compromised," she wrote in a dismissal order.

Jones signed all her orders in handwriting that slanted to the right and displayed loops from penmanship learned as a Catholic school girl in a wealthy and nearly all-white San Antonio suburb. Almost none of the orders signed by Jones (or by other chiefs) held the name of either the accused judge or accuser. The names were all kept secret except in very unusual cases.

Complainants are often generally described in those orders as a "prisoner," a "litigant," or, more rarely, as an attorney or a federal government employee. Almost no complaints that Jones reviewed were described as having been filed by a federal court employee, such as Cathy McBroom. Jones clearly had a hard time believing the allegations in the judicial misconduct complaint McBroom filed in May 2007. The complaint might have seemed like another fabrication, except that McBroom included details about specific federal employees as witnesses who had seen the aftermath of both attacks. McBroom, an eight-year veteran, also named two other court employees who, she claimed, had been targeted. And she alleged that court security guards had actively protected the judge. Back in her attorney days, Jones had specialized in bankruptcies and civil disputes. She had no experience investigating criminal matters or sexual misconduct. But it would fall to her to lead the investigation and decide how to proceed.

Even in 2007, most of America's circuit courts were still dominated by white men, though Jones was the Fifth Circuit's second female chief judge. Her predecessor, Chief Judge Carolyn Dineen King, serving from 1999 to 2006, had been another trailblazer. King became a circuit judge in 1979, nominated by President Jimmy Carter, who fulfilled a campaign promise to help diversify the courts.

Way back in 1934, Florence Allen, a suffragist, had become the first woman appointed to a lifetime federal judgeship. In 1958, she became the first female chief judge of a circuit. But during her lifetime, Allen remained one of a handful of women on the circuit courts. When Carter entered office, only six women served among the nation's five hundred district and circuit judges. Largely through Carter's nominations, forty women had earned lifetime judicial appointments by 1981. But they still accounted for less than 10 percent of all federal judges, according to information compiled by Lynn Hecht Schafran, the long-time director of the National Judicial Education Program to Promote Equality for Women and Men in the Courts.

At first, Carolyn King, then known as Carolyn Dineen Randall, balked at accepting Carter's support for a circuit court appointment, not wanting to abandon her prosperous Houston law practice. Later, King and two other Carter nominees, Mary Schroeder, of the Ninth Circuit, and Stephanie Seymour, of the Tenth Circuit, all became circuit chiefs. (And an upstart feminist named Ruth Bader Ginsburg joined the DC Circuit as a Carter appointee.) Over the years, King has been candid in oral histories and speeches to women's legal groups about her struggles with sexism. As a top Yale Law School graduate in 1962, she'd struggled to find a job in Houston and believed she had been denied a position as assistant US attorney because of her gender. Even after becoming a top-producing corporate attorney, she had been passed up repeatedly for partnerships in her firm—a senior partner had told her he expected her to resign after becoming a mother. Instead, she left the firm and launched her own practice.

In the 1980s President Ronald Reagan made more steps to diversify the conservatives on the courts, nominating Sandra Day O'Connor as the first female member of the US Supreme Court in 1981 and Jones to the Fifth Circuit four years later. (Carter's appointment of Ginsburg as circuit judge later paved the way for her subsequent nomination to the high court.) Though gender obviously played a role in Jones's appointment, she herself was no fan of affirmative action. Jones sometimes boasted about how she'd received the offer to become the first female partner at her Houston law firm while on maternity leave with her second child. In a profile published in 2012, she was quoted as saying, "The biggest 'obstacle' I had to overcome in ascending the ladder to partnership at Andrews, Kurth, Campbell and Jones was myself, as I attempted to manage career and family."[2] As a circuit judge, some of Jones's rulings were considered hostile to claims of sex discrimination.

Jones's reputation as a foe of sexual harassment claims was solidified in 1988, when Jones and King participated in a three-judge panel for an appeal brought by Susan Waltman, a Louisiana native who'd filed a lawsuit against her former employer, a paper mill in the town of Bossier. The case, *Waltman v. International Paper*, drew national attention as part of legal efforts in the 1970s and 1980s to extend caselaw and workplace rules under Title VII of the Civil Rights Act, to protect women from sexual harassment on the job.

Discrimination on the basis of "race, color, religion, sex and national origin" had already been banned in 1964 under Title VII. Under that law, employment could not be denied on the basis of gender alone. But that protection had first been extended to ban sexual harassment in the workplace in 1977, in an opinion issued by the DC Circuit Court of Appeals, only after Paulette Barnes, a former employee of the federal government, sued the Environmental Protection Agency. Barnes presented proof that her EPA position was eliminated after she repeatedly refused to grant sexual favors to her boss, who happened to be the head of the agency's office of Equal Employment Opportunity and thus its point man for running antidiscrimination and hiring programs.

It was in 1986—twenty-two years after the passage of Title VII— that the Supreme Court finally issued its first landmark anti–sexual harassment opinion. In that case, a woman named Mechelle Vinson presented evidence that her predatory boss at a branch of Meritor Savings Bank in Washington, DC, had repeatedly extracted sexual favors from her and other employees during the four years she worked for him first as teller and later as assistant manager. Unlike Barnes, Vinson had felt compelled to succumb to sexual pressure from her boss in order to keep her job and detailed a long-standing pattern of verbal and sexual abuse, including episodes of what she described as being forced to submit to sex inside a vault. Vinson was fired after she took sick leave to escape him. The landmark ruling in *Meritor Savings Bank v. Vinson* established that creating such a "hostile work environment" was illegal, a violation of the Civil Rights Act. The decision established that no employer could permit a "hostile workplace," in which supervisors could extract sexual favors in exchange for work or employment benefits.

The challenge for lawyers involved in subsequent sexual harassment cases—including a matter involving a papermill worker named Susan Waltman in Louisiana—was figuring out exactly what patterns of on-the-job behavior fit the courts' evolving definition of a "hostile workplace."[3]

The first time Susan Waltman heard her coworkers' obscene propositions broadcast over an intercom occurred soon after she started her job at International Paper, one of the largest employers in Bossier, a suburb of Shreveport on the banks of the Red River in northwest Louisiana's piney woods. Young, attractive, and ambitious, Waltman loved her hometown and initially hoped the mill would be the place to build a career. Her aspirations faltered after one of her supervisors suggested Waltman have sex with a coworker, then "pinched her buttocks with pliers" and tried to shove "his hands in her back pockets." Waltman tried to ignore coworkers' crude comments and offensive stunts, but three different managers she approached did little to help. One supervisor told her simply to "expect this behavior working with men." Another manager called a meeting and read the company anti-harassment policy aloud—an effort that backfired when, right after the lecture, another coworker "grabbed Waltman's breasts and directed a high-pressure hose at her crotch." Meanwhile, anonymous tormentors kept drawing penises and scribbling sexual graffiti on the walls, slipped her dirty notes, and strung used tampons on her employee locker. Waltman continued to complain, but attacks only turned more violent. One contract worker grabbed Waltman and held her while another stuck his tongue in her ear. Finally, a different coworker threatened to "cut off her breast and shove it down her throat" and in a subsequent episode, picked her up and held her dangling thirty feet above a stairwell.

In all, Waltman endured a string of ugly episodes for two and a half years before she finally quit. Then she found a civil rights lawyer, Laurie Lyons, who helped her file both a formal complaint and a federal lawsuit in the district court in Shreveport, in which she alleged she'd been forced out because of a long pattern of illegal sexual harassment in the workplace. However, the district court judge rejected her claim, finding insufficient evidence of a "hostile workplace," the standard for protection under Title VII. At that time, some federal judges believed that the only type of behavior that should be banned was if a supervisor demanded sex in exchange for work or other employment benefits, not the kind of pervasive harassment Waltman faced from multiple aggressors. The key questions were: How bad did that behavior have to be? How much did a woman have to complain and to document those complaints in order to establish a pattern of illegal behavior? And under what circumstances was the employer liable for harassment?

Lyons quickly appealed the ruling from the US district court in Shreveport to the Fifth Circuit US Court of Appeals. In October 1988, Lyons and her husband, who doubled as her law partner, drove five hours southeast along the winding blacktop highways that traverse the state's thick forests and swamplands to New Orleans, where Lyons would deliver her very first oral argument before the Fifth Circuit. Lyons learned early that the panel hearing the case would feature three Texas-based judges: Carolyn Dineen King, Edith Hollan Jones, and a seventy-nine-year-old senior jurist named William Homer Thornberry. Lyons considered herself both a conservative and a feminist and had initially been thrilled to draw two women for a three-judge panel in a sexual harassment case. She figured her biggest obstacle would be Thornberry, the lone man. Then a friend who practiced regularly in the Fifth Circuit told her that Thornberry, an ex-congressman appointed to the bench by President Lyndon B. Johnson, would be open-minded and reasonable. Edith Jones would be the problem.

On the eve of the argument, October 3, 1988, Lyons and her husband, both longtime New Orleans Saints fans, went to see their team play a hated rival at the Superdome. The game was still tied when Lyons left to get a good night's sleep for her big day in court, so she missed the dramatic forty-nine-yard field goal that gave her team a big win. For her, winning a victory for women in court was more important.

The next morning, Lyons donned her most severe suit and drove to the John Minor Wisdom Court of Appeals Building. The Italian Renaissance Revival courthouse, ringed with columns and statues, had a granite base topped with marble. Built in the early 1900s, it had been renamed for Wisdom, who in the 1950s and 1960s, had bravely stood with the so-called Fifth Circuit Four, a group of white male jurists who issued landmark opinions that mandated school desegregation and voting rights for African Americans despite widespread opposition in the Deep South.

Lyons hoped her case could help improve civil rights for women. A crowd of about twenty—mostly lawyers, law clerks, and a leader from the Washington, DC–based Equal Employment Opportunity Commission—gathered to hear arguments inside the ornate space, featuring paneling carved from the Louisiana gum tree and hung with shimmering bronze chandeliers. All rose when the three judges entered. The jurists took their seats in oversized office chairs on an elevated dais and stared down as Lyons began her oral argument, which was limited to thirty minutes. Lyons opened by saying that she believed that her client had been subjected to virtually every type of sexual harassment imaginable.

"Well, your client wasn't raped!" Jones interjected in a sharp tone that sounded more like her native Philadelphia than Texas, where she'd spent most of her life.[4]

Behind her, Lyons heard audible gasps from sympathetic members of the crowd. Feeling rattled, Lyons went on to emphasize how a parade of coworkers had propositioned Waltman, poked her with pliers, and grabbed her breasts.

Jones interrupted again to insist that the male coworker who'd grabbed Waltman's breasts had apologized and that he and others were Waltman's "friends."

Thornberry, who had been silent, reacted by blurting out, "That doesn't matter."

Lyons took a breath and told herself to stay calm. Perhaps Jones's pointed questions were part of a sincere effort to understand the facts of the case. Back and forth comments were common in oral arguments. But Lyons soon realized that Jones "was just going to attack," launching arguments of a type that Lyons would have expected from International Paper's attorneys.

At one point, Jones declared that it was impossible to make male employees want to have females around. "Well, you know we would not tolerate this kind of behavior in the Fifth Circuit! But what can you expect when you've got a plant full of men?" Jones said.

Judge King visibly reacted, swiveling her huge chair and turning her back on Jones. "That sounds like the same arguments we heard in the 1960s on race discrimination," King said.

Jones interrupted so often that Lyons's time expired before she finished. Without being asked, King granted Lyons additional minutes. By the end of the day, Lyons began to hope that King and Thornberry might consider her arguments. But Jones was clearly on the side of the mill, convinced that elements such as graffiti could never be interpreted as personal or harassment, even though one message read "Sue is a Whore" and another specified in a vulgar way the sexual services Waltman supposedly provided.

In 1989, King and Thornberry issued a decision (voting 2–1 against Jones) that awarded Waltman a new hearing based on evidence of what appeared to be pervasive harassment prohibited under Title VII. In the aftermath, International Paper settled the case. Waltman used the money to return to school and later became a veterinarian in Bossier.

In contrast, Jones wrote a long dissent declaring that in her view nothing short of rape or serious injury should be considered illegal workplace harassment. "We have so little social consensus in sexual mores nowadays that . . . it is impossible generally to categorize unacceptable sexual etiquette," Jones wrote. She declared it "impossible to eradicate sexual conduct from the workplace without unthinkable intrusiveness."

In 1990, Jones's youthful vigor and her unflinching ultraconservatism put her on President George H. W. Bush's short list for the Supreme Court. Raised Catholic, Jones vigorously opposed abortion. As a jurist, she'd repeated Justice Byron White's dissent in *Roe v. Wade* in which he labeled the ruling in favor of abortion rights an "exercise of raw judicial power," which earned her supporters on the right. But her nomination drew strong attacks from women's groups, in part because the Waltman decision that Jones had so zealously opposed gained mainstream support.

The Waltman case was part of a series of decisions that helped establish the definition of a hostile workplace, though legal disputes have continued and protections have eroded. In 1993 the Supreme Court, in an opinion written by O'Connor, ruled in *Harris v. Forklift Systems Inc.* that harassment had to be sufficiently "severe or pervasive" to constitute a hostile workplace. Then, in 1998, in response to another pair of cases, the Supreme Court ruled that employers could limit their liability by demonstrating either that they took "reasonable care to prevent and correct promptly any sexually harassing behavior" or that the plaintiff "unreasonably failed to take advantage of any preventative or corrective opportunities provided by the employer."[5]

Outside the courts, the concept of sexual harassment gradually became embedded in American workers' minds. Soon nearly every US private company with more than fifteen employees (the size to which employment laws generally apply) established policies and offered training. Experts continue to disagree on whether those programs really worked to prevent sexual harassment or simply to limit employers' legal liability.

Jones's long opposition to claims of both gender bias and abortion rights made her the kind of ultraconservative powerhouse that supporters of the Federalist Society would later successfully promote for other court openings. But Jones's opinions proved too polarizing for her to win a Supreme Court nomination either from George H. W. Bush in the 1990s or from subsequent Republican presidents. Though her fans kept mentioning her as a potential Supreme, feminists kept quoting Jones's comments in the Waltman case. Jones won other supporters elsewhere. She remained a popular speaker for campus chapters of the Federalist Society, which ultimately founded chapters in accredited law schools nationwide. Jones appeared at elite law schools across the country, including Harvard, Penn, and her alma mater, the University of Texas.

The University of Texas School of Law occupies a gleaming white complex perched on a hill on the north side of a forty-acre campus and serves as the undisputed educational center of Lone Star State legal power. Hung along its halls are the portraits of its most illustrious graduates, and one of these is Edith Hollan Jones. In 2001, students who were members of the Federalist Society gathered at lunchtime in an auditorium to eat pizza, consume Cokes, and hear Jones speak. Most of the mainly conservative crowd clapped politely as she spoke. But around that same time, Jones had raised the ire of opponents of the death penalty with another controversial dissent in which she had urged rejecting the appeal of a death row inmate, Calvin Burdine, despite evidence that Burdine's elderly defense attorney repeatedly dozed throughout his trial. During her speech, a handful of activists from the Coalition to End the Death Penalty extracted pillows from backpacks and pretended to snooze in a silent sleeping protest.

Jones ignored the nappers as she shared some of her favorite legal history, touching on famous figures from President George Washington to Kenneth Starr, a native Texan and former DC Circuit Court of Appeals judge who was celebrated by many conservatives as the special prosecutor who'd investigated Clinton in the 1990s. In her speech, Jones didn't dwell on allegations against Clinton, who had been impeached in part for lying under oath in responses to a federal sexual harassment case filed by a former Arkansas state employee. But Jones expressed her general dislike of all sexual harassment lawsuits. She declared those cases to be a waste of federal judges' time and resources. Litigants would be better off getting a "second job instead of filing suit," she said.

Clearly, Jones's speeches and rulings made it seem exceedingly unlikely that she would take any interest in Cathy McBroom's 2007 judicial misconduct complaint involving allegations of sexual harassment and physical sexual abuse in a workplace run by Judge Samuel Bristow Kent.

By the time Jones began to review McBroom's complaint, Jones had known Kent for more than three decades. They were nearly the same age: both were born in 1949 and attended UT Law, finishing only six months apart. Back in the early 1970s, when Jones and Kent roamed its halls as students, UT Law classrooms were dominated by men. Vietnam War veterans sat beside left-wing antiwar protesters with shaggy hair and muttonchop sideburns. Among the small cadre of female students and the tinier band of female professors, many supported the Women's Law Caucus, a fledgling group of feminists who helped convince Texans to ratify the Equal Rights Amendment in 1972. Jones didn't join. She opposed the ERA.

Classmates recall that Jones, a graduate of Cornell University, seemed unfazed by the competition in UT Law's type A male–dominated courses and clubs. Neither Jones nor Kent frequented either the regular campus antiwar protests or the beer busts, where, according to the yearbook, law students "quaffed suds" and "floated kegs" out on the lawn. Neither showed up in yearbook photos of a 1974 Halloween party during which one student wore a Nixon mask and flashed the then president's trademark double peace signs, while another turned out as a Playboy Bunny with rabbit ears, a cotton tail, hot pants, and black tights. Instead Jones focused on polishing her prose as a member of the law review, joined the (then) tiny Texas Republican Party, dated an older student, and finished near the top of her class when she graduated in May 1974.

Nearly 250 law firms visited UT Law that year to recruit. Most firms sent male representatives. Despite mandates to end gender and racial discrimination incorporated in the 1964 Civil Rights Act, some recruiters made it clear they had no jobs for women. Nationwide, law firms routinely refused to promote women associates to partnerships in the 1970s, a practice that remained legal until a 1983 Supreme Court decision written by O'Connor in a little-known case, *Hishon v. King & Spalding*. Her decision confirmed that "Title VII protections applied to the partnership decisions of law firms as well as to the hiring and promotion practices of corporations," Justice O'Connor later wrote in an article for the New York Bar Association.[6] Entrenched discrimination against promoting women to partnerships and the lack of women jurists appointed or elected to state courts made it harder for them to gain experience needed to win federal court appointments.

Despite those obstacles, Jones quickly received a job offer and later became the first female partner at the Houston firm of Andrews, Kurth, Campbell and Jones. Former classmates say they might even have picked Jones as a future federal judge.

Fewer would have bet on such a bright future for Kent. Dark-haired and square-jawed, Kent stood out as larger and more handsome than most of his classmates in the yearbook photos but earned average grades. Kent was already married by the time he attended law school; he mowed lawns and worked in the library to support his family, leaving little time for extracurricular activities. Still, Kent could be charming and charismatic, and he had an impressive memory and a knack for maritime law. He left law school early, passed the bar exam, and in 1975 accepted an offer from one of the state's oldest firms, Royston, Razor, in Galveston.

Jones's and Kent's trajectories started to align more as they pursued their careers in the law. As attorneys, both Jones and Kent won early praise from legal peers and from Republican Party leaders. Both were nominated and confirmed as federal judges while still in their thirties. Both belonged to interlocking elite legal circles: "Texas Exes" (graduates of UT) and Article III judges whose lifetime appointments were constitutionally guaranteed. As judges, Kent and Jones wrote opinions that were widely circulated by law school professors and legal commentators. But unlike Jones, Kent carved out centrist or even populist stands. In fact, he'd often been openly angry when some of his decisions were overturned by Jones and her allies in the Fifth Circuit's ultraconservative wing. The two jurists were not friends.

As chief judge, Jones had the authority to dismiss the misconduct complaint against Kent outright if she'd found it "frivolous." McBroom's complaint might have seemed to Jones like just another outlandish rant, except that McBroom provided details of Kent's alleged misconduct and named potential witnesses too. As a court employee since 1999, she had worked with other powerful federal judges and also had other coworkers who could vouch for her. As part of her limited review, Jones determined that the facts were "reasonably in dispute." Jones formed a three-judge Special Investigatory Committee, and she shared the complaint confidentially with

Kent. Kent's response was never shared with the public—or with McBroom. He later publicly proclaimed through an attorney that all contact with McBroom had been "enthusiastically consensual." Jones certainly wanted to believe that Kent, a fellow federal judge, was telling the truth.

Many circuit chief judges complete their seven-year terms without ever forming a single investigatory committee or taking any disciplinary action, according to statistics federal courts provide about secret probes. (Unanswered is whether some of those judges ignored serious complaints or simply never receive any that merited investigation.) Earlier that same year, however, Jones had formed a committee to investigate US District Judge G. Thomas Porteous Jr. of New Orleans. A whiskey-drinking fixture at the Big Easy's riverboat casinos and a former state judge, Porteous had long been accused of being a player in a corrupt clique of Jefferson Parish lawyers and judges who acted in league with a powerful bail bondsman. Some of his friends already had been convicted of criminal charges, though prosecutors had never filed charges against Porteous. Instead prosecutors filed a formal judicial misconduct complaint. That meant he, too, was Jones's problem.

Even for Jones, a meticulous workaholic, simultaneously running two misconduct investigations on top of her other duties would be difficult, though she hired outside attorneys to assist. Ultimately, one of her investigations would be considered a model, and the other, a flop.

CHAPTER 8

A Botched Investigation

Galveston and Houston, Texas, 2007

Donna Wilkerson had been working for US District Judge Samuel Kent in the Galveston courthouse for six years when her boss received via Federal Express a formal copy of the misconduct complaint Mc-Broom filed in May 2007. Kent was unsurprised—Judge Head had phoned ahead to alert him that a complaint had been filed, Wilkerson later said. Wilkerson was immediately summoned into Kent's office, where Kent loudly insisted that McBroom was lying again, just as she had done in her request for an emergency transfer. Then he told Wilkerson to read the complaint aloud. As she read, Wilkerson felt growing shock: the complaint not only described Kent's two attacks on McBroom but also included excerpts from the conversation Wilkerson shared with McBroom at the Seawall café. Wilkerson "admitted at that time she had experienced the same abuse from [Kent] on a regular basis, but that she could not afford to leave her 'good deal.'" McBroom's complaint also alleged that Wilkerson and Gore had covered up Kent's misconduct and that Wilkerson had specifically requested to keep their conversation about Kent's misbehavior secret because Wilkerson did not want to lose her "rice bowl"—"Judge Kent was allowing Wilkerson to work extremely reduced hours and still receive full-time pay."

Wilkerson was furious. She remembered their conversation differently and believed that McBroom had violated a pact they'd made to keep each other's confidences and the oaths they'd taken as federal employees to safeguard court confidentiality. *This is going to expose me too*, Wilkerson thought. McBroom had to do what she had to do. But Wilkerson would not participate.

The wedge that McBroom's complaint drove between the two was common in workplace reports of sexual harassment. Many American women experienced some form of sexual harassment—unwanted physical contact, propositions, offensive and suggestive remarks, or even sexual assault in their careers, survey data from the Equal Employment Opportunity Commission shows. Yet women—and men, too—remain reluctant to report sexual harassment, because of embarrassment, fear of retaliation, or of not being believed. The Southern District of Texas's own policy supposedly protected complainants and witnesses against retaliation related to sexual harassment complaints. But neither McBroom nor Wilkerson believed that either of them would be protected as a participant in a judicial misconduct matter.

Kent leaned even more heavily than usual on Wilkerson that summer as the Fifth Circuit's investigatory committee began. H. Alston Johnson III, a Baton Rouge-based attorney hired by Jones and her committee, had already begun contacting court employees to interview them. All were sworn to secrecy as witnesses in the judiciary's ongoing top secret judicial misconduct investigation of Kent. Kent had long been blurring the lines between his personal and professional talks with Wilkerson, and now he began calling his secretary at home at odd hours. Sometimes he called at midnight or at 2 a.m. to say that his life was over and that he was going to lose his bench. Mixed with the oddly timed outbursts were suggestions about what Wilkerson should tell the investigatory committee of judges and Johnson, the attorney assisting with the probe. Kent suggested that McBroom was a flirt and a liar. He also suggested that Wilkerson might admit he had hugged and kissed her once.

In July 2007, the judges on the judicial investigatory committee and their attorney arrived in Galveston to question Wilkerson in person and under oath in a closed hearing. Wilkerson knew many lawyers but asked no one for advice before facing the investigatory panel in a conference room at a beachfront hotel. Its members asked directly about Kent's behavior and about McBroom's allegations. Her inquisitors included Edith Jones, the formidable chief judge of the Fifth Circuit, and two other judges, Wilkerson later recalled, though the transcript of the secret hearing has never been released. Under questioning, Kent's loyal secretary stuck to a pared-down version of events. Wilkerson acknowledged the judge "kissed and hugged her a couple of times." The contact was unwanted. The witness statement remained secret, but Wilkerson later recalled saying, "Yes, he was inappropriate with me, but it stopped. I handled it."

That statement hid the full truth. Though Kent did stop his advances "off and on," Wilkerson much later admitted to federal criminal investigators that Kent had intermittently propositioned and groped her on the days he'd been drinking over a period of five years, according to 2009 federal court and congressional records related to the Kent case. Sometimes he came behind her chair and grabbed her breasts. Other times he pressed her into a hug and grabbed her bottom.

There had been episodes of full-on sexual assault that Wilkerson did not mention to the judges at the July 2007 meeting either. But investigatory committee members had not pressed her for details of Kent's "inappropriate behavior" and did not seem all that interested in his behavior toward her, Wilkerson thought. Instead, they wanted to know all about McBroom. How did she act at work in Galveston? How did she dress? Was she a flirt? Though Wilkerson supported her judge, she found their questions odd. Later, Wilkerson wondered why no one asked whether Kent, her boss, had pressured her not to testify or whether she'd like a transfer. "No one ever came to my rescue," she later said. "No one asked me: 'Do you want to be reassigned?'"

That month, some of the same investigatory committee members also traveled to the Hyatt Hotel in downtown Houston to question McBroom privately. McBroom arrived with her husband, Rex, who'd taken a day off to accompany her. Nervous and unsure about what to expect, the pair rode an escalator encased in the hotel's towering glass atrium and found their way to a small conference room.

Minutes later, two judges entered through another door. US Circuit Judge W. Eugene Davis, a bespectacled gray-haired jurist, was based in Louisiana and had served on the court of appeals for twenty-four years with Jones. US District Judge Sarah S. Vance was based in the Eastern District of Louisiana courthouse in New Orleans along with Porteous. Both wore street clothes instead of their usual black robes. They introduced themselves, as did the panel's attorney, Alston Johnson III. Three chairs were set up for jurists at a conference table, but one seat remained empty. Davis and Vance had traveled about 350 miles from New Orleans for the meeting. But Chief Judge Jones, whose office was only blocks away, was inexplicably absent.

Johnson took the lead in questioning. A senior partner with his firm, Johnson had handled depositions and arguments in hundreds of civil cases, though Johnson generally specialized in insurance and regulatory matters. During his law professor days, Johnson had defended the firm he later joined in a racial discrimination case, but it's unclear whether he had ever handled a sexual harassment matter, and he did not practice criminal law. At the time of Judge Jones's investigation, Johnson's firm was appealing a decision of a maritime case from Kent's court, a matter that might have made it awkward for the firm if he played a role that embarrassed or angered Kent. (Long after his work in the confidential probe had ended, Johnson declined requests to respond to questions about his work in the Kent case or his firm's potential conflict of interest.)

Jones's decision as chief judge to hire an attorney who lacked specialized training in investigating sexual harassment or sexual assault still stuns Lynn Hecht Schafran, an attorney who for four decades has trained federal and state judges on how to tackle gender bias issues. "That is so far wide of the mark of how that [investigation] should have been conducted," she said. "It's safe to say—there were firms that could have investigated it. There were attorneys who specialized in sexual harassment; there's no question that the right kind of people were out there." In their secret hotel hearing in July 2007, Johnson and the two judges inquired directly about McBroom's professional and personal relationship with Kent. They wanted her to describe the outfits she wore to work and to exercise. Were her clothes revealing? They asked whether she'd dated other court employees and whether she'd cheated on her husband. They wanted to know about outings to happy hours at local clubs and restaurants.

McBroom was perplexed by the investigators' seeming obsession with her wardrobe. On the day she'd been attacked in 2007, she remembered wearing a pair of black pinstriped pants and a blue sweater with a black cardigan over the top. She'd also been carrying a pile of court orders for Kent to sign. *What did that have to do with anything?* When members of the panel got around to asking about details of the March 2007 attack in Kent's chambers—which McBroom already had described in her testimony and in her written complaint—they asked McBroom and her husband to stand and provide a demonstration. They wanted McBroom to guide her husband so that he could physically reenact the way Kent had grabbed and groped her.

Rex McBroom had heard all those sordid details directly from his wife. But being asked to perform a kind of play in which he depicted the judge he abhorred was horribly awkward—and emotionally painful. Though Rex had accompanied his wife and continued to support her, the McBrooms were still living apart. Now the McBrooms felt they were being compelled to recreate an event whose trauma had strained their relationship to the extent that both feared their marriage would not survive. Rex was so reserved that communication had been a serious problem in the marriage. He wanted Kent held accountable but disliked feeling forced to perform before such an audience. He thought judges overseeing the probe had assumed a self-protective posture. "It seemed like a secret society. . . . They were trying to interrogate her to protect their secret society," he later said.

By the end of the summer, Johnson had completed his part of the probe. He interviewed at least a dozen witnesses, including court security officers and other employees who interacted directly with McBroom after the incidents she described that took place in 2003 and 2007. Several had seen or heard things that could have corroborated her allegations, but several later said they believed that Kent would read their supposedly confidential statements and retaliate. Even coworkers who liked McBroom generally stuck to answering questions in a fashion that some later described as "narrow" or "slanted."

Johnson tracked down a few former court employees too, including the former law clerk who described being forcibly French-kissed by Kent in the late 1990s, when she was a twenty-six-year-old. But curiously, Johnson never interviewed two senior law enforcement officials, both employees of the US Marshals Service who'd worked closely with Kent for years and who'd heard about that incident and witnessed other episodes of misbehavior.

A few months later, a retired homicide detective who worked for McBroom's attorneys conducted his own investigation. He tracked down twenty witnesses, only half of whom had previously been interviewed. One witness told him, "The lawyer who was asking the questions for the judges did not ask the right questions. . . . The whole building had a defeatist attitude about the judge and everyone was afraid of him."[1]

Outwardly, Kent remained confident. His version of events appeared to be that McBroom was lying and had exaggerated a few caresses and comments. Some staffers overheard Kent loudly tell a US magistrate judge based in Galveston about his version of McBroom's unusual departure. In interviews, former and current court employees later summarized his version of the conversation as: "Cathy and I have been having an affair. She came to me and said she made this mistake and told me that I needed to fix it and I told her, 'Hell no, I'm not fixing it.' And Cathy told me, 'If I am going to get into trouble, then you are going to get into trouble.'"

In the misconduct matter, Kent hired a powerful female attorney, Maria Wyckoff Boyce, to represent him. Boyce was a partner at Baker Botts, a legendary Houston law firm founded in 1840 when Texas was an independent republic. The judge's legal bills were never disclosed. Indeed, there's no way for the press or the public to "follow the money" to learn about the judicial misconduct system, which generally covers legal fees for accused judges but not for complainants, even when the alleged victim is a federal court employee. The attorneys who represent judges in misconduct matters have far greater access to documents and a right to privately respond to allegations, while complainants usually remain in the dark.

Judge Jones wanted everything wrapped up fast. Within 90 to 120 days, Jones expected the panel of three judges that she led to finish the probe, review any information collected by Johnson, and complete a full report with secret findings and recommendations for consideration by the members of the Fifth Circuit Judicial Council, the circuit's policymaking body of judges. The council would then hold a secret hearing and vote whether to take action—or not.

Eventually Jones summoned McBroom for a brief meeting in her neat office in the Houston federal courthouse located inside an enclave reserved for circuit court business. It felt to McBroom like being summoned to the principal's office. In a dispassionate and somewhat disapproving tone, Jones told McBroom that the judicial council planned to meet in New Orleans that September and might need her to testify. It was possible that Kent's attorney might want to cross-examine McBroom under oath, Jones said.

McBroom quietly asked if she needed her own lawyer.

"I could not advise you on that," was Jones's reply.

As McBroom returned to her less elite space in the same courthouse, she again felt overcome by a now-familiar wave of panic. The stress of dealing with the assault, changing jobs, and pursuing a formal complaint pressed down. McBroom was like many other victims of sexual abuse: Many struggle with anxiety or depression, and may develop post-traumatic stress disorder. Health and mental health bills uncovered by insurance and lost wages are common concerns for victims according to data collected by the Centers for Disease Control and Prevention. In order to quickly master her new job and avoid losing pay, McBroom had continued to work full-time all summer without taking any real breaks. She'd been seeing a counselor and took pills to sleep and to combat anxiety attacks that continued nearly six months after her transfer.

Filing a complaint about Kent had only increased the pressure on McBroom, as it so often does for sexual assault victims who report abusers. In surveys of survivors of domestic violence and sexual abuse, Judith Lewis Herman, a Harvard University–based psychiatrist, has found: "Victims who file civil or criminal complaints are subject to the rules and procedures of a complex legal system, where their mental health and safety may be of marginal concern and where the potential for re-traumatization may be high."[2] The US Constitution provides more protections for the accused, but guarantees little or none for the complainant. As Herman has written: "Victims understand all too well that what awaits them in the legal system is a theatre of shame."[3]

That September, McBroom felt like she was "falling apart." Her daughter was about to deliver a baby, but uncertainty and stress clouded even the happiness over the anticipated arrival of her first grandchild. She worried that she might be summoned to testify and miss the birth.

The prospect of testifying before an entire council of federal judges felt terrifying. McBroom feared for her career, and for her mental stability. She needed help but lacked money for an attorney, and Jones had made it clear that the federal government would provide no legal assistance. She mentioned her dilemma to a colleague, who suggested contacting Rusty Hardin, a nationally known criminal defense attorney based in Houston. Hardin often argued aggressively in complex federal cases and didn't seem like a man who'd be easily intimidated, her lawyer friend thought. McBroom requested an appointment with Hardin, whom she'd never met and could not afford to pay.

Dressed in a blue three-piece suit, McBroom arrived on September 12, 2007, at the law firm of Rusty Hardin & Associates, on the twenty-second floor of a cluster of skyscrapers in the Houston Center complex. She entered a waiting area with a domed, stained-glass ceiling, and then was escorted to Hardin's private office. Hardin ushered her into a room with a long brag wall filled with framed front-page stories and legal awards. He asked her to call him Rusty and invited her to sit in an overstuffed chair. McBroom's perch had a sweeping view of downtown Houston, including the domes and squares of the Harris County Criminal Justice Center, where Hardin had gotten his start as a state prosecutor years before. Joining them at the table were Hardin's top federal attorney, Joe Roden, a savvy Marine and Gulf War veteran who grew up in East Texas; the firm's seasoned investigator, Jim Yarbrough, a retired Houston homicide detective; yet another attorney; and a paralegal.

For the next hour, McBroom painfully repeated the events that had forced her to request an immediate transfer, prompted her to separate from her husband, and still kept her awake at night. They all listened as she struggled to summarize the judge's bizarre behavior, the two most serious attacks, and her attempts to alert court authorities. McBroom still felt too traumatized to repeat the details aloud. Instead, she numbly handed over paperwork: her formal judicial misconduct complaint and the transfer request she'd written in the immediate aftermath of the March incident. The more emotional request letter included a minute-by-minute summary of her final encounter with Kent.

Hardin collected the documents, told McBroom he'd like to help, and later escorted her out. Then he returned to the table where his team members waited. The firm had handled many high-profile white-collar crimes and was about to accept a complex case defending a prominent major league baseball pitcher accused of illegally using performance-enhancing drugs. Still, to different degrees, all those present felt shocked by what McBroom had told them about a federal judge.

Hardin already had accepted the story as true. He thought that McBroom wore the haunted look of a sexual assault victim, still so familiar from his state prosecutor days.

"Well," Hardin asked, leveling a stare so intense it felt like being poked. "Do you believe her?" He knew Kent and figured the judge had other victims, but he sought a consensus before agreeing to take a case that would pay nothing and could cost the firm all the goodwill they'd ever earned in federal courts.

Everyone agreed McBroom seemed to be telling the truth. And they all wanted to help. "I don't care if he is a federal judge," Hardin said loudly, letting his emotions show. "We can't let him get away with that. That is just wrong."

Later McBroom got a follow-up call from Hardin, confirming his support. She suddenly felt better than she had in months. She had never expected that any attorney would back her against Kent, especially not for free. The day after the meeting, on September 13, 2007, McBroom's granddaughter Sara was born, and McBroom managed to will away her anxiety long enough to celebrate. "It was so wonderful to be believed by someone. It was such a relief," she later said.

In his years first as a prosecutor and later as a defense attorney, Rusty Hardin had come to dislike judicial corruption so intensely that he'd volunteered to help pro bono on some matters as special counsel for the State Commission on Judicial Conduct. But that commission only reviewed complaints about state judges—men and women who were mostly elected to judicial jobs, from lowly justices of the peace to members of the State Supreme Court. In Texas, as in many other states, some of the most serious judicial ethics investigations ended with closed hearings that featured witnesses and resembled trials. But if disciplinary action was taken, all records and transcripts generally became public. Given his experience with state disciplinary hearings, Hardin told McBroom that he felt certain the Fifth Circuit Judicial Council members would personally want to hear her testify, given the criminal nature of her allegations against Kent. Hardin also assumed that he, as her attorney, would be allowed to address the council.

But Hardin and his seasoned team knew almost nothing in September 2007 about the federal judicial complaint system. In fact, few people in the United States had any experience with it. Only a handful of people seemed able to decode the federal judicial disciplinary process. Professor Arthur Hellman, of the University of Pittsburgh Law School, described problems with the insider review process in several articles for law journals, including one he called "Judges Judging Judges."[4] Lara Bazelon, a law professor at the University of San Francisco, analyzed the system in an article titled "Putting the Mice in Charge of the Cheese." They and others have urged reforms and greater transparency in the inconsistent and highly secretive reviews. "In an institution as large as the federal judiciary, which counts more than a thousand judges among its members, it is not surprising that there are a few bad apples. Nor is it surprising that if, left unchecked, those few could exact a cost disproportionate to their number by damaging the integrity as a whole," Bazelon wrote. "Unfortunately, thorough investigations and appropriate sanctions are not always forthcoming because federal judges, whose job is to police their colleagues, often fail to do so."[5]

At a closed meeting in New Orleans, Fifth Circuit Judicial Council members were asked to review and vote on the investigatory committee's secret report and confidential recommendations on Kent. All deliberations were conducted and votes cast behind closed doors. To Hardin's astonishment, McBroom was never called to testify, nor was he allowed to attend. Neither got to read or rebut Kent's statements. The hearing records and the investigatory committee's secret report were never disclosed to McBroom or to the public.

In the closed meeting, a majority of judges voted to impose a rare public reprimand for Kent. Like everyone else, McBroom first saw that reprimand on September 28, 2007, when a brief public order signed by Jones appeared on the Fifth Circuit website.

Federal judicial disciplinary orders are rare. But in those unusual and important cases, chief judges generally include a fairly detailed summary of the complaint and the findings of any investigation in their orders. In Kent's case, almost no information was provided. The order featured a terse and cryptic description. It said Kent had committed "sexual harassment" toward an unnamed court "employee" and added that the investigatory committee also had reviewed "instances of alleged inappropriate behavior toward other employees." Kent was reprimanded for conduct further described in a confidential report, which "shall not be disclosed." After four months of paid leave and some counseling, Kent would return to the federal bench, though he would be reassigned to Houston instead of returning to his beloved island.

In a series on the dysfunctional federal judicial misconduct system, the *Houston Chronicle* later found that Kent was one of only seven judges to receive any formal disciplinary action in response to more than six thousand complaints filed from 1999 to 2009. According to federal court statistics, one judge was punished anonymously, shielded from shame by the same peers who voted secretly for disciplinary action.[6]

Kent's punishment seemed more like a paid vacation to McBroom and other critics: he would receive four months off with full pay— around $55,000 in paid leave, calculated on the basis of his $165,000 annual salary. Kent was a public figure. His peers had reprimanded him. But he retained his powerful lifetime appointment. And no one really knew what he had done. The language used in the disciplinary order was so vague that it left many wondering whether Kent did anything wrong at all. Had he hurled a few misplaced f-bombs? Pinched someone's butt? Told off-color jokes? A few weeks later, Kent hired Dick DeGuerin, a prominent criminal defense attorney in Houston. DeGuerin, who had special access as the accused judge's attorney, provided the only description of the investigative report ever revealed to the public. In subsequent interviews with the press, DeGuerin said that the report identified issues with McBroom's credibility and found "no probable cause" to believe that any crime had been committed by Kent.[7]

Lara Bazelon, among others, was critical of the Fifth Circuit Judicial Council's decision-making process in the Kent case, which kept "McBroom in the dark while providing Kent with access to the very information it denied her. . . . The judges appeared to be playing favorites—siding with a privileged colleague against his far less powerful accuser."[8] Furthermore, the council's failure to divulge even basic information about the complaint in its reprimand appeared to violate the federal judicial misconduct statute, which states, "Unless contrary to the interests of justice, each such order shall be accompanied by written reasons therefor." In the information void, the *Houston Chronicle* and other media ended up becoming the authority on the misconduct case.

The Exposé

Houston Chronicle *Newsroom, September 2007*

I panicked when I saw the reprimand posted on the Fifth Circuit website while working in the *Houston Chronicle* newsroom late on another busy Friday afternoon. Harvey Rice and I had been investigating McBroom's allegations for months. A lot of the statements we had gathered were provided off the record or on background because so many people were afraid of Kent—and of Jones. Now we rushed to publish whatever we could to avoid being scooped by national media and bloggers who were now swarming on the explosive story of a federal judge who'd been disciplined for sexually harassing unidentified members of his staff. We knew the shocking facts were worse than the dry legalistic summary supplied by the circuit court. We reported for the first time that a case manager named Cathy McBroom had been seen fleeing from Kent's chambers in March 2007 "crying and visibly upset."[1] And we knew she had never returned to her Galveston office, instead requesting an immediate transfer and filing a formal complaint.

We were now convinced that McBroom's allegations involved at least one sexual assault, and I worried about including her name in the story. As part of its code of ethics, the *Houston Chronicle* generally withholds the names of sexual assault victims, unless they have agreed to be identified. So, I called Hardin. He told me that Mc-Broom was already convinced that she could not keep her identity secret. I still worried that the story would likely make McBroom's life worse, especially if she was still dealing with the psychological effects of being sexually assaulted. But I also thought the public had the right to know about the serious allegations she and other women were making against a federal judge with a lifetime appointment.

We knew that some of our sources, including Felicia Williams, Kent's former case manager, had testified before the judges' secret investigatory committee. Williams told me she'd shared three specific incidents with the panel, including the time Kent propositioned her. She considered Kent's punishment too light. "It seems like maybe a slap on the hand," Williams said. "It's not going to mean anything to him." Our story also quoted experts who described Kent's reprimand as incredibly vague. All of the experts agreed they could not recall any other federal judge ever being disciplined for sexual misconduct at all. Indeed, Kent was the first.

That first story posted that same day. Though more complete than anyone else's, it still felt like a failure to me. We could not report what I believed to be the shocking truth: a federal judge had been accused of sexual assault inside a federal courthouse, and other judges who voted to reprimand him had hidden the serious nature of those allegations.

There was no paper trail to follow. The complaint itself was not public, nor was the investigative report nor even the budget. Everything about the probe seemed locked down. None of the federal judges would talk about their secret investigation. I called Judge Jones, whose staff referred me to Joseph St. Amant, a senior staff attorney for the Fifth Circuit based in New Orleans. St. Amant said that under federal law neither Jones nor Kent could comment about the misconduct matter. "But what was their obligation if Kent had actually committed a crime against a federal court employee?" I asked. St. Amant said only, "That's a complicated matter."

I remained obsessed with how I could reveal the specific allegations behind Kent's reprimand. Back in May 2007, McBroom and all current federal court employees involved as witnesses in the judicial investigation process had been ordered to remain silent by Jones and other court officials investigating the complaint. For that reason, I'd focused on tracking down former court employees who could still talk. But surely McBroom had told someone else about what happened before receiving that order? Two months separated the date of the alleged attack and the date she filed the complaint.

The following week, I called someone who could relay a message to McBroom. "I'm not asking for an interview," I said. Then I made my pitch. I didn't see how anyone whom McBroom told in the immediate aftermath of the attack could face legal consequences for doing an interview (unless they, too, were federal court employees). "Under the First Amendment, her friends and family have freedom of speech like all Americans, even if she's been ordered to stay silent," I said. "And if Cathy McBroom was sexually assaulted and the judges who investigated Kent reprimanded him only for undefined 'harassment,' I figure her mother, her best friend or other family might *want* to talk." Then I provided my direct work and cell numbers.

A few days later, I received a call from a woman who identified herself as Mary Ann Schopp. Her voice quavered. She'd never spoken to a reporter before. "I'm Cathy McBroom's mother," she said. "What do you want to ask me?" Gradually, Schopp began to explain how Kent had attacked her daughter not once but twice inside the courthouse. The call didn't last long, but Schopp confirmed dates and facts about two different incidents. Before hanging up, Schopp also provided a phone number for Charlene Clark, McBroom's best friend.

I quickly reached Clark, who naturally expressed concern about granting an interview in which she might publicly accuse a federal judge of a crime. What protection from Kent could I offer? It was an excellent question. I told Clark that she didn't seem to be legally barred from discussing the allegations, given that she was not a judicial employee (and especially since her friend, McBroom, had spoken to Clark prior to filing any formal complaint). Her story matched up with Schopp's account. In the first of several interviews, Clark told me that she believed the 2003 and 2007 attacks were only the worst in a series of at least ten incidents during which Kent had forcibly cornered and caressed McBroom or made inappropriate sexual remarks at work.

Finally, I had two on-the-record sources I needed. On November 11, 2007, I published an investigative story for the *Houston Chronicle* that revealed to the public for the first time that McBroom alleged that Kent, a federal judge, had touched her under her clothing and tried to force her to perform a sex act inside the courthouse in March 2007.[2] I shared how McBroom had reported a previous attack by the judge in 2003, but had received no help from a supervisor. I also described Kent's behavior toward two former court employees I'd found: He'd grabbed and French-kissed a law clerk and crudely propositioned Williams. In a phone interview, the law clerk verified the allegations but asked not to be identified by name. For years, she told me she'd never spoken about the experience, even with her husband. Williams also said she had never previously shared stories about Kent's misbehavior out of loyalty and out of fear that Kent would retaliate. It was true that Williams had been involuntarily transferred and demoted by Kent, but she remained a very credible source: She was praised both by other court officials and prosecutors who had been her bosses and had worked for the federal government until her retirement in 2006, after thirty-three years of service.

After leaving Galveston, Williams also had befriended McBroom. "I need to relay how Cathy and I felt threatened due to [Kent's] power and authority and were always concerned about our positions and knew we could be dismissed at a moment's notice," Williams told me. "Since [I] no longer work for him, I feel more comfortable talking but will always feel the emotional pain."

I knew that my story, entitled "How Far Did This Federal Judge Go?," would likely embarrass McBroom, who remained a federal court employee, but that first investigative story also brought her unexpected support. Two days later, on November 13, 2007, three members of Congress—the ranking Republican and Democratic leaders of the House Judiciary Committee—held a press conference expressing outrage and calling for new investigations based on the *Houston Chronicle*'s detailed account of Kent's misconduct. "The recently publicized charges against United States District Judge Samuel Kent are shocking and cause grave concern for all of us," said the statement co-signed by committee chairman John Conyers Jr., a Michigan Democrat; courts subcommittee chairman Howard Berman, a California

Democrat; and ranking member Lamar Smith, a Texas Republican. Though written in politician-ese, their bipartisan message was clear: they strongly suggested that the Fifth Circuit Judicial Council had erred. Powerful congressmen had publicly declared that they believed McBroom's complaint merited further investigation—and a criminal probe. They called on McBroom to file a criminal complaint with the US Department of Justice. Furthermore, the congressmen calling for action were the same men who wielded the power to impeach Kent, when and if that became necessary.

Within days, McBroom's attorneys privately wrote to both the Fifth Circuit Judicial Council and to Michael B. Mukasey, then attorney general of the United States, requesting reconsideration of McBroom's complaint and a criminal probe. They enclosed copies of McBroom's transfer letter, her complaint, and the *Houston Chronicle* story.

CHAPTER 9

A Corrupt Judge

Pennsylvania, 1930s, and New Orleans, Louisiana, 2007

Legal scholars who have documented the darker side of America's courts know that for over two centuries nearly all the best-known federal judicial scandals—some seventy congressional investigations, fifteen impeachments, and sundry prosecutions and resignations—have involved jurists who took bribes or committed other corrupt acts. Some accepted gifts or cash from high-rolling attorneys or sleazy crime bosses that they failed to report, while others lied under oath to conceal their misdeeds. But signs of racial or sexual misconduct tended to be overlooked. Sometimes, even the most corrupt of the nation's politically connected federal judges could survive. For more than a century, none went to prison.

Back in the 1930s, US District Judge Albert W. Johnson converted his appointment on the Pennsylvania Middle District Court into a lucrative family business by blatantly dispensing bankruptcy appointments to friends and family and by soliciting bribes directly too. In 1931, Johnson founded the Tea Springs Lodge, an exclusive preserve mainly for the judge, his family, and friends of the court. Fifty-one members received court appointments that earned them more than $265,000 in fees, more than $4.2 million in 2021 dollars. A grand jury and a subcommittee of the House Judiciary Committee spent fifteen years investigating. But no Pennsylvania attorney seemed willing to help "clean up the most corrupt situation that has existed or could possibly exist in any judicial district," lamented Representative Carey Estes Kefauver, the crime-fighting Tennessee lawmaker who ran the congressional probe as a member of the House Judicial Committee. Johnson eventually became the first Article III federal judge ever to be indicted, and he resigned from office. But criminal charges were dropped and he went free after two key government witnesses refused to testify.

Johnson's antics were later chronicled in a 1962 book, *The Corrupt Judge*, by an attorney, Joseph Borkin, who summarized foibles of flawed federal judges over nearly two centuries. Johnson became Exhibit A for how even "corrupt and venal" federal jurists sometimes seemed immune from punishment.[1] Over the years, the House Judiciary Committee struggled to untangle complex corruption complaints in dozens of cases involving corrupt or crooked jurists, Borkin argued in his book. That judicial disciplinary system, for years overseen by various members of that same house committee, became further stretched as the judiciary grew over two centuries from only a handful of judges in colonial times to more than a thousand judges with lifetime appointments, including both those who serve as active judges and those who have taken senior status but still hear cases. The 1980 Judicial Conduct and Disability Act, passed by Congress and which enabled judges to judge one another, was meant to boost the involvement of chief judges and judicial councils in determining remedies or punishments for errant peers. But the House of Representatives retained its investigation and impeachment powers for the most serious cases.

Separately, the US Department of Justice created the Public Integrity Section in 1976 to handle criminal investigations of elite office holders, including federal judges. The unit typically handles politically charged cases that raise conflict-of-interest issues for local US attorneys. In the 1980s, prosecutors investigated three federal judges, two of whom went to prison for felonies. By 2007, members of the thirty-person unit were busy unraveling another string of judicial scandals. In Colorado, Chief District Judge Edward Nottingham Jr. (later dubbed Judge Naughty in the Denver press) was facing two separate judicial misconduct probes involving potentially criminal allegations of abuse of power, of lying under oath about bills from a topless bar, and of frequenting a Denver escort service under investigation by the FBI as a front for prostitution.

Meanwhile, in Louisiana, the group had already spent years reviewing complex corruption allegations against US District Judge G. Thomas Porteous Jr. In February 2007, Chief Judge Jones traveled to Washington, DC, to attend an unusual meeting at Main Justice, the building that houses the headquarters of the US Department of Justice. In a wood-paneled room equipped with a fireplace and lined with portraits of top assistant US attorneys, Jones was informed about the long-running criminal probe that had targeted Porteous among other attorneys and state court officials in Louisiana. Jones brought along with her an experienced former prosecutor to the meeting: Ronald Woods, a former US attorney from Houston. The briefing came from prosecutors involved in a broader corruption probe in Jefferson Parish, where Porteous served as a state judge before being elevated to the federal bench in the Eastern District of Louisiana. By 2007, several of Porteous's courthouse cronies already had gone to prison for being part of a network that directed lucrative business to a powerful bondsman in exchange for gifts or kickbacks. Many people expected Porteous, an avuncular jurist with an offbeat sense of humor, to be indicted too. Porteous, a master of mockery, had publicly predicted it.

But DOJ prosecutors struggled with the question of whether they could use evidence from "Operation Wrinkled Robe" against Porteous in a criminal case. Most of it was now too old under statutes of limitations, they told Jones and Wood. Separately, FBI agents found that Porteous, after becoming a federal judge, had accepted more gifts and cash and had failed to disclose them as required by law. Other records suggested that Porteous, again as a federal judge, may have committed perjury by filing for bankruptcy under a fake name. Those more recent acts, if proven, were also felonies, yet Porteous had never been indicted. Instead, prosecutors were planning to file a formal federal judicial misconduct complaint. This meant that deciding what to do with Porteous would soon be Jones's problem.

It turned out that Porteous had already been the subject of another judicial misconduct complaint filed at the very beginning of his federal judicial career. But that complaint had never been formally investigated.

It is said that federal judges are superior to the lowlier breed of state jurists, who generally must solicit campaign contributions, stump for office, or schmooze to win a political appointment. In contrast, federal judges undergo intense bipartisan scrutiny. They are nominated by presidents, vetted by the FBI and by congressional committees, and only then confirmed in the Senate. Anyone with the moxie and pedigree to pass inspection is generally deemed worthy. Even New Orleans lawyers who considered Porteous corrupt also described the man as likeable and charming. His 1994 nomination, supported by President Bill Clinton, had been rapidly approved, though congressional records show that the background check described Porteous as an alcoholic and as possibly on the take. Porteous filled a post vacated by US District Judge Robert Collins, who was convicted of bribery in 1991 after a dope dealer paid cash to win a lighter sentence. Collins collected his $133,600 annual pay as a prisoner until 1993, when he resigned under threat of impeachment.

In October 1994, Porteous prepared to occupy Collins's former chambers in the Eastern District of New Orleans courthouse, on a square adjacent to the Fifth Circuit's headquarters. Porteous was no patrician. He'd ascended from a modest upbringing, endured the suicide of his father, become a standout athlete at his Catholic high school, graduated from law school in Baton Rouge, and chosen public service. He'd worked first as a prosecutor, then as an elected judge. He promised not to be one of those stuffy federal judges who walled himself off and forgot old friends. Before he left state office, Porteous told a newly elected judge (who would later be indicted) that being a judge meant "you'll never have to buy lunch again." He'd added this tip: "Always wash your rear end so the attorneys will have a clean place to kiss."

Courthouse insiders knew that, with a stay-at-home spouse and four children, Porteous had often struggled to get by on a government salary. As a state judge, he had quietly accepted gifts from a bail bondsman and lawyer friends: free car repair, fence repair and painting at his home, baskets brimming with shrimp and crawdads, fine food and drink at New Orleans restaurants, trips to Vegas, as well as cash, often tucked inside unmarked envelopes. For decades, two of his closest friends—attorneys Robert Creely and Jacob Amato Jr., known to Porteous's kids as Uncle Bob and Uncle Jake— had picked up restaurant and bar tabs and had given him more than twenty thousand dollars in cash to help with personal bills. (Many years later, both men cooperated with congressional investigations of Porteous, and in 2010, they gave up their law licenses in lieu of submitting to professional disciplinary action, Louisiana court records show.)

The first formal complaint filed against Porteous as a federal judge arrived as Porteous and his staff were still unpacking boxes. The tipster had initially contacted the Metropolitan Crime Commission, a New Orleans nonprofit that guarantees whistleblowers' anonymity. (The MCC, a revered New Orleans crime-fighting institution, was founded in 1952 by businessmen and civic leaders who were fed up with the abundant local corruption.) The tipster feared retribution and initially sought confidentiality, though his identity would later be disclosed as Mike Reynolds, then a Jefferson Parish prosecutor.[2]

Back when he was a state judge, Porteous broke a Louisiana state law to do a favor for the employee of a bail bonding firm owned by Porteous's friend, Louis Marcotte, a snappy dresser who wore his jet-black hair slicked back and regularly dispensed gifts to Porteous and other officials, Reynolds alleged. As part of a criminal case, Reynolds said that Porteous had issued a ruling that enabled Marcotte's employee, a convicted burglar, to receive a light punishment as a so-called "first offender" even after being convicted of his second felony. Porteous surely knew his ruling violated the Louisiana code of criminal procedure, which did not allow any judge to modify someone's prior criminal conviction outside of the normal appeal process.

The tip involved Porteous's behavior as a state judge and arrived too late to affect Porteous's federal judicial nomination. The US Senate had already voted to confirm him. Still, Rafael Goyeneche III, a former state prosecutor who served as president of the MCC, decided to investigate and later pursue a formal misconduct complaint. Goyeneche might not have been so concerned if Porteous had performed just one illegal favor for a convicted criminal working for a local bondsman. Instead, Goyeneche worried that Porteous and others in Jefferson Parish, one of the largest in Louisiana, were routinely performing other favors for the same bondsman as part of a massive corrupt scheme. Marcotte's company held an unusual monopoly over jail bonds in Jefferson Parish. The bondsman controlled 94 percent of a $44 million annual business, raking in around $4.4 million in annual profits, Goyeneche later learned. (Indeed, the unusually close relationship between the bondsman and other Jefferson Parish officials would later spark the Wrinkled Robe investigation.) Goyeneche figured he should speak directly to Porteous and called his office for an appointment. "I was surprised he took the meeting—he knew what we were," Goyeneche later said. The MCC's employees already had launched its own investigation, making phone calls and requesting records. They weren't "flying below the radar screen," he explained.

Goyeneche went to visit Porteous in chambers, along with the MCC's vice president, a former New Orleans police officer, Anthony Radosti, on November 9, 1994, according to a memo Goyeneche later prepared. Radosti was a seasoned veteran of showdowns, including deadly gun battles. Porteous's secretary ushered them inside. Goyeneche figured Porteous would quickly brush them off.

Instead, Porteous greeted the two warmly as if they were paying a social call. Then he got down to business. "Let's not sugarcoat anything," Porteous said, according to a written summary of the meeting the MCC later provided.[3] "In other words, you think I'm dirty."

Both men demurred, adding they simply had "some questions" about the odd ruling regarding the ex-con and "welcomed an explanation of his reasoning."

Porteous said he'd known the bondsman, Marcotte, for "a number of years," had traveled with him to Las Vegas to gamble, and considered him "a friend." He also acknowledged that the bondsman's employee, a convicted burglar, likely violated probation with his second offense. But Porteous described the employee as a "likeable . . . fuck-up" who deserved "a break."

Outwardly, Goyeneche's professional shell remained intact, but inside he felt flummoxed. Porteous's attitude seemed flippant. In the meeting, Porteous basically admitted to misusing his power as a state judge to clean up the record of a man he called a "fuck-up" who worked for Marcotte, his "friend." Goyeneche told Porteous his actions seemed "improper."

Porteous argued that if his ruling had been illegal, the prosecutor should have appealed. "Do what you think you have to do," Porteous said, dismissing them.

The judge's final words sounded like a dare, Goyeneche thought. Porteous appeared to believe that he, a federal judge, was untouchable. In 1994, Goyeneche filed a formal complaint with the Louisiana Judiciary Commission, which did nothing. It concluded that Porteous was not subject to their review because he was no longer a state judge. Goyeneche said he separately alerted federal district court authorities but got brushed off. That complaint fell into a black hole.

It would take years before similar allegations generated investigations of Porteous by the FBI, a federal grand jury, the Department of Justice's Public Integrity Section, and eventually Jones. By then, even Goyeneche, whose nonprofit is dedicated to fighting corruption, felt shocked that someone in "a position of such prominence could sink to such depths. But federal judges are human just like anybody else," he concluded. Some seem "to forget that they're public servants."

Porteous's problems continued and were compounded, he and his advocates would later argue, by personal losses and by disabling addictions to alcohol and gambling, vices fed by his indulgent hometown. Porteous often drank at lunch, a custom common among the courthouse crowd in New Orleans. During his early years as a federal judge, Harrah's opened an immense casino only blocks from the courthouse. Another temptation for his gambling habit, the Treasure Chest riverboat, with three decks filled with clanging slot machines and bars stocked with cocktails, was docked near his home. The temptations proved irresistible for Porteous. Between June 1995 and July 2000, he accumulated more than $66,000 in casino markers, and his credit card debts ballooned to $180,000. His problems seemed to peak in 2001, when he initially filed for bankruptcy under "Ortous," a fractured version of his name, in a failed attempt to avoid embarrassing publicity that in the end only delayed coverage and provoked even more public ridicule.

Thanks to the Washington, DC, briefing, Jones had been expecting the formal judicial misconduct complaint about Porteous that arrived in May 2007 from Deputy Assistant Attorney General John C. Keeney, who asked her to launch a misconduct investigation. His twenty-two-page complaint, divided into seven sections, accused Porteous of a long list of corrupt or illegal acts, summarized as "evidence of pervasive misconduct." Eventually grand jury testimony, public records, statements, and other material collected by prosecutors and FBI agents were unsealed and forwarded to Jones too. Those documents contained proof of many seemingly illegal acts, some of which dated back to the 1990s and could have been too old to prosecute but could still be considered judicial misconduct. Other allegations were newer. The complaint failed to answer the question: Why had the US Department of Justice decided not to prosecute Porteous, a federal judge, for failing to report gifts? Nor for bankruptcy fraud? After all, the Public Integrity Section had far more investigative resources than Jones, who began the review on top of her many other duties. She also would simultaneously investigate Kent.

Jones moved more swiftly on the Kent complaint, perhaps because the allegations seemed simpler and most witnesses were readily accessible court employees. That dispute, like so many matters involving sex crimes, turned on the credibility of two people. For that probe, Jones relied on a single attorney whose firm bio describes him as having "extensive experience in legislative and regulatory and governmental matters."

In the Porteous matter, Jones had recruited Ronald Woods, a gray-haired attorney who specialized for decades in white-collar crime. Woods, a former prosecutor and an ex-Special Agent for the FBI, prepared the case as the court's special investigator; later, Lawrence Finder, another seasoned former federal prosecutor, helped Woods prep for the disciplinary hearing. Together they made a synchronous and formidable team who built an investigation atop the already massive archive provided by the Public Integrity Section prosecutors. In five months, the pair reviewed dozens of documents and grand jury testimony and interviewed witnesses. On October 18, 2017, they filed a list, "Charges of Judicial Misconduct," on behalf of the investigatory committee, just six days before the hearing. Operating on a tight budget, the two loaded an SUV with exhibits and hand-delivered copies to Porteous, who had never responded to invitations to come to Houston to review the evidence. Any one of the charges was potentially career ending, unless Porteous could mount a formidable defense, but Porteous couldn't seem to keep an attorney long. When the day of the hearing arrived, he represented himself.

On October 29, 2007, Porteous was preparing to testify in his closed judicial disciplinary hearing in New Orleans when he received an unusual phone call. Normally, judges move freely through secure federal buildings without having to undergo the indignities of producing IDs and undergoing the scrutiny of armed guards and x-ray machines. A staff member from the Fifth Circuit courthouse next door phoned to explain that prior to the hearing Porteous would be required to pass through security. Minutes before the 10 a.m. hearing began, Porteous found himself emptying his pockets at the public entrance of the John Minor Wisdom Court of Appeals Building. Some friends saw it as a deliberate insult ordered by Jones. Others wondered whether Porteous was deemed a security or suicide risk because of his self-described mental impairments.

As part of his defense, Porteous portrayed himself as a tragic figure. In 2005, Porteous and his wife were among an estimated three hundred thousand families who lost homes to floods caused by Hurricane Katrina, according to a December 2008 Government Accountability Office report; other estimates were even higher. Their two-story brick home on Lake Ponchatrain was wrecked, and a few months later, in the chaotic aftermath, Porteous's beloved wife died of a heart attack. In 2006, Porteous recused himself from criminal cases because of the grand jury investigation of "Operation Wrinkled Robe." He then requested and received a year-long leave, claiming to be too ill and impaired from personal losses to perform judicial duties. He had returned to his bench only weeks before the hearing.

Normally, testimony that accused judges such as Porteous offer in response to judicial misconduct complaints is never provided to outsiders nor even to complainants. But an archive and hearing transcript released by Fifth Circuit officials a few months later provided an unusual window into how the secret system of investigating judicial misconduct complaints tackled the corruption allegations against him. It's possible that Porteous agreed to make those disciplinary documents available, since federal law gives the accused judge some discretion over disclosing disciplinary records. The Judicial Conduct and Disability Act says that unless the judge who is the subject of the accusation authorizes the disclosure, "all papers, documents, and records of proceedings related to investigations conducted under [the law] shall be confidential and shall not be disclosed by any person." By making so much of the archive public, the Fifth Circuit also facilitated access to the records for members of Congress who would soon be considering whether to impeach Porteous, as his own peers would later recommend.

In their October hearing, judicial investigators only had to determine whether Porteous had committed "conduct prejudicial to the effective and expeditious administration of the business of the court." But so many interrelated accusations were lodged against him that his disciplinary hearing resembled a trial, featuring two full days of witness testimony and dozens of exhibits.

Presiding was Jones, flanked by US Circuit Judge Fortunato Pedro "Pete" Benavides, based in Austin, and US District Judge Sim Lake in Houston. All three were Texans. Even the court reporter was imported from Houston. As Fifth Circuit appellate judges, Jones and Benavides did not normally oversee trials, but Lake, a trial veteran, had recently presided over the criminal trial of Jeff Skilling, the highest-ranking executive to be convicted in the complex Houston-based Enron scandal. Jones began the hearing by reminding Porteous that he was being granted immunity from prosecution but remained under oath. Jones also urged Porteous to offer his resignation. She called him a disgrace and asked him to save them all time and taxpayer money.

Porteous was used to presiding over hearings, not testifying or standing accused. Porteous protested he'd been offered immunity only orally and lacked any written guarantee. Jones insisted her promise was enough. At one point Porteous boldly asked Jones to recuse herself. Clearly, he suggested, she was not objective.

Jones refused. In a judicial misconduct probe, Jones played multiple roles. As chief circuit judge she was the senior investigating judge and would recommend punishment as an investigatory committee member, almost like a prosecutor. Yet she was presiding over the hearing in more or less a regular judicial role. In a follow-up meeting, she would vote on a punishment as a member of the Fifth Circuit Judicial Council. Some of Porteous's allies thought Jones seemed openly hostile. Patrick Fanning, a New Orleans attorney who attended the hearing to represent a witness, later said, "A guilty man had an unfair trial." The witnesses included Porteous's friends and his longtime legal secretary. But some of the invited spectators, including two prosecutors from the Public Integrity Section, made Porteous uncomfortable.

In 2007, the Fifth Circuit Court of Appeals courtroom held the usual wooden benches and a stage with elevated seats for the judges. The room normally lacked any audio-visual equipment, but a projector had been brought in for Porteous's hearing: Finder and Woods planned to present eighty-five exhibits, including credit card bills, casino records, federal disclosure reports, and federal codes of conduct. The evidence sat in banker's boxes piled next to Porteous.

As a young prosecutor, Finder had cut his teeth in his native Chicago by playing a supporting role in a 1984 judicial corruption probe called "Operation Greylord," named for the curly wigs worn by British judges. Investigators used undercover methods to help root out ninety-two corrupt officials in Cook County, Illinois, including state judges, lawyers, cops, and a state legislator in what was considered a landmark case in cleaning up state courts. The experience helped shape Finder's character as an attorney. By 2007, he'd accumulated more than two decades' experience of investigating corruption and white-collar crime first as a prosecutor and later as a defense attorney. Finder still saw judicial corruption as the ultimate betrayal of the justice system by people sworn to uphold and protect the nation's constitution and laws.

Finder looks the part of a tough ex-fed. He has an intense gaze and coal-black hair. But his style is soft-spoken. He began his interrogation with a gentle question: "Judge Porteous, a little background information, please." Finder took Porteous through his rise through the Louisiana legal hierarchy to the lofty post of a US district judge. Finder then adjusted the courtroom projector to display the oath every federal judge is legally required to take, to "faithfully and impartially discharge and perform all the duties incumbent upon me . . . under the Constitution and laws of the United States."

Next, he displayed on the screen the Code of Conduct for United States Judges—the ethical canons all judges agree to uphold. "Are you familiar with Canon One, Your Honor, that a judge should uphold the integrity and independence of the judiciary?" he asked.

"Yes," Porteous said.

Without making accusations, Finder kept reminding Porteous of the many promises he and other judges make and that he'd failed to keep.

The judges on the investigatory committee listened. Then, abruptly, Benavides spoke, requesting clarification on the offer of immunity from prosecution that Porteous had received prior to testifying in the disciplinary probe. Like Porteous, Benavides was a Clinton nominee who also became a federal judge in 1994. His request seemed designed to reawaken Porteous to the lingering risks of a criminal prosecution.

Finder reminded Porteous that he could still be prosecuted if he lied under oath to the investigatory panel. "As long as you bring it up, Your Honor, I do need to make certain that the witness knows that, while this is a grant of use immunity coextensive with his Fifth Amendment rights, it would not [provide] him any kind of immunity from false statement or perjury."

In other words, Porteous could admit committing bankruptcy fraud, concealing gifts in sworn disclosures, underreporting income to the IRS, and other kinds of criminal activity to his fellow judges and expect immunity, as long as he didn't lie under oath. Telling a lie could still put Porteous in prison for perjury.

"And you're aware of that, Judge Porteous?" Jones asked.

"Yes ma'am." Porteous's mouth must have gone dry. A few minutes later, he requested a glass of water. Benavides suggested someone bring over the entire pitcher.

For hours, Finder proceeded to take Porteous through his flawed bankruptcy filings, his casino markers, and his many failures to accurately declare debts, assets, and income, all in apparent violation of federal laws. He then dug deeper into his boxes and displayed official forms that Porteous had filed beginning in 1995, the first year he was required to disclose gifts, trips, and outside income as a federal judge.

The annual disclosure requirements were first established for judges under the Ethics in Government Act of 1978. Each year, judges are required to list outside income, as well as trips, gifts, or honoraria that they or their spouses accept and sign those disclosure forms under penalty of perjury. The forms were meant "to ensure confidence in the integrity of the federal government by demonstrating that they are able to carry out their duties without compromising the public trust," according to the judiciary's own disclosure regulations.

But many jurists filed incomplete or empty forms and the requirements were largely unenforced. In the 2000s, a huge archive of public disclosures filed by Porteous, Kent, and other federal judges each year had been posted online by the nonprofit Judicial Watch in an effort to spotlight how few judges accurately filled out the forms as required by federal law. Federal disclosure requirements are designed in part to keep judges from hearing cases that present conflicts of interest and from accepting unreported gifts from litigants or lawyers, which could be seen as bribes. In essence, the law exists to protect the public from corruption and conflicts of interest. In theory, failure to properly fill out those forms could be prosecuted under federal statutes. But many disclosure forms filed by judges were blank or contained obviously incomplete information.

For those reasons, a single slip might be something other jurists would excuse as an inadvertent error, but in twelve years, Porteous had disclosed only two hunting trips. He'd failed to report many other trips, services, and cash he'd taken from lawyers and litigants with business in his court. Under questioning, Porteous admitted accepting at least two thousand dollars in cash from two close attorney friends. The "gifts" had never been repaid—nor reported to the IRS as income, he testified.

Later, at yet another secret hearing in New Orleans in December 2007, the full membership of the Fifth Circuit Judicial Council would review Porteous's statements at the hearing and the investigatory committee's report. A majority voted to reprimand Porteous and strip him of all of his cases as district judge. The council also recommended that Porteous be considered for impeachment by the House of Representatives. At the same time, the group released records and a transcript of its normally secret hearing. Legal experts and members of Congress praised the Fifth Circuit Judicial Council's action as a model effort to share information about a normally closed judicial misconduct review. Many observers applauded Jones for the quality of the probe, though they were less complimentary of the work she did in 2007 on investigating the Kent complaint.

Complainants are usually not allowed to attend disciplinary hearings. But the transcript shows that Jones made an exception in Porteous's case. Federal prosecutors, representatives of the Department of Justice that filed the complaint, were allowed to listen to Porteous testify. Among those in the audience was Dan Petalas, a young federal prosecutor who had previously spent months on the criminal investigation of Porteous but had never gotten to question the judge. Sitting nearby was Peter Ainsworth, deputy chief for litigation in the Public Integrity Section. Ainsworth, only a spectator at Porteous's disciplinary hearing, would soon form a team and launch a criminal investigation of Kent.

Still, there was no guarantee that Kent would ever be indicted. No criminal charges were ever filed against Porteous, though he would later be impeached.

Another US District judge whom the Public Integrity Section had been investigating in 2007, Nottingham, was never disciplined or indicted. Instead, Nottingham agreed to resign as a federal judge in 2008 and as a result, all complaints against him were dismissed and the results of two separate judicial misconduct investigations that had been launched were never revealed. Nottingham resumed his law practice in Denver. Maybe Kent, too, could survive his own alcohol-soaked scandals without being indicted or impeached. In January 2008, Kent returned to work at the same Houston courthouse where Jones was based.

PART III

Judgment Day for Judges

CHAPTER 10

The Keeper of Secrets

Texas, 2007–2008

A pair of FBI agents were assigned to undertake a criminal probe of US District Judge Samuel Bristow Kent in the fall of 2007. That investigation began soon after McBroom's attorney forwarded a formal request—along with a copy of the *Houston Chronicle* investigation and the congressmen's press release—to the US Department of Justice. Externally as confident as ever, Kent called an agent he knew at the FBI office in Texas City and volunteered to "sit down" and discuss the case. Kent arrived on November 30, 2007, alone without counsel. During the unusual meeting, the judge seemed his jovial self. A small group of agents, including the one Kent knew and others who were formally assigned to the case, allowed Kent to say whatever he liked and asked few questions. It was an odd situation for them, listening to a supremely confident federal judge expound on potentially criminal allegations against himself.

The two agents officially assigned to the Kent case were David Baker, tall and muscular, and Joe Garcia, a shorter but tough-looking investigator with large dark eyes and thinning black hair. Baker, the senior agent, was particularly outgoing and would later become an FBI recruiter. Both were polite and tenacious enough to confront multimillionaire trial attorneys and egotistical federal judges, yet versatile enough to quickly fade into the background when necessary. Each man knew Kent by reputation; neither wanted to give the impression that the bureau was favoring Kent, a sitting federal judge.

Kent spoke in his usual booming voice as he told them that McBroom was an attractive and sexually adventurous woman. To him, she had seemed both flirtatious and receptive to his attentions, despite her subsequent complaints. Kent later would admit that he'd been drinking prior to the physical assaults McBroom described and that he was relatively strongly affected by alcohol because of his type 2 diabetes. But in the interview, his view of his own desirability—and his innocence—remained unshakable. Afterward, Kent told others that the agents asked "all the right questions."

Wilkerson repeatedly declined invitations to speak to the FBI. Eventually, frustrated investigators approached McBroom and urged her to try to persuade Wilkerson to cooperate by phone. McBroom finally agreed, since she didn't want to appear unwilling to cooperate with the FBI. Agents didn't need Wilkerson's permission to secretly record the call, since Texas was a one-party state.

Wilkerson was reflexively courteous and cordial when she answered the phone, but bristled when she recognized McBroom's voice. "What's the reason for this call?" she said.

"We need some help and we need you to do something for us," McBroom said. She didn't define "we" or "us." McBroom felt uncomfortable. The pair hadn't spoken in months. She knew Wilkerson must have been furious about being named in her misconduct complaint.

"What do you want me to do, Cathy? Hasn't he already been punished enough?" Wilkerson said of Kent. Obviously irritated, Wilkerson asked if McBroom was calling on behalf of the feds. "We know the FBI is tracking people. We know the FBI is there or asking us to meet so they can overhear. I'm not stupid!"

"Donna, you know you're a victim of this too!" McBroom countered.

There was only silence. Wilkerson said nothing.

McBroom hung up and refused agents' requests to try calling Wilkerson again.

In December 2007, Wilkerson was out Christmas shopping with her teenaged son and daughter at busy Baybrook Mall when she received a call directly from an FBI agent. He told Wilkerson she was about to receive an unwelcome gift: a subpoena ordering her to testify before the federal grand jury. Wilkerson pleaded with him not to serve her at home. She did not want her children—or her husband—to wonder why she was being targeted as a witness. "Just meet us outside Macy's in five minutes," the agent said. Wilkerson felt even more freaked out to know he was that close. *Was she being followed? At the mall?* Her usual holiday spirit vanished as she detoured to meet the agent and retrieve the subpoena. She became a nervous wreck.

Wilkerson had begun to sink into what her therapist later diagnosed as severe depression. Only much later, after years of counseling, did she begin to realize to what extent she'd been controlled by Kent. Her therapist has described the pattern of trauma Wilkerson experienced as similar to Stockholm Syndrome, a disorder in which victims of kidnappings become so controlled by their captors and tormentors that they end up being brainwashed into forming an attachment for them. In a last-ditch effort to restore her composure before delivering the dreaded testimony, Wilkerson scheduled a trip to the salon.

Judge Susan Criss's roots were starting to show. The busy Galveston County district judge was overdue for her cut and color in December 2007, and with holidays ahead, it took some wrangling to land a weekday slot at the popular Genesis Salon. Criss made her way through rush-hour traffic and then sat through the goop and odor of the tedious tinting process, after which she would reemerge as a brassy blond. She had just gotten settled under a hair dryer when she spotted a familiar face. Beside her, with her hair similarly encased in a heated globe, sat Donna Wilkerson—a woman who in the legal world of Galveston County felt to Criss like a shirttail relative: for years, Wilkerson had served as secretary to Criss's former husband, a local lawyer. She had forever endeared herself by remaining just as pleasant and friendly to Criss after the divorce.

Criss hadn't seen Wilkerson for months but knew from island gossip and newspapers that her friend was in an uncomfortable position. Their heads under dryer globes, the two friends were sequestered in side-by-side faux leather seats. A hug was temporarily out of the question, so Criss reached out a freshly manicured hand in greeting.

Wearing her usual toothy smile and impeccable makeup, Wilkerson smiled back, and then seemed to crumble. Wilkerson kept her voice just loud enough to be heard over the dryer as she confided that she was preparing for an ordeal. The next day she had to testify to a federal grand jury. Wilkerson wondered if Criss, as an attorney and a friend, had any advice.

"Just tell the truth," Criss replied. "They're not investigating you!"

The assurances didn't seem to make Wilkerson feel any better.

Criss had long known Wilkerson's current boss. Kent was a prominent fixture in the Galveston legal scene. He moved in the same circles as Criss, though she was an elected state judge and a Democrat and he'd won his federal bench under a Republican president. Though she had mostly practiced as a prosecutor before being elected judge in 1998, Criss also had served as a defense attorney and had had one particularly memorable case before Kent. It hadn't gone well. Through a calendar mix-up, Criss somehow failed to realize she had cases simultaneously scheduled for hearings in two different courts on the same day—a jury trial in state court and a sentencing in federal court.

Criss was making closing arguments to a Galveston jury, when she received an urgent message that Kent was looking for her. Criss had wrongly believed the federal matter to be canceled, but soon realized her mistake. She finished her argument, requested a break, explained herself to the state judge, and then called Kent's staff to admit she'd failed to notice the conflict. Half afraid Kent might send a marshal to "lock me up for contempt of court," Criss left the Galveston County courthouse as soon as the jury began deliberating and raced to federal court. Their exchange remained burned into her memory years later.

When she arrived, Kent screamed, "Who do you think you are, not showing up?"

"I told you I messed up on my calendar, but there's no excuse," Criss replied. "I shouldn't have done that."

Kent seemed ready to explode. He often raged at lawyers who dared arrive even a few minutes late and was known for issuing thousand-dollar fines for tardiness, yet he seemed to appreciate Criss's candor. He found her in contempt but fined her only one hundred dollars. Then, he gave her client what Criss considered a fair sentence. After that episode, they'd remained more or less cordial, though not close.

In December 2007, Criss was a regular at the Genesis Salon, a business cofounded by three women who chose the first book of the Bible to signal that their place would inspire fresh starts. The cozy spot was full of women prepping for holiday parties. In that atmosphere, Criss hesitated to ask too many questions about Kent or the grand jury, especially when others might overhear, despite the blasts of blow dryers. "You might want to get a lawyer yourself," Criss told Wilkerson. "But mainly, you just need to tell the truth."

Wilkerson remained agitated. She had continued to report to work to Kent's empty chambers at the Galveston federal courthouse after his reprimand, and she and his law clerk had fumbled for things to do for four months. Meanwhile, the grand jury investigating Kent began meeting in the Houston federal courthouse, where Wilkerson, too, expected to be transferred when Kent returned to work.

Wilkerson told Criss that when Kent learned she'd been subpoenaed, he had called her and threatened to kill himself.

Why was Kent so worried about her friend's testimony? Criss wondered. Beyond her nervousness, Wilkerson offered no hint whether Kent had sexually harassed or assaulted her. Criss didn't press. She knew from her own experience that sussing out the truth about sexual misconduct could be tricky, especially when the alleged perpetrator was a powerful man.

As a young prosecutor in the 1990s, Criss had felt threatened by a Texas City detective who had called to proposition her late one night and then pushed to visit her home uninvited. Criss filed a confidential internal affairs complaint only after she learned that the same officer had forcibly groped and kissed other women, including lawyers and police officers. Despite her position as a county prosecutor, she heard nothing regarding her complaint. About a decade later, when the same officer was up for a promotion to police chief, Criss, by then a judge, decided to make the older allegations public.[1] The officer later pleaded guilty to a misdemeanor and received deferred prosecution for harassing another woman, and agreed to surrender his badge in a 2004 plea deal.

Criss didn't know what to think about Judge Kent. She knew he could be crude and enjoyed dirty jokes, but other attorneys in Texas's male-dominated legal world acted much the same way. Some Texans tried to pass off coarse behavior as a variation on the region's complex Southern gentleman–cowboy brand of what some considered charm and others saw as outright sexism. In its most innocuous forms, Southern traditions dictated that gentlemen open the door for a woman and say "Yes, ma'am" and "No, ma'am" and fetch food or drinks for ladies—courtesies many Texas women still appreciated or even expected. But some so-called gentlemen still addressed grown women as "girls," "gals" or even "little ladies" in formal settings, including courtrooms.

Some attorneys (including law professors, legislators, and judges) greeted women they barely knew with lingering hugs, kisses, and caresses. Others sought sexual favors from junior employees or law clerks in return for gifts or mentoring. Many women attorneys quietly exchanged information about harassers through whisper networks. Few dared to complain. When a federal prosecutor later dared to challenge a judge in Houston who referred to federal agents as "girls," he banned her from his courtroom.

Criss didn't know Cathy McBroom, but figured all the publicity about a federal judge like Kent might generate more allegations—perhaps some true and others false or exaggerated. Criss knew firsthand about an embarrassing episode involving Kent that happened at a Christmas party in 2001. At that time, Criss was already serving as an elected state district judge, a position that she felt kept her perpetually in the public eye.

The event, hosted by a Texas City law firm, was attended by a who's who of the Galveston legal community. The firm offered a generous buffet with a sous-chef carving roast beef, a gulf seafood buffet, fresh strawberries piled beside a chocolate fountain, and an open bar. Many people were drinking heavily, and Kent seemed truly hammered. Criss remembered seeing the big judge sway. At one point another lawyer nudged Criss, who turned to see Kent locked in an embrace with one of her court employees beside the buffet. Minutes later the woman approached Criss, claiming that Kent had forced his tongue into her mouth. Yet to Criss it looked as though her employee had been flattered by the judge's attention. She later spotted the pair talking again. But when Kent pushed her employee into an empty office and closed the door, others felt compelled to carry out a rescue.

Criss considered Kent not guilty in the Christmas party incident. "I ultimately didn't think Kent had done anything wrong," she said later. Back then, Kent was a widower who'd just watched his first wife slowly die of cancer. Criss thought even federal judges had a right to a little fun. In fact, she thought her married employee had been largely to blame by getting drunk at a professional event and then playing "grab ass" with a federal judge. "She'd put me and herself in a bad position," Criss said.

When FBI agents eventually asked her about Kent's behavior, Criss offered up the same opinion. But that didn't mean Criss automatically believed what Kent's defense attorney later claimed: his client had never molested or sexually harassed any woman on the job. In the judicial misconduct matter, Criss lacked sufficient information to form an opinion as to whether Kent was innocent or guilty.

That night at the salon, she was more worried about her friend, who kept tearing up as they talked. She hoped Donna Wilkerson would be okay. In her decades as a prosecutor and a judge, Criss had worked with many rape victims. She didn't suspect from Wilkerson's demeanor that Kent had sexually assaulted his secretary. But it was clear that when Wilkerson left the salon with her newly tinted blond hair and blow-out, she still seemed just as frightened.

Wilkerson had been keeping Kent's secrets a long time. She had first begun working for him in 2001, a year she'd felt vulnerable and devastated by a terrible loss.

Wilkerson grew up on a small farm near the Galveston County railroad town of Santa Fe. She was just eleven when her mother died and her teenage sister, Pat, stepped in as a surrogate mother. With Pat watching out for her, Wilkerson maintained a relentlessly sunny nature, much like the South Texas climate. She married her high school sweetheart and remained happily married for more than two decades and through many jobs. But when Wilkerson first met Kent, she had spent about a year commuting between her job as a legal secretary at a Houston law firm, her Santa Fe home, and the island hospital where her beloved sister Pat, then only fifty-one, was dying of a rare disorder that continued to ravage her lungs even after a transplant. Pat's last wish had been for her baby sister to "quit the rat race."

"You work too much, you're too far away from home," Pat said before she died in May 2001.

A few months later, Wilkerson spotted the job opening at Kent's island federal courthouse, only twenty minutes from Santa Fe, and the opportunity seemed like a miracle. After so much grief, hope surged. Wilkerson thought: *I still have it. I am still worthy, and I'm going to be OK.*

Wilkerson knew that Kent was considered powerful by her lawyer bosses, and came away impressed by her first visit to his chambers. Wilkerson had never seen Washington, DC, and she figured a US senator's office could hardly be fancier. In their first conversation, Kent warned Wilkerson that there were three things he'd never tolerate: disloyalty, talking out of school, or engaging in behavior that could be an "embarrassment to the court." Any infractions would be grounds for "immediate dismissal." Then Kent broke the ice by warning that he cussed like a sailor. "Frankly, I like the way it sounds. So, if you have a problem with cussin', you need to tell me now," he said, according to Wilkerson's recollections.

Wilkerson burst out laughing. "That stuff doesn't bother me," she declared. If anything, Kent's salty talk made the job more appealing. Kent seemed like "somebody out of an old southern novel about an old southern judge," especially with that stogie in his mouth, she thought.

Donna Wilkerson needed a secure post to support her family in 2001. Her husband had a position with what had been a stable employer, Enron, until the prosecution of top executives for corruption forced the break-up of the Houston pipeline behemoth. Although

Wilkerson's husband kept a job with a corporate spin-off company, his Enron retirement and benefits disappeared. After learning that the federal court position would offer a salary better than her current post, Wilkerson agreed when Kent asked her to start immediately.

In December 2001, Wilkerson replaced Kent's secretary, Gerry Henry, who had worked beside Kent since his early lawyering days. A tough chain-smoking mother figure to Kent, Henry had been the only courthouse employee to regularly challenge the big judge. In the five days the two secretaries overlapped, Henry found time to warn Wilkerson that Kent could be a real handful, especially after long drinking lunches with lawyer friends.

On the Friday of her first week, Wilkerson got a sneak preview. Kent had recently remarried and he brought along his new wife, Sarah, to Henry's retirement luncheon at a local restaurant. Kent already seemed drunk when he began making crude remarks and then bent over to grab his wife's breasts and bottom before an astonished crowd, Wilkerson later recalled.

Later, when the staff returned to the courthouse, Kent summoned Wilkerson inside his office and closed the door. He sat down behind his massive desk and told Wilkerson he was "very excited to have [her] coming on board to take Ms. Henry's place." He said he thought she would "be an asset to him and the operations of the court." And then he added a more personal compliment: "You are so beautiful and so smart and we are going to make a great team."

Then, in what seemed like a gentlemanly gesture, Kent rose from his desk and walked over to open the door and usher her out. But as Wilkerson reached the threshold, Kent pivoted, placed his hands on either side of her body, leaned forward, lowered his huge head, and shoved his tongue inside her mouth.

Wilkerson froze. She didn't know how else to respond. Her new boss, the federal judge, was French-kissing her. The experience seemed surreal, so she pretended it wasn't happening. "On the other side of the door was a room full of people . . . and I said nothing." Flustered, Wilkerson exited the office, wondering, *What in the world was that?*

A decade younger than Kent and far more vulnerable than Henry, Wilkerson was groomed as Kent's confidante, counselor, and, as she realized only much later, his primary victim. Many of his first comments and jokes fell into what Wilkerson considered a "gray area" of sexual harassment. In nineteen years as a legal assistant, Wilkerson had previously encountered powerful men who felt free to extend compliments or to make inappropriate gestures. The pattern had begun with her first boss, who dubbed her Little Donna and asked why she wore such baggy pants when she had such a fine figure. From the beginning, Kent used their working relationship as an excuse to shower Wilkerson with "hugs and kisses" and comments about what he called her "cutest titties" and "cutest ass." She tolerated it.

Wilkerson didn't dare complain. Her salary was by far the best money she'd ever made; she thought of it as her "rice bowl." Wilkerson remained happily married to a hard-working, macho man. But, temporarily at least, she'd become her family's biggest wage earner and the provider of health benefits. Wilkerson did not share her troubles with her husband. If he knew the judge had touched her, she feared he might try to kill Kent—an act that surely would end with her spouse in prison or dead. Kent carried a concealed handgun and as a federal judge was constantly surrounded by armed guards, one of whom was a former member of the Galveston Police Department SWAT team.

Over the next six years, Wilkerson learned to put up with Kent's remarks and his idiosyncrasies—serving him his coffee every day in the mug emblazoned with the "Lion King" logo. In return, he promised her: "Loyalty for loyalty—you will have a job until you die." On those afternoons after he drank, she developed evasive maneuvers: slapping away his hand, objecting and darting under her desk, or leaving work early. Wilkerson had trouble seeing herself as a victim. Fundamentally, she felt sorry for Kent: he was a flawed, lonely alcoholic, she thought. She somehow hoped to "fix him." It took many years of therapy before Wilkerson later felt able to analyze Kent's manipulative behavior. She eventually came to believe that Kent deliberately compromised, cultivated, and brainwashed her as his most loyal confidante and most frequent target for sexual harassment and sexual assault. Each time he strayed further, with a hug, kiss, caress or worse, Kent offered apologies and additional perks. And each time she asked herself, *How can this continue to happen?*

Wilkerson was tougher than her sharply dressed soccer mom exterior suggested. As a motherless girl, she'd frequently sprawled on the floor watching World Wrestling Federation bouts on TV with her dad. Like McBroom, she figured she was tough enough to laugh off or fend off Kent's crude remarks and advances. But Wilkerson also began requesting to go home early on Fridays or whenever Kent headed out for those long drinking lunches. Usually, Kent would agree. She got to spend more time with her children that way.

As the keeper of Kent's secrets, Wilkerson became hypersensitive to the judge's shifting moods. She heard Kent tell how as a teen, he watched his father die of cancer. She heard him angrily rail against his mother, an elegant commercial real estate broker who had raised Kent and his four siblings alone after that death. She heard him complain about his own two daughters as "hardhearted." She knew both daughters had cut off contact with him after their mother's death, because, according to Kent, he'd written them out of his will. He told Wilkerson that his new will included a bequest for her. Wilkerson didn't know whether the stories were true, though Kent certainly seemed to believe them. She appreciated his trust, but repeatedly saw how Kent's allies could become his foes. Soon after she arrived, Kent had banished his longtime case manager, Felicia Williams. Cathy McBroom, Williams's successor, had at first seemed slated to become Kent's favorite. Wilkerson saw Kent hug and compliment McBroom. Kent described McBroom as "flirty" and "breathy," and told Wilkerson, "She's after me."

After McBroom sought and received her emergency transfer to Houston, Wilkerson felt upset and then relieved. She figured Kent's behavior would surely improve. But she worried when McBroom later followed up with a formal misconduct complaint in May. As witnesses in the secret federal judicial misconduct probe in the summer of 2007, both Wilkerson and Kent were instructed never to discuss the investigation. So Wilkerson said nothing when she heard Kent tell others at the Galveston courthouse that McBroom was a liar, a flirt, and a disgruntled employee or when Kent described his relationship with McBroom as "consensual." She overheard Kent and one of the court security officers trade salty stories about how McBroom got drunk with and dated coworkers. She heard Kent and others claim that McBroom wore low-cut blouses and fishnet stockings and had shown off an intimate tattoo at work. Even when Kent began calling his accuser McWhore, Wilkerson did not object.

The reprimand issued to Kent in September 2007 came as another shock. The reprimand cited Kent for sexual harassment of court employees, though it didn't name her. Even though she was among his unnamed victims, Wilkerson believed that after Kent completed his leave (and some much-needed therapy) they'd resume working together. The idea that the FBI would get involved and poke holes in conflicting statements she and Kent had provided to the investigatory committee of judges never occurred to her, until November, when the *Houston Chronicle* reported that McBroom's lawyer, Hardin, was pushing for a criminal probe.

As the Christmas holidays approached, Kent's leave and the FBI investigation continued. On sunny days, neighbors sometimes spotted Kent outside working on a deck on his wooded property near Santa Fe. He remained in close touch with Wilkerson, who lived only two miles away in the town with a population of about ten thousand. Wilkerson kept her own ranch-style home spotless and filled it with highly polished furniture and hand-selected décor that varied with the seasons. One emerald-green wall held oversized portraits of her husband and children in golden frames. Her place held the floral and spicy scents of candles she sold and stored in an immaculate garage. Kent's calls and visits injected chaos into her well-ordered life. Even during his leave, Kent regularly called or pulled his gray Toyota Solara up in the drive for an unannounced visit. He kept worrying aloud about the criminal probe into McBroom's complaint. "I know I've been a bad boy and misbehaved," he repeatedly said. But then he would minimize his past contact with Wilkerson as if it had been a one-time thing that immediately ceased.

Wilkerson always listened to Kent's declarations, though her own recollections differed. Even during her first round of grand jury testimony she held back. She remained under Kent's control.

In January 2008, Wilkerson and Kent reported to his new chambers inside the Sugar Cube, the squat courthouse with rows of small square windows that looks like a prison but is a power center for the federal judiciary in Texas. Exiled from his kingdom on Galveston Island, Kent used Wilkerson and other staff members as a shield. He arrived and departed with Wilkerson each day. He ordered her and the rest of his staff to dine with him in chambers, instead of in the courthouse cafeteria or in one of an array of tempting downtown Houston restaurants that were only blocks away. But Kent was no longer the only judge in this courthouse: the vast edifice was filled with jurists with far more seniority and power, including Jones.

Kent kept Wilkerson particularly close as the FBI's criminal probe continued. They commuted to and from work together on the hour-long drive from their homes in Santa Fe. Kent often drove them in his Ford Explorer or in his Toyota Solara (which got better gas mileage), sometimes weaving through traffic at eighty-five miles an hour on the busy Gulf Freeway. He parked in the judges' private walled lot, used a hidden high security entrance and an exclusive elevator.

Wilkerson hoped to find new friends at the Houston courthouse. Instead, she felt shunned. Even when she addressed other employees directly on judicial business, some avoided looking her in the eye. Then, in mid-January, Wilkerson was subpoenaed to testify before the grand jury again. She had been preparing to leave Kent's office that morning when he transmitted more distress signals. "If anyone from [my doctor's office] calls, please put them through right away," he said. "You know they have me on suicide watch again, right?" A few minutes later, he loudly asked his law clerk to review his life insurance policy and verify that if he did kill himself, his widow could still collect benefits. As Wilkerson stepped out of the office, she worried that her testimony would put Kent's blood on her hands.

That second round of questioning lasted seven hours. Many questions centered on allegations of Kent's favoritism toward certain attorneys and on gifts he'd accepted, as well as Kent's behavior toward her. Wilkerson later said that she figured prosecutors knew she was "skating around" some questions, but she couldn't make herself talk. The details were humiliating and potentially explosive. She still hoped the investigation would soon end and her life would return to normal. And she felt certain nothing would happen to Kent even if she dared to speak out. Sure, other employees had seen Kent kiss or hug her, but that was relatively innocuous. Only two people knew more about what Kent had done to her behind closed doors. Both had worked as Kent's law clerks. Like her, they had taken oaths in their time as judicial employees to safeguard the confidentiality of the court.

CHAPTER 11

A Criminal Probe

Houston, 2008

In 2008, Sam Kent no longer appeared at his regular table at the Pelican Club in Galveston for long drinking lunches with his court-house cronies. But behind the scenes, wealthy and well-connected attorney friends still supported him and gathered in private dinner parties to strategize. One of his former law clerks, Kurt Arnold, now a powerful Houston-based trial attorney, recommended that Kent hire Dick DeGuerin, a prominent criminal defense lawyer who had handled Arnold's mother's divorce years before. Kent already knew DeGuerin, a high-powered attorney who also happened to be a member of the Pelican Club.

A quintessential Texan who's as comfortable on a horse as in a courtroom, DeGuerin is legendary for representing both the famous and the infamous. He delights in being provocative and relishes a challenge. The lean Austin native with a razor-sharp wit had made national news in 2003 after winning an acquittal for Robert Durst, a Manhattan real estate heir who had killed, beheaded, and hacked up a Galveston Island neighbor. ("A real head case," and "Run for your lives!" were headlines featured in news articles from New York City newspapers that were framed and hung on DeGuerin's office brag wall.) After listening to DeGuerin's masterful argument of self-defense, a jury had found Durst not guilty of murdering his seventy-one-year-old neighbor.

DeGuerin grew up among Texas's legal elite. He was the son of a prominent Austin attorney and the older brother of another power-house Houston lawyer. Family friends included former president Lyndon B. Johnson. A self-described yellow-dog Democrat, DeGuerin didn't play party politics when he decided whom to represent. He'd successfully defended US senator Kay Bailey Hutchison, a Texas Republican, winning her 1994 acquittal from political ethics charges, and he later handled the defense of powerful US representative Tom "The Hammer" DeLay against 2005 charges of money laundering and conspiracy, which related to DeLay's alleged misuse of campaign contributions to redraw Texas districts in a way that favored GOP candidates. Though DeLay, the former House Majority Leader, had initially been convicted, he later prevailed in an appeal.

Like Kent, his latest high-profile Republican client, DeGuerin was one of the Texas Exes, part of the powerful band of alumni of the University of Texas. He had once considered becoming an FBI agent, though that dream had ended, he said, because of drunken behavior in his frat-boy days that had resulted in a misdemeanor alcohol-related arrest. That incident subsequently rendered him unattractive to the bureau when he later applied. DeGuerin, however, considered himself a master negotiator: he had even tried to peacefully end the ill-fated stand-off between David Koresh and federal agents at Waco in 1993 by entering the heavily fortified Branch Davidian compound without body armor and repeatedly negotiating with the cult leader at the urging of Koresh's mother. Over the years, DeGuerin's name had appeared in national news reports about the deadly Waco siege as well as many other celebrated cases.

After DeGuerin entered the fray, he immediately ramped up the public rhetoric on behalf of Kent, who apparently remained muzzled by court confidentiality rules that applied to all judicial disciplinary matters. *Texas Lawyer* magazine published a cover story featuring DeGuerin and Rusty Hardin: two of Houston's best-known defense lawyers were duking it out on opposite sides in the Kent case. "When Rusty Hardin became involved and started saying a crime had been committed it became obvious [Kent] needed some advice about that," DeGuerin told the magazine.[1] Hardin v. DeGuerin seemed like a dream matchup of Houston legal heavyweights.

In interviews, DeGuerin repeatedly described McBroom as a woman scorned whose intimate encounters with Kent were "enthusiastically consensual." DeGuerin offered that Kent would take a lie detector test anytime, anywhere to prove it, although research had shown that polygraph test results could be unreliable and thus were inadmissible as evidence in federal court. The tests were still used as investigative tools but could be misleading depending on the skill of the operator, the personality of the accused, and the way questions were asked. For example, a narcissist who believed his or her own falsehoods might pass, whereas a nervous innocent person might fail.

That mantra about the contact between Kent and McBroom being "enthusiastically consensual" infuriated Hardin and McBroom and her family and friends. But it reflected DeGuerin's client's point of view: Kent seemed convinced that he was attractive to women of all ages, and that his compliments, kisses, and propositions were welcome even to employees.

An aggressive and strong-willed master of criminal defense, DeGuerin pledged to defend Kent's claim of innocence by every means possible: he would dig deep into McBroom's sexual history, sordid courthouse gossip, Kent's unshakable belief in himself, his client's depression and diabetes (a condition known to mask or enhance symptoms of inebriation), and even Kent's embarrassing bouts of impotence to find evidence to bolster Kent's credibility or to attack McBroom's. His team approached McBroom's friends, current and former courthouse colleagues, and even her estranged husband in hopes of finding material to help his client.

DeGuerin's strategy followed a playbook that researchers say is often used by criminal defense attorneys in sexual assault cases. Perpetrators of sexual assault and their allies typically do all they can to silence or discredit complainants. Nearly every case provokes predictable responses: "It never happened; the victim lies; the victim exaggerates; the victim brought it upon herself," Judith Lewis Herman, the Harvard-based expert in the field of sexual trauma, has written.[2] In a related 1992 book, Herman concluded: "The more powerful the perpetrator, the greater is his prerogative to name and define reality and the more completely his arguments prevail."[3]

As the winter and spring of 2008 progressed, McBroom continued to juggle her responsibilities as a courthouse employee, working mother, and new grandmother with her ongoing meetings with prosecutors, FBI agents, and her own lawyers. Sometimes she felt like the accused criminal. Everything she did or said seemed to be scrutinized under a microscope. Her financial records, emails, and telephone records were all eventually subpoenaed. McBroom had provided a long preliminary interview to FBI agents, and initially thought that agents were respectful and that they really listened and took her allegations seriously. Then, as months passed, McBroom worried. Though she had named the judge's secretary as another victim, she knew Wilkerson was refusing to cooperate. McBroom's complaint also had described how her former boss, Gore, had been kissed by Kent and had covered up his misconduct. But Gore, too, seemed to have taken Kent's side.

Still, McBroom no longer stood alone. She'd won an important ally in Rusty Hardin. Hardin knew how to argue a case in court—and also in the court of public opinion. His high-powered firm was simultaneously earning national publicity for its defense of the major league baseball pitcher Roger Clemens, who'd played for both the New York Yankees and the Houston Astros, against allegations of lying about illegal steroid use. A *New York Times* story on the Clemens case described Hardin as "a charmer of juries and journalists and a lawyer whose preparation and aggressive tactics draw in celebrity clients and often send them home with their names cleared."[4] But in McBroom's case, Hardin was taking the prosecution's side. He began publicly declaring that a federal judge had committed "several felonies," on the basis of his client's statements and other evidence. Meanwhile, DeGuerin claimed Hardin was misusing the media to publicize McBroom's allegations and attack Kent, who was forced to keep silent under an agreement struck during the secret judicial disciplinary probe.

Beginning in January 2008, Kent presided over a courtroom in Houston only three floors above the office where Cathy McBroom had worked since requesting an emergency transfer to escape from him. As a judge, Kent used a private elevator and rarely left his en-clave. He and McBroom never saw each other there.

That de facto separation didn't stop McBroom's best friend, Charlene Clark, the San Antonio schoolteacher, from organizing a public protest over his reassignment. McBroom's mother, father, stepfather, her two sons, son-in-law, daughter, and first grandchild were among those Clark organized to parade back and forth with hand-made signs outside the federal courthouse in downtown Houston on January 2, 2008, the day Kent returned to work. "Impeach Judge Kent" one homemade sign said, alongside a big photo of Kent's face. Another read "Warning: Sexual Predator Lurking Under Judicial Robe." Freezing gusts of wind blew through the canyons created by Houston's skyscrapers on the morning of the protest but did little to discourage the group. They simply yelled louder to be heard by motorists who passed the busy intersection beside the courthouse, located adjacent to Houston's bustling city hall complex, a public park, and the theater district.

Clark took a day off from teaching and traveled two hundred miles to organize the protest. She carried a sign and handed out fly-ers and copies of a press release she'd written for reporters and any-one else who happened to walk or drive by that morning. "It is time to put a stop to his criminal and unethical behavior before another female employee falls victim," Clark's press release said. "We must insist on impeachment now!"

McBroom's daughter Evelyn marched and held up a sign as she pushed a stroller on the sidewalk with tiny Sara, the four-month-old baby bundled in thick blankets. McBroom's youngest son, Caleb, then fourteen, wore a long parka that flapped in the gusts of wind as he stood on the sidewalk near the stoplight at Rusk and Smith Streets and shouted about what Kent had done to his mom. Caleb stretched his arm to hand out flyers to curious motorists and pedes-trians. The flyer said that the Southern District of Texas's 2003 policy against sexual harassment banned any "unwelcome sexual advances, requests of sexual favors and other verbal or physical contact." It alleged that "Judge Kent has blatantly disregarded this policy and routinely made unwelcome sexual advances on the female employees of the Galveston federal court system" and that "the Fifth Circuit's solution to this criminal behavior is to transfer Judge Kent (after a 4-month paid leave) to the very same building where his victims work! He returns to work today 1/02/2008."

Protesters urged passers-by to insist that Congress take action with signs that said "Impeachment Now!" and provided phone numbers for representatives empowered to initiate such a review. "Mrs. McBroom is not Judge Kent's first or last victim! He has a long-standing reputation for sexually abusive behavior. This behavior cannot be tolerated! It is time to stop using the taxpayers' money to pay for and allow this man to behave as if he is 'above the law,'" their handouts declared.

McBroom did not parade on the sidewalk that morning. Indeed, she felt forced to quickly pass protesting friends and family as she entered the courthouse on one of the coldest days of the year. When a judge later urged her to stop them she quietly explained she would never try to keep her loved ones from exercising their constitutional rights.

Inside the Sugar Cube, other federal court employees and attorneys wondered why McBroom and her allies were pushing for more punishment. To insiders, Kent's 2007 public reprimand seemed sufficient punishment. The very short list of public disciplinary actions taken against federal judges nationwide in a decade included the reprimand to US District Judge McBryde in Fort Worth in 1999, a long-delayed reprimand to Senior US District Judge Real in Los Angeles, approved in 2006 but not issued until 2008, and the admonishment of Ninth Circuit Chief Judge Alex Kozinski in 2009. Kent had also agreed to other conditions: He'd undergone counseling. He'd given up civil cases involving sexual harassment. Nor was Kent handling any criminal matters, since he was still being investigated both by the FBI and by that special unit of prosecutors called the Public Integrity Section.

Cathy McBroom knew that Kent's attorneys, led by DeGuerin, were deploying private investigators in efforts to discredit her. His team had been calling friends, former friends, and past and present courthouse colleagues, as well as former classmates and former co-workers from other jobs. DeGuerin's team seemed bent on a quest to uncover her entire sexual life, her social drinking history, and her character as far back as puberty, she thought. DeGuerin even sent a packet of questions via FedEx to McBroom's estranged husband, Rex McBroom, at the chemical plant where he worked. He refused to sign for the package.

Three prosecutors from the Department of Justice's Washington, DC–based Public Integrity Section had begun working regularly in Houston in 2008—and they were pushing FBI agents to investigate McBroom's credibility too. In March 2008, prosecutors summoned McBroom to the FBI headquarters, then in an office building off Houston's busy Loop, Interstate 610, for an unusual interview that McBroom said focused largely on her sexual history. The FBI agents she'd met attended the meeting, but John Pearson, one of the Public Integrity Section prosecutors, posed most of the questions. Pearson, like Kent and Jones, was a graduate of the University of Texas School of Law, but he received his law degree in 2003, just four years before being assigned to the Kent case. He was younger even than Mc-Broom's oldest daughter.

McBroom found Pearson both aggressive and annoying as he blasted her with questions. It seemed to her that he was pushing her to list every sexual encounter she'd ever had in her life outside of her marriages as well as any other embarrassing facts that could possibly be used by Kent's defense team to attack her credibility. "They had called all my former friends, and people I used to go to happy hours with," she remembered much later. "They wanted to know every-thing I had ever done since high school." As she stumbled through a few anecdotes in a conference room full of men in suits, McBroom felt utterly humiliated. McBroom had married and gotten divorced young, and later remarried. She'd been having a rocky time with her second husband for several years and would soon be divorced again. She liked to laugh, dance, and drink wine and margaritas. She'd dated a lot before and between her marriages and easily attracted men. Some stories she felt ashamed to tell. She'd been unfaithful to her es-tranged husband and had partied with other men, including federal court colleagues. But she didn't understand why these very personal choices were relevant to her complaint about Kent. Pearson, who struck her as a clean-cut goody-two-shoes type, offended her with a tone that seemed judgmental. If she stumbled or misremembered a date or an ex-boyfriend's name, government lawyers prompted her with information they'd collected from others. "They knew things about me that I had already forgotten," McBroom later said.

After the interview Hardin called Pearson and began to deliver what would be a series of lectures. He was furious that McBroom, as a crime victim and complaining witness, had been attacked in that interrogation as if she were the suspect. "I have never seen a victim treated this way. You're not going to have a witness," he warned. "You're going to break her. Leave her alone." Hardin also phoned the other prosecutors to complain. In some conversations Hardin lost his temper. Hardin thought Pearson seemed green. Hardin knew Pearson's parents, who lived in Houston, and considered him a junior lawyer liable to lose his nerve in a legal fight with a judge backed by an aggressive attorney like DeGuerin.

Two of the three prosecutors assigned to the Kent case were relatively young. Pearson had spent most of the year in Houston, though he normally lived and worked in Washington, DC. His partner on the case was another talented prosecutor named AnnaLou Tirol, a marathon runner like McBroom, who had been brought in from California. Tirol, in contrast to Pearson, knew how to make McBroom "feel confident" and "feel heard," McBroom said. Both Pearson and Tirol were rising stars who would later earn promotions: in a few more years, Tirol would run the Public Integrity Section as acting chief from September 2016 to September 2019. At the time, they were overseen by a seasoned veteran from Washington, DC, Peter Ainsworth, an expert who frequently gave presentations on his corruption fighting efforts at conferences around the globe.

In Hardin's mind, all three prosecutors had become distracted in their search for evidence of bribery, influence peddling, or illegal gifts involving Kent and his entourage of attorney friends—the kinds of cases the Public Integrity Section typically investigated against high-profile targets like members of Congress, other federal judges, and high-powered political elites. "They're missing the point," he said.

Hardin grew more agitated when no indictments had yet been issued by June 2008. He knew the five-year statute of limitations on the first of the two sexual assaults McBroom had described—the 2003 attack—would soon expire. If that happened, it would weaken any chance of a successful prosecution of Kent. Hardin feared the federal prosecutors were too inexperienced or unmotivated to build a strong case for sexual assault, the kind of crime normally handled by local district attorneys. As a former state prosecutor, he knew those cases required gaining the trust of an often fragile or psychologically damaged witness, and then gathering supporting evidence to help her survive an intensely emotional courtroom conflict. In a private meeting, he berated them, saying, "Even a gorilla would have indicted Kent by now!"

Behind the scenes, Dick DeGuerin was putting on pressure too. On August 11, 2008, he and Kent flew to Washington to meet directly at Main Justice with high-ranking prosecutors who oversaw the probe. Their meeting included FBI agents, the case prosecutors, the head of the Public Integrity Section, and senior prosecutors at the US Department of Justice. As before, Kent insisted that McBroom was lying. Kent said that "any attempt to characterize the conduct between him and [McBroom] as nonconsensual was absolute nonsense."[5]

McBroom waited all day in Hardin's office on August 28, 2008, knowing the statute of limitations of the 2003 attack would expire in only hours. Finally, a phone call arrived. Kent had been indicted on two counts of "abusive sexual contact" and another count of "attempted aggravated sexual abuse" for attacks carried out in 2003 and 2007 on "Person A." Person A, of course, was Cathy McBroom.

CHAPTER 12

Person B

Houston, 2008–2009

In the weeks after Kent's indictment, Public Integrity Section prosecutors and witnesses kept filing in and out of the Houston federal
courthouse's grand jury room. Officials refused to discuss the ongoing secret investigation, but investigators still seemed focused on gifts
and trips Kent received from lawyer friends and any favors the judge
might have performed in return. FBI agents don't often investigate
sexual assaults, which are typically handled in state courts, but they
can be masters at unraveling fraud schemes and other complex forms
of corruption. They inquired about Kent's limo rides and excur-
sions aboard yachts as well as trips to London, Colorado, and Civil
War battlefields. They also wanted to know about Kent's behavior
at haunts like Heartbreakers, the so-called "gentleman's club" on
the Gulf Freeway. Ultimately, eight of Kent's closest attorney friends
were subpoenaed to produce receipts, credit card statements, and
financial records from as far back as 2001. Two were trial lawyers
who had once been Kent's law clerks: Tony Buzbee and Kurt Arnold.

By 2007 Tony Buzbee was a high-rolling millionaire trial attorney
with a penthouse suite on the seventy-third floor of the Chase Tower.
Buzbee had gotten his first real legal job as Kent's law clerk after

graduating from University of Houston Law in 1997. An ex-Marine and a Gulf War veteran, Buzbee had a blunt manner of speaking. He'd handled enough high-profile cases and thrown enough flamboyant Houston society parties with A-list celebrity musicians to feel very comfortable with press attention. (He also flirted with politics, later running unsuccessfully to become Houston's mayor.) In an interview, Buzbee confirmed that agents asked about Kent and requested financial records, too, but said he'd gotten no favors from Kent. Yes, some of his clients benefitted from settlements and verdicts in Kent's court, Buzbee said, but he lost plenty of cases there too.

Another subpoena went to Kurt Arnold, another more recent ex-clerk, who had attended Kent's alma mater, the UT School of Law. Considered something of a child prodigy, Arnold graduated from college at only nineteen and later finished in the top 5 percent of his law school class in 2002. During his clerkship, from 2002 to 2003, Arnold really clicked with Kent. Even after Arnold established his own law firm in Houston, he and Kent remained close. Arnold didn't want to discuss Kent with reporters.

The credit card statements and other records various lawyers were providing to prosecutors weren't made public, but Kent had listed a few interesting gifts on federal disclosure forms. In 2001, Kent reported that a huge insurance company had reimbursed him an unspecified amount for "round trip transportation only" to speak at a conference in London, though Kent did not specify who'd paid for his stay at a posh London hotel and other travel expenses. That same year, Melancon, his attorney friend, had thrown a wedding reception for the judge, his new wife, and about a hundred guests. Kent reported the catered party with seafood, drinks, and live music as worth only a thousand dollars. In 2002, Kent listed one more present: a three-hundred-dollar crystal bowl from a different attorney friend. Although Kent disclosed nothing more from 2003 to 2007, former court employees and attorneys said in interviews that Kent received a stream of expensive lunches, cocktails, and other freebies. Federal agents were asking about those undisclosed items.

Then, in July 2008, a source called the *Houston Chronicle* newsroom with information about another favor Kent allegedly received that seemed far more valuable than free lunches or even deluxe

London lodgings. After his first wife's death, Kent had been saddled with medical bills and had complained aloud of debts. His second wife wanted to move off-island, but he couldn't sell his old house. So an attorney friend offered to buy the judge's Galveston place for an inflated price, the tipster said. The tipster lacked details but thought the buyer had been one of Kent's former law clerks. Both the house he sold and the one he bought were in Galveston County, so part of the story could likely be confirmed in public records.

The clerk's office in Galveston County holds a treasure trove of intricate hand-drawn maps and shelves lined with bound deeds dating back to the 1800s. For investigative reporters, genealogists, and other researchers, it can be a place of rich discoveries. By the 2000s, employees had scanned many documents and a computer search turned up two recent records for Samuel Kent: a deed for a house Kent bought in Santa Fe in 2006 and another for the island place sold that same year. Both appeared to be cash transactions; no mortgage records were associated with those deeds.

One deed listed the sales price for Kent's former home, a two-story red-brick house in the Denver Court neighborhood, as $339,500. Another search of that address showed its assessed value for tax purposes that same year was just $224,090. According to tax records the Galveston house was sixty-two years old, with no recent remodeling or central air conditioning. So far, the tip seemed to be checking out: Kent seemed to have gotten a great price—more than $100,000 over the property's assessed value—in what looked like a cash deal. But the buyer was not an attorney; she was an orthodontist from Corpus Christi who had once lived in Houston. There were no other records in Galveston County under her name, yet the house, obviously run-down from the outside, didn't look like a beach getaway or an attractive rental property.

But there was more information about the orthodontist in the Harris County clerk's archives, located in 2007 in an eerie half-abandoned former jail in downtown Houston near Buffalo Bayou—a gloomy place with massive concrete walls. The archives held an old divorce case listed under the orthodontist's name. Inside a yellow-backed folder was a thin sheaf of papers: the record of the division of assets and severing of ties between two people who'd wed and had children together. One child's name was familiar: the buyer of Kent's old house was also the mother of Kurt Arnold, Kent's ex-clerk.

Arnold referred further questions about the house to his criminal defense lawyer, Randy Schaffer. Schaffer's son, Josh, also an attorney, was a personal friend of Arnold's—they had been UT law classmates. In an interview, Randy Schaffer acknowledged that Kent's house had become part of the federal probe but insisted that Arnold had violated no laws. "I think this is essentially a situation where a young lawyer has been caught in the crossfire of the government going after Kent."[1]

Buzbee, another trial lawyer who had been one of Kent's other former clerks, said Kent also had urged him to buy the old house. But Buzbee, who at that time owned a real estate management company, said the house did not meet his investment standards. It was too outdated, too far from the beach, and too expensive. "I told him 'No' in no uncertain terms. It's not a good rental house. It doesn't have central heat or air conditioning," he said.

Kent's lawyer, Dick DeGuerin, was very busy in 2008: he was simultaneously seeking a new trial for a former Katy football coach whom DeGuerin believed had been wrongfully convicted of murder and representing the wife of a state supreme court justice in another high-profile case. Still, DeGuerin took time to provide the *Houston Chronicle* with a thick stack of documents. In interviews, DeGuerin insisted there was nothing wrong with Kent's selling real estate to an attorney or to an attorney's mother. The house had been Kent and his first wife's dream home, he explained. But it was also where Mary Ann had slowly and painfully died. Kent's second wife wanted no part of it. Six years after his first wife's death, DeGuerin estimated that Kent remained $80,000 in debt because of medical expenses that were not covered by his federal health insurance. Kent put the house on the market but had no money to spruce up the place. At first no buyers seemed interested.

Except Arnold. Arnold just helped arrange for his mother to buy the place, DeGuerin explained. Arnold's mother did not take out a loan to buy Kent's house, because Arnold provided money for the sale, DeGuerin confirmed. Before doing so, Arnold had told Kent he worried about how such a deal might look to outsiders, since

Arnold's firm regularly handled cases in Kent's court. So Kent had asked his law clerk at that time, a recent Harvard Law graduate, to review the facts and provide a formal legal opinion on the proposed sale, DeGuerin said as he handed over the opinion.

It hardly seemed possible that Kent's current law clerk could have provided an objective legal opinion for her mentor and boss on the ethics of a real estate deal that involved the judge and one of his ex-clerks. But she had done so on Kent's orders. The clerk wrote that an arm's-length sale involving a real estate agent and a fair and well-documented price might be acceptable, but could be questioned under a federal judicial canon according to which judges should avoid "impropriety and the appearance of impropriety in all actions." That canon, she wrote, "contains the only language that is arguably critical of the contemplated transaction." Prosecutors' interest in the unusual house sale prompted another front-page story in the *Houston Chronicle*.[2]

Behind the scenes, Pearson, one of the prosecutors, assembled a file of legal precedents for Schaffer, Arnold's attorney. The documents showed that other people who used so-called straw buyers to purchase real estate from judges or other public officials had later been convicted of criminal charges. After reviewing the cases, Schaffer contacted DeGuerin and asked to speak to Kent. Schaffer believed the federal judge had knowingly put his own law clerks on the hot seat through his own "greed and selfishness," Schaffer later said. "I wanted to get him to man up and save the kids."

Kent showed up for the meeting in blue jeans and a work shirt. Schaffer and Kent, both about the same age, began discussing basketball as they waited in a small reception area in DeGuerin's office, a homey space in a historic building in downtown Houston that is filled with rustic wooden furniture, Texas memorabilia, and items from the attorney's ranch in far West Texas. Initially, Kent was adamant that he'd done nothing wrong, Schaffer later recalled. That changed when Schaffer shared the file he'd gotten from prosecutors. Using a middle man—effectively a "straw buyer"—made the "house transaction look pretty seedy," he told Kent. "I think you should seriously consider your situation." After reviewing several cases, Kent began "crying like a baby," Schaffer said.

A few months later, Arnold, under pressure from prosecutors, hired another criminal defense attorney to help him: Reid Weingarten, a Washington, DC, lawyer who also happened to be a former Public Integrity Section prosecutor. In the 1980s, Weingarten had prosecuted Judge Nixon, who had been criminally convicted and subsequently impeached. With Weingarten's assistance, Arnold cut a deal to cooperate with Kent's prosecution and was never charged himself.

Arnold has never discussed the arrangement. But DeGuerin later said the younger lawyer worked out a deal to protect himself, his mother, and his law license. "They told him he was going to be indicted and the only way he could stay out of prison was to turn against Sam," DeGuerin said. DeGuerin continued to publicly defend the sale as legal and said he considered that to have been an empty threat, merely a prosecutors' trick. "But it scared the shit out of that weasel." DeGuerin thought prosecutors would never have been able to prove Arnold got favorable rulings or anything else from Kent in return.

Among other documents, Arnold supplied investigators with a copy of a bill for about two thousand dollars that he'd paid at Heartbreakers for a group that included Kent, DeGuerin said. The windowless club off of I-45 South had been one of Kent's longtime hangouts. The club's dancers wore low-cut scarlet gowns, and supposedly some of them offered extra services for a price. Prosecutors argued that the tab Arnold paid included a lap dance or a blowjob for Kent, DeGuerin said, though Kent denied that.

The alleged blowjob receipt must have looked like valuable evidence for prosecutors and potentially damaging to Kent's defense. In her statement about the March 2007 incident, McBroom had said that Kent had a visible erection when he tried to force her to perform oral sex. But as part of his attack on McBroom's credibility, DeGuerin had claimed that Kent suffered erectile dysfunction. Behind the scenes, federal prosecutors already had begun trying to locate expert witnesses on erectile dysfunction who could provide testimony about potential "triggers." However, the Heartbreakers' bill was less valuable to prosecutors than another secret Arnold shared with them: Kent repeatedly had unwanted sexual contact with another female court employee—Donna Wilkerson.

Wilkerson first discovered that Arnold had talked to federal investigators directly from Kent, who pulled into her driveway one night in mid-2008 and asked her to climb inside his silver Toyota Solara. When she refused, Kent blurted out that Arnold had turned against him. Kent said Arnold had talked about her, too, and said they "needed to circle the wagons," Wilkerson later recalled.

Wilkerson worried that Arnold had been targeted partly because of their long friendship. She and Arnold had gotten close during his clerkship—she'd considered him a smart, sweet, and funny kid. For years, they'd stayed in touch by exchanging texts and chatting on days when Arnold had cases in Kent's court. She trusted Arnold and she shared information with him about Kent's misbehavior that she had told no one else. Arnold, like Wilkerson, had been part of Kent's inner circle and had sworn an oath in his year as a judicial employee to keep the judge's secrets. Arnold knew what Kent had done to Wilkerson. He knew things she'd never told anyone in her own family.

The surreal scene in the driveway got stranger when Wilkerson's husband came out to greet Kent. Wilkerson listened as the two men exchanged pleasantries. Then Kent began repeating lies he'd told others. He mentioned that he'd approached Wilkerson a couple of times and that she'd rebuffed him. Then he offered up an awkward apology for his behavior, blurting out some of what he'd done to her and long concealed from others in an erratic way that she found frightening. Wilkerson had never before told her husband any details about Kent's misbehavior. The visit made Wilkerson worry whether Kent had become unhinged.

Santa Fe was a relatively small town, and over the years, Wilkerson and her husband had socialized with Kent and his wife and attended flashy parties thrown by attorneys who practiced in his court. Sometimes she'd seen Kent get plastered at those parties and hit on lawyers' girlfriends or wives. At one particularly elaborate event at Tony Buzbee's mansion in Friendswood, she'd watched as Kent stood over a chocolate fountain, drunkenly dipped his fingers into the liquid and slowly licked them. Later he delivered a weird speech in a fake English accent, but Kent had been careful never to approach

Wilkerson in front of her husband. Now Wilkerson realized that everything was "going to hit the fan." Slowly she began feeding information to her husband about Kent's attacks. The incidents had been
more numerous and worse than even Arnold knew. The judge had
begun by dispensing unwelcome kisses, hugs, and suggestive compliments. Then he'd started touching Wilkerson in chambers after
his long drinking lunches, even though she'd repeatedly pushed him
away and urged him to stop. Soon, she would feel compelled to describe the details of those attacks first to investigators and later in
court and in congressional testimony.[3]

From her first days at work, Kent regularly watched Wilkerson as
she sat in her office, connected to his, and remarked on her beauty
and sensuality as she applied lotion to her arms or drank bottled
water—after which she ceased doing both in his presence. On Fridays, or whenever he'd gone out for one of those long lunches, he
began coming up behind her chair unexpectedly and reaching inside
her blouse. She started to wear turtleneck sweaters to thwart his efforts. She wore one so often that it became pilled and ratty. "Cut it
out. Cut that shit out. Quit acting like a pig," she'd sometimes felt
forced to say to Kent. For weeks, or months, he would behave. Still,
she feared that if she protested, she'd jeopardize her career. As a high
school graduate, she was unlikely to get another job that paid more
than $70,000 a year plus benefits. Nor did she want to provoke a
conflict that could prompt her own husband—a man with a "fairly
short fuse"—to confront Kent.

The worst episodes, the ones she never wanted to think about,
occurred in her third and fourth years of working for Kent, and always on afternoons when Kent had gone out for two- or three-hour
lunches and returned to the office intoxicated and out of control.
He'd usually begin by unleashing obscene suggestions and invent-
ing a work-related reason for her to come into his office. She tried
to avoid him, but when he felt determined to grab her in chambers,
Wilkerson—less than half his weight and a foot shorter—found it impossible to escape. "Once caught, cornered or pinned, there was no
getting away," she later said, though she tried putting furniture in between them or "talking him down." At times he trapped her behind
her desk or on the floor, pushed aside her clothing and sucked her

breasts or attempted to shove his fingers inside her. She tried to suppress memories of how he'd also forced her down on the floor, shimmied down her pants, and spread her legs to perform unwanted oral sex, attacks she later felt forced to describe to federal investigators.

By the end of 2008, Wilkerson felt sure that because she'd minimized Kent's misbehavior before the grand jury—and because Arnold had told the truth—she could be a target for a perjury prosecution. Both FBI agents and prosecutors continued to pressure her to cooperate. She wasn't speaking to Kent anymore, but he managed to send a message. His law clerk told her that Kent claimed that if "Donna rolled on him, it would be all he could take and he would kill himself."

Finally, Wilkerson called an attorney friend and former employer for advice. He immediately asked, "What are you doing?!!!" He was shocked when she admitted she'd already spoken twice to a federal grand jury without seeking counsel and urged her to obtain her own attorney. Terry Yates agreed to represent her. In a meeting, Yates laid out two options: bluff and live with the secret for the rest of your life, or get on board. Then he gave her some badly needed counsel that she never forgot: "If Kent has been doing all of those things to you against your will for all these years, then the judge really isn't your friend and you don't owe him your loyalty."

In the end Wilkerson agreed to voluntarily grant an interview to the FBI. She spoke for eight hours. Wilkerson described five years of episodes involving Kent that included repeated unwanted sexual contact that had gone as far as oral and digital sex. "I spilled it all out," she later remembered. "And I slept better that night than I did in years because I was finally free." At the meeting, agents told Wilkerson that she and McBroom were not the only women who claimed to be Kent's victims: At least six other women had agreed to testify against him.

On January 6, 2009, the grand jury re-indicted Kent. The new indictment added two new felony charges related to sexual attacks on a woman identified only as "Person B." Kent was charged with sexual abuse for forcibly assaulting Person B with his finger and hands and with aggravated sexual abuse for extensive unwanted sexual contact on one or more occasions between 2004 and 2005. The new indictment added a felony charge of obstruction of justice for lying to the Fifth Circuit investigatory committee. Prosecutors now considered the federal judges who'd investigated Kent to be additional victims of his crimes, because he'd lied to them under oath.

McBroom broke down and cried when she saw the new indictments with allegations of sexual attacks on "Person B." This person, whoever it was, also had suffered and been forced to repeatedly submit to forced sexual contact. McBroom finally had an ally. An anonymous ally. "It was no longer a 'he said, she said,' case. . . . It was a 'he said, they said,'" McBroom later said. She believed Person B to be Wilkerson, though prosecutors refused to reveal the other victim's identity. McBroom knew nothing about other women who'd also agreed to testify if the case ever went to trial.

Kent already faced three felony charges for the attacks on McBroom. He now had been charged with three more. If convicted on all six charges, the maximum sentence could put him in prison for life.

DeGuerin attempted one last counteroffensive. He granted another round of interviews and characterized Wilkerson and Kent's relationship as "an affair of the heart." Under threat of prosecution, two of Kent's closest friends had been compelled to embellish and twist the truth, he insisted. "They cut away all of his support system," DeGuerin said. "They scared everyone who wanted to help him and they all left like rats." Ultimately, the additional charges deflated Kent's interest in fighting to defend himself. Kent could win only by discrediting McBroom, Arnold, Wilkerson, and potentially six more women.

DeGuerin and his legal team could still help Kent negotiate. In February 2009 Kent received a plea deal that allowed the federal judge to avoid becoming a registered sex offender. Under the deal, all five of the sexual abuse–related charges were dropped, though Kent was required to admit that the facts underlying those charges were true. In a voice that had dropped from a boom to a whisper, Kent pled guilty to one count of obstruction of justice.

On May 11, 2009, Senior US District Judge Roger Vinson, who'd been specially assigned to the case from Florida, returned to the Houston federal courthouse one more time for the sentencing.

When Cathy McBroom walked into the courtroom to give her victim's statement that day, she knew she would finally meet Person B. All alone on one of the benches sat Donna Wilkerson, who was dressed to the nines as usual. McBroom didn't cross the room to greet her. She figured Wilkerson probably still "hates my guts—because her life has been ruined too." Both McBroom and Wilkerson had prepared statements about Kent's impact on their lives and how the federal judge had deliberately exploited his power to harm them.

McBroom took the stand first. It felt strange to testify as a witness after so many years as an active participant and organizer of hearings. Kent was no longer sitting on an elevated bench but in the defendant's chair. "When I think of the events leading up to his conviction, I'm consumed with emotion. Even though I have been able to move on in both my personal life and my career, I will forever be scarred by what happened in Galveston," she said. McBroom recounted the details of the attacks and their lasting impact on her and on her children, who'd read Kent's claims that all of that unwanted contact had been "enthusiastically consensual." McBroom said she'd been shocked by Kent's "evil and deliberate manipulation" of the truth in his efforts to defend himself. "He bragged about his gift of manipulation, which he thought would save him from conviction. People were asking him to just resign and he would tell them that if he had just fifteen minutes with a jury he would be exonerated," she said. "This judge has hurt so many people in so many ways. Every employee in Galveston has been afraid of his power and control."[4]

Wilkerson testified next. Slowly, she began to describe how for seven years she had been "sexually and psychologically abused and manipulated," beginning on her very first week at work. For so long she had done the tasks Kent had requested—and now she wondered whether all of his kingly commands were fueled by hidden motives to facilitate abusive and criminal activities. "I would like to tell you about the real Sam Kent," she said. "Sam Kent has spent his life manipulating people and abusing his relationships with people. Certainly, this has been my experience the time I have known him. He has also spent this time lying to everyone. He will never acknowledge what he has done to the people around him. He continues to try to manipulate the system and make excuses for his aberrant behavior."

Dick DeGuerin then addressed the court, requesting that Kent be sentenced to a medical facility and receive court-ordered drug and alcohol counseling. "Although Sam Kent says that he is not an alcoholic, he is an alcoholic," DeGuerin added.

Finally, Judge Kent stood. He said he was a "completely broken man, but in some ways a better person." Kent apologized to "his staff," though he did not mention McBroom or Wilkerson by name, and to "my wife and family and to my marriage, all of whom and which I have likely irretrievably lost." He also apologized "to all who seek redress in the federal system for tarnishing its image and because never again can I vouchsafe their interest." He concluded: "I have had the benefit of twenty-six months of absolute sobriety, a wonderful pretrial officer, a sensitive and thoughtful presentencing officer, terrific attorneys and excellent medical help. Through their assistance, I have come to see what a flawed, selfish, thoughtless and indulgent person I have been, and I have already begun to try and put myself right and emerge from this a better person."

Then the prosecutor spoke, summarizing Judge Kent's conduct and requesting a thirty-six-month sentence, consistent with the plea agreement.

Judge Vinson addressed Judge Kent last. "The consequence to you of your wrongful conduct is not only the loss of a job which many [people] feel is the best job in the world, but also punishment under the law. And as you well know, the law is no respecter of persons, and everyone stands equal in this Court. And former judges are no exception. Your wrongful conduct is a huge black X on your own record. It's a smear on the legal profession, and, of course, it's a stain on the justice system itself. And, importantly, it is a matter of grave concern within the federal courts." Vinson imposed a thirty-three-month sentence, three months less than prosecutors requested. He told Kent to surrender voluntarily to the federal Bureau of Prisons no later than noon on June 15, 2009.

Person A and Person B—Cathy McBroom and Donna Wilkerson—left the courtroom that day without speaking to each other.

Each had mixed feelings about the plea deal. Kent was a convicted felon. He'd admitted to unwanted nonconsensual sexual contact with them. But he'd only been convicted of obstruction of justice for lying to the Fifth Circuit's investigatory committee and to federal investigators. He remained a US district judge. And he had never really apologized to them.

CHAPTER 13

The Path to Impeachment

Washington, DC, 2009

James Sensenbrenner, a firebrand Republican congressman from Wisconsin and longtime advocate of judicial reforms, was one of several lawmakers angered by a federal judge's refusal to resign even as a convicted felon and admitted sexual abuser. Sensenbrenner spoke in a flat Midwestern accent, but could quickly turn up the volume. On June 9, 2009, a few weeks after Kent's sentencing in Texas, he and other members of the House of Representatives introduced a resolution to launch impeachment proceedings. In all of American history, only thirteen federal judges had ever been impeached, but in 2009, the House had two impeachments in the works. Members of Congress already had established a task force to consider impeaching Porteous. Now they would look at Kent too.

Federal judges' lifetime power arose from Article III of the Constitution, which was drafted in 1787 in Philadelphia, then the nation's largest city with forty thousand souls. The Constitution states that judicial power "shall be vested in one supreme Court and in such inferior Courts as the Congress may from time to time ordain and establish." Federal judges were to be appointed for life "during good

Behaviour"—which was not defined—and were to receive a "Compensation, which shall not be diminished during their Continuance in Office." Impeachment was envisioned as a way to dispatch only the most errant federal judges and elite office holders, such as congressmen, cabinet members, and presidents. However, after the first messy attempted impeachment of a sitting senator in 1799, Congress had only once impeached a cabinet member and rarely used the tool against presidents. Three presidents have been impeached: Andrew Johnson in 1868, Bill Clinton in 1998, and Donald Trump in 2019 and again in January 2021. None was convicted by the Senate and removed from office. Only Clinton's impeachment had anything to do with sexual misconduct (he was impeached in part for perjury after the House found that he had lied under oath about sexual encounters with a White House intern named Monica Lewinsky).

All other successful House impeachments targeted federal judges. Rules have been streamlined over the centuries, but the process remains complex. First, representatives must investigate, draw up formal charges, and then vote on whether to approve each charge. Next, House managers—congressmen who act as prosecutors—present their case to the Senate, or a Senate committee, in a trial.

Back in the 1780s, impeachment possibly fit the need for judicial oversight in America. The new nation under President George Washington was only beginning to expand its original footprint and was run by a single political party dominated by white Revolutionary War veterans who favored knee breeches and powdered wigs. Back then, in most states the vote was restricted to white male property owners, a tiny fraction of the nation's population of 2.7 million. The first federal courts began days after the passage of the Judiciary Act of 1789 with only a dozen judges.

One of George Washington's judicial appointees was John Pickering, another patriot of the Revolutionary War. As a former state supreme court justice who had read law at Harvard College, Pickering initially seemed well qualified to serve the District of New Hampshire. A miniature of him shows a proper gent with a tight-lipped smile, a hook nose, and the requisite wig.[1] Washington didn't seem to notice that Pickering suffered from what some called a nervous disorder prior to his 1795 appointment, though his behavior had prompted complaints. By 1801, Pickering failed to show up to federal court so often that other judges were begged to send a permanent substitute to compensate for Pickering's so-called "derangement."

If any federal jurist turned foul in those days, congressmen in the compact sixteen United States could quickly detect it. Pickering's antics spawned press coverage and public ridicule, but the partisan nomination process and deference to judicial independence protected Pickering until the Federalist Party, of which he was a member, lost power in 1800 with the election of Thomas Jefferson as president. Jefferson had formed a rival party, the Jeffersonian Republicans (or the Democratic Republicans). He decried the Constitution's lifetime appointments for federal judges, claiming those tenures bestowed excessive power.

In 1802, Pickering presided over a federal government case seeking unpaid taxes from the owner of the merchant ship *Eliza*, with four sets of sails and masts that seemingly stretched to the sky. As a district judge, Pickering had the duty of ruling on the government's effort to seize and sell the ship for taxes that the owner failed to pay after unloading imported goods in the nearby port of Portsmouth, New Hampshire. Pickering took the bench "in a state of total intoxication, produced by the free and intemperate use of intoxicating liquors and did then and there frequently, in a most profane and indecent manner, invoke the name of the Supreme Being, to the evil example of all good citizens," according to congressional records. He ignored rules during the herky-jerky proceeding, prompting spectators to jeer as the courtroom became a "bedlam of confusion and laughter."[2] Before the government finished presenting its case, Pickering ordered the ship restored to its owner, a member of his Federalist Party. When the prosecutor beseeched Pickering to hear remaining witnesses, Pickering said, "We will hear everything—swear every damn scoundrel that can be produced—but if we sit here four thousand years the ship will still be restored."[3]

Pickering's bizarre behavior prompted the secretary of the treasury to report to Jefferson that the judge was acting in a manner "which showed total unfitness for the office."[4] Jefferson pushed to use impeachment for the first time against a judge. But members of the House of Representatives dithered. They approved a resolution on their intent to impeach, then adjourned. Finally, in March 1803, representatives approved articles of impeachment, a list of misdeeds resembling a criminal indictment. Pickering would later stand trial in the Senate on those charges, including allegations of inappropriate behavior in the *Eliza* case, of "absence of temperance" and incompetence in court. But Pickering failed to show up or hire an attorney to respond, spawning more havoc.

At trial, the most compelling argument for the defense came from Pickering's son, Jacob, who claimed that for two years before the alleged offenses and ever since his father "has been and now is insane, his mind wholly deranged and altogether incapable of transacting any kind of business which requires the exercise of judgment, or the faculties of reason and therefore . . . is incapable of corruption," according to the official record of "The Impeachment and Trial of John Pickering."[5] In that context, Jacob Pickering said that his father's "obscene behavior" should serve as "irresistible evidence of his deranged state of mind," because his father had previously been known "for the purity of his language and the correctness of his habits." The judge's loyal son thus attempted a disability defense to impeachment in his petition. The tactic proved unsuccessful. In March 1804, John Pickering became the nation's first judge to be found guilty of impeachment charges and removed by the Senate.

More than two hundred years later, attorney Dick DeGuerin in 2009 attempted to convince court leaders that Samuel B. Kent deserved a disability retirement and not impeachment, citing Kent's depression, physical impairments, and problems with alcohol. Kent, at fifty-nine, was not old enough to qualify for a federal pension, an option that otherwise might have allowed him to avoid further scrutiny and retire with full pay. On May 27, 2009, Chief Judge Jones declined his disability retirement request. In her ruling Jones said that Kent's alcoholism was a "catalyst" for some of his criminal misbehavior and he would be unable to serve the court even as a senior judge. "Kent has forfeited his claim to such status by pleading guilty to a felony," she wrote. "Further, the interpretation [of federal law] must be influenced by public policy that a claimant should not profit from his own wrongdoing by engaging in criminal misconduct and then collecting a federal retirement salary."

Sensenbrenner and other senior congressmen had plenty of experience with impeachment. They'd participated in back-to-back judicial impeachments in the 1980s. Three came quickly on the heels of the 1980 Judicial Conduct and Disability Act. All involved corruption allegations against district judges: Harry E. Claiborne of Nevada, Walter Nixon of Mississippi, and Alcee Hastings of Florida. Like Kent, those jurists were first criminally prosecuted by the Public Integrity Section, then a relatively new unit of the Department of Justice. Sensenbrenner and other members of the House Judiciary Committee remembered well the agonizing and polarizing debates of the 1980s when they'd been stuck for months in hearings involving federal judges' alleged misbehavior with a colorful cast of characters: Claiborne's with a Nevada brothel owner, Hastings's with a representative of "mob-connected felons," and Nixon's with a Mississippi businessman who had bestowed an unusually generous gift.

In 1984, Claiborne, chief district judge in Nevada and a former prosecutor, beat other charges against him but was convicted of falsifying income tax returns. In 1986, Nixon, also chief judge in his district, was convicted of perjury for lying to a grand jury that asked about oil and gas rights worth $60,000 that he'd allegedly gotten in exchange for helping to influence the drug prosecution of a business associate's son. Both refused to resign and became the first federal judges ever to continue to collect judicial pay as prisoners. But with criminal convictions in hand, there was little debate in the House about whether either judge had committed an "impeachable offense." Claiborne was impeached and then removed from office by the Senate in 1986, seven months into his two-year prison sentence. Nixon appealed and kept his pay for three years after his conviction, until his removal in 1989.

The prosecution and impeachment of District Judge Alcee Hastings, of Florida, overlapped with Nixon's, but took a different path. Hastings, a dynamic and popular ex-politician, was nominated through President Carter's efforts to diversify the courts and became the first African American federal district judge in Florida in 1979. A bearded man with a bald pate and a wide smile, Hastings had been a district judge for just two years when scandal cast a cloud over his judicial service. Hastings was indicted alongside an attorney friend,

William A. Borders, and charged with conspiracy and obstruction of justice after allegedly soliciting a $150,000 bribe in return for reducing sentences of mob-connected felons. Borders was convicted of conspiracy, but Hastings was acquitted in 1983. In his defense Hastings used recordings from the government's undercover sting to show that although he had made self-incriminating statements, he had never actually accepted a bribe. Hastings argued that he'd been entrapped by a Department of Justice loyal to President Reagan and hostile to judges nominated by President Carter. His defenders attacked the case assembled by the Public Integrity Section, which found itself stretched to prosecute three federal judges in succession. His acquittal represented a defeat for the unit, which won convictions against Claiborne and Nixon only by bringing lesser charges, which they were able to make stick.

After the failed prosecution of Hastings, procedures outlined by the 1980 Judicial Conduct and Disability Act kicked in. Two judges from the Atlanta-based Eleventh Circuit Court of Appeals, the circuit that includes Florida, initiated a formal misconduct complaint based on information from Hastings's prosecution. Judicial leaders spent three more years investigating whether Hastings lied and falsified evidence to win his acquittal. Following that secret probe, the Eleventh Circuit Judicial Council voted to discipline Hastings for committing perjury, tampering with evidence, and conspiracy to accept bribes. Then the judicial council leaders recommended that Congress consider impeachment too.

Hastings was outraged. He argued that since he'd been acquitted by a jury, any judicial discipline or impeachment for the same offenses amounted to illegal double jeopardy, though Congress previously had impeached others for offenses that were never prosecuted at all. He also claimed that the efforts were racially motivated. At the time, Congressman John Conyers, a prominent Michigan Democrat and a cofounder of the Congressional Black Caucus, belonged to the House Judiciary Committee. Conyers and others investigated the claim. As colleagues prepared to vote on Hastings's impeachment in August 1988, Conyers declared in a speech to fellow members of Congress that he'd found no trace of racism and urged the Senate to remove Hastings as unfit. "I looked for any scintilla of racism,"

Conyers told colleagues. "I could not find any."[6] Hastings was subsequently impeached for seventeen forms of misconduct and was removed by the Senate in October 1989. Hastings, who had been under investigation during most of his tenure as judge, earned a place in history as one of only eight jurists ever to be both impeached and removed from office.

Under the Constitution, the Senate can also disqualify public officials who are removed from office from ever holding "any office of honor, trust or profit under the United States." Even by 2020, that measure had been used against only three of twenty impeached officials, all federal judges: West Humphreys, a jurist who was impeached and removed for treason after he abandoned his position and joined the Confederacy, as well as Robert Archbald and Porteous, who were both impeached for corruption. It was not used against Nixon, Claiborne, or Hastings.

In the aftermath of the 1980s impeachments, both Nixon and Hastings appealed their Senate convictions to the Supreme Court but lost. On January 13, 1993, Chief Justice William Rehnquist wrote on behalf of a unanimous court in the Nixon case that authority over impeachment trials "is reposed in the Senate and nowhere else." Upon release from prison, Nixon petitioned to regain his license and returned to practicing law.

Hastings did even better. He ran for Congress and won, taking office as representative for Florida's Twentieth Congressional District in 1993. Hastings had represented Floridians for sixteen years when the House began its efforts to impeach Judge Kent.

Wilkerson and McBroom traveled to Washington, DC, to testify on June 3, 2009, when the House Judiciary Committee convened to consider Kent's impeachment. They stayed together in the same small hotel. By then the pair had made peace. Both were astonished that Kent, as a convicted felon, could remain a federal judge and continue to draw his $174,000 annual salary unless he was both impeached and removed. By then Wilkerson had apologized to McBroom for prolonging the process by refusing to come forward sooner. "I said I was sorry because I had understood she could probably hate me and be upset with me and she had every right to do so, but I hoped she would understand the position I was in," Wilkerson later said. "My life had been a living hell for a long time because of my involvement with this."

McBroom told Wilkerson she understood, and appreciated why Wilkerson initially felt so upset about being outed as another victim in a misconduct complaint. Those awkward conversations became the foundation of a friendship.

Donna Wilkerson feared addressing such a large body as the House of Representatives about Kent. Too nervous to speak spontaneously, she read from a prepared speech, using blunt language to convey how she'd been attacked and why she'd remained with Kent for so long even after being repeatedly victimized. Wilkerson labeled her former boss a narcissistic liar who was incapable of admitting he'd done wrong:

> I have explained in the past that the severity of the sexual abuse can be described using a Bell curve as an example—starting with the most minor of incidents of hugs and kisses, then escalating to worse incidents of touching me inappropriately, groping me outside my clothes, then inside my clothes (top and bottom), then attempting to and gaining penetration of my genitals with his hand, placing my hand on my crotch, and then topping the curve at the most severe episode of once, and possibly twice, pulling down my pants and performing oral sex on me. These episodes always occurred inside of his chambers—sometimes in his office, and sometimes in the reception area or wherever in chambers he could corner me.[7]

Cathy McBroom had prepared nothing in advance. Her attorney, Rusty Hardin, accompanied her to Washington and suggested that she speak from the heart. As she waited nervously in the House meeting room, she thought again of Anita Hill, the only other woman she knew of who'd testified before a roomful of congressmen about a judge accused of sexual harassment. She wished she'd brought friends and family along for support, as Hill had done, but after two long years she finally felt strong enough to publicly share her story. When her turn came, she scanned each representative's face as she spoke about how she'd been subjected to a string of abuse and attacks at the hands of a seemingly untouchable judge. She was distracted by a Texas representative, who kept munching from a bag of corn chips in the otherwise quiet room. McBroom drew a deep breath and then spoke about how she continued to feel under attack even after daring to file a formal complaint.

"Judge Kent used his power to manipulate people for his own selfish desires," McBroom testified, her voice pulsating with remembered pain and outrage. "He told his staff members that I was the one who pursued him. He told other judges whom I have to face every day that it was just an affair gone bad. Being molested by a drunken giant is not my idea of an affair! Finally, he bragged about his gift for manipulation. He told his staff that if he had fifteen minutes with a jury, he would be exonerated. Judge Kent is unfit to be a United States district judge."[8]

Over the centuries, some of the most common grounds for impeachment in the United States have involved abuse of power, lying under oath, and other kinds of corruption—allegations of which both Kent and Porteous stood accused. But Kent's case for the first time involved serial sexual abuse of court employees. Were those subsumed under what the Constitution meant by "high crimes and misdemeanors?" To help them decide, members of Congress turned to one of the few experts in the country who understood both impeachment and judicial misconduct reviews: Professor Arthur Hellman, of the University of Pittsburgh Law School.

Hellman delivered a brief history of the phrase "high crimes and misdemeanors," including views of the Framers, constitutional scholars, and citations from previous impeachment cases over two centuries. He explained that the phrase had long been understood to cover "serious abuses of power" and underscored that testimony from McBroom and Wilkerson, if found credible by Congress, provided a "strong case" for impeachment. Indeed, Hellman, used to conducting research in a law school setting, had been sitting beside the women at the witness table as they delivered their statements. He later said he felt that he'd just witnessed an important, though disturbing, chapter in judicial history. The evidence indicated that "Judge Kent relied on his position of authority and control in the

Galveston Division of the District Court to coerce employees of that court to engage in sexual acts for his personal gratification and to remain silent rather than to report his attacks to a higher authority," Hellman testified. "It is a high crime and misdemeanor."

Kent didn't appear to testify in person but sent the closest thing to a written apology he would ever give McBroom or Wilkerson. It read in part: "For several years, influenced by misguided emotions that probably stemmed from innate personality flaws exacerbated by alcohol abuse and a series of life tragedies . . . I began relating to Mrs. McBroom and Mrs. Wilkerson in inappropriate ways. . . . In doing so, I allowed myself to maintain unrealistic views of how they perceived me and my actions. I sincerely regret that my actions caused them and their families so much emotional distress." Kent also wrote separately to President Barack Obama, offering to resign in one year. He sought mercy—and another year's salary. And Kent reminded lawmakers that he was not the only federal judge with problems. He claimed there were many others like him.

Instead, the House Judiciary Committee moved quickly to unanimously approve impeachment charges, and House members voted on June 19, 2009, to impeach Kent on all four counts. For the first time in US history, a federal judge had been impeached on the basis of evidence that he'd abused his power in order to commit sexual abuse and sexual assault and had lied to federal judges and agents to hide his crimes. On the following Monday morning, Sensenbrenner, the Republican from Wisconsin and a veteran of other impeachments, hand-carried the articles of impeachment to the Senate along with four other US representatives chosen as managers for Kent's anticipated Senate trial. Sensenbrenner also issued a press release urging immediate action: "This man violated the very laws he took an oath to uphold and is currently serving out his 33-month sentence in prison. However, he is still collecting nearly $477 a day, $174,000 a year. . . . The House managers call upon the Senate to immediately begin the necessary next steps of having the case tried and the Senate vote to remove Judge Kent from office; thereby stopping him from collecting another taxpayer-funded paycheck."

A few days later, Senator Harry Reid, then the Senate majority leader, dispatched an emissary to visit Kent, who had reported to prison as ordered. Federal prisoner no. 45225–079, a fifty-nine-year-old white male, already had been tallied by passing guards for the fourth time on June 24, 2009, when some high-profile visitors arrived in the late afternoon. Kent was initially assigned to Federal Medical Center Devens, a compound of brick buildings on the bucolic wooded grounds of what was originally a military base in Ayer, Massachusetts. The facility serves male prisoners requiring specialized long-term medical and psychiatric treatment. No one there called him Your Honor.

His official visitors were wearing suits, and the stern expressions of high-level government security officials. They were led by Terrance W. Gainer, the Senate sergeant at arms who often opens sessions of the Senate with the traditional cry "Hear ye, hear ye." Gainer, a balding veteran police officer with a big brushy mustache, brought official paperwork: a summons from the Senate and a one-page fill-in-the-blank resignation letter. Senate Majority Leader Reid had moved quickly to send Gainer. That's how badly Reid wanted this prisoner to give up his position.

Kent, whose wife was suffering health problems and who also had a stepdaughter to support, had hoped to hold on to his judicial salary longer. But as a prisoner he lost his resolve. He was likely depressed. He'd just entered "A & O," the month-long admission and orientation period, during which many prisoners experience a crisis and fall into hopelessness or express suicidal thoughts. Wearing prison garb instead of his usual black robe, Kent scribbled his name at the bottom of the resignation form. The signature was barely legible.

Kent's action avoided the additional expense of a Senate trial that otherwise would have been necessary for his removal. The resignation, effective June 30, 2009, was applauded by Representative Lamar Smith, a Republican from San Antonio who served on the House Judiciary Committee. "Earlier this month, the House's Impeachment Task Force heard the testimony from Judge Kent's two victims," Smith wrote in a letter to the *Houston Chronicle*. Smith had been deeply troubled by Wilkerson and McBroom's testimony about "the living nightmare they experienced while working for Judge Kent," including episodes of physical and verbal sexual abuse that continued for years. Smith said he found the Kent case disturbing for many reasons. "These women should have felt safe to file complaints without fear of retribution. Judge Kent's alcohol abuse should have been reported. And court security officers who were fully aware of the abusive actions of the Judge should have spoken up sooner." Smith credited the *Houston Chronicle's* coverage with finally giving victims a voice and helping to uncover the truth. He only wished Kent had resigned "sooner and spared his victims the pain, the taxpayers the money and Congress the need to impeach him."

Porteous was less cooperative than Kent. Though many would argue that Porteous should have gone to prison for crimes he had committed, he had never been charged or prosecuted. Porteous, like Kent, requested a disability retirement, but his request, like Kent's, was denied. Prior to impeachment proceedings, he won representation from a prominent law professor, who formed a defense team. That team, like others who had defended federal judges in impeachments in the past, hoped to exploit historical differences of opinion that had developed over time regarding what the Constitution really meant by "impeachable offenses." Ethics experts, authors, and even other federal judges disagreed about whether Porteous deserved to be impeached, despite his admission of having committed a long list of illegal and unethical acts. Four federal judges who belonged to the Fifth Circuit Judicial Council voted against recommending impeachment and subsequently published a forty-nine-page dissent—an action that helped Porteous defend himself before Congress. But House members found a long list of reasons to impeach Porteous, including fraud, perjury, failure to report gifts, and other offenses. His removal in 2010 came after a trial in the Senate that included evidence and testimony from some of the same witnesses featured in the judiciary's misconduct hearing in New Orleans.

Federal Bureau of Prisons policy says that victims identified in federal cases should be informed in advance of a prisoner's release: on furlough, on house arrest, or to a halfway house. Former judge Kent's furlough came on July 27, 2011. He was allowed to leave prison, after serving twenty-five months of his thirty-three-month sentence, to accompany his family to Pearland, a Houston suburb, where he checked into a hotel with his wife and prepared for the wedding of his stepdaughter. But he would not be returning to prison after his "furlough." Instead he would report home to complete his sentence on house arrest.

Kent's victims were easy to find so that they could be informed. Cathy McBroom and Donna Wilkerson were still federal court employees in 2011. By then McBroom and Wilkerson had both returned to work at the Galveston federal courthouse, where McBroom had received a promotion and become Wilkerson's supervisor. But Kent had been out for two full days staying in a hotel near where the two women lived and worked before either received any warning. Cathy McBroom was on her way home from visiting a college campus with her youngest son, Caleb, when a prison official called to say someone had goofed. As a crime victim, McBroom was supposed to have gotten advance notice, but Kent was already out, the official said. The news filled her with panic. Meanwhile, Donna Wilkerson received an email from a victim case manager in Florida: "Our VNS [victim notification] system failed to notify you of inmate Kent's furlough to the Houston & Pearland, TX area. Please accept our apologies. He was released from the institution on 7/27/11 on a furlough in the Houston area." Wilkerson was shocked to learn that Kent wasn't returning to prison. The email said Kent would finish his sentence on "home detention" at a place he and his wife owned in Fort Davis in the wide-open spaces of Texas's Big Bend Country and that he would be released on November 5, 2011.

The news of Kent's early release shook both women deeply. In the phone calls they made, their voices trembled with an emotional mix of outrage, fear, and helplessness about being informed after the fact. Their protests had some impact: Kent was ordered to temporarily report back to prison for several days, and missed his stepdaughter's rehearsal dinner and wedding, his angry wife later told a reporter for the *Texas Lawyer*.[9]

The unusual slip made both Wilkerson and McBroom wonder whether Kent, an ex-judge, could still pull strings even as a prisoner. Neither considered Kent's original sentence to be sufficient punishment for what he'd done. Neither understood why most federal prisoners served full sentences without parole, while Kent won early release. Kent had been required to surrender his Texas law license as a felon, but could do paralegal work for other attorneys. His wife, who supported him throughout, welcomed him home. Under the plea deal, he was not required to register as a sex offender.

For years McBroom continued to wonder what, if any, lessons had been learned from the scandal and from years of personal and professional pain she'd suffered by speaking out to expose Kent and federal judicial corruption. Yes, Kent had been forced to admit to imposing unwanted sexual contact on her and Wilkerson and had pleaded guilty to obstruction of justice. But his admissions came only after he had branded her a liar. The only public statement Chief Judge Jones made about the matter appeared in *Texas Lawyer* magazine in 2009: "The whole thing is a huge embarrassment to everybody in the federal judiciary, and we know that Judge Kent is an outlier," Jones wrote. "And that said, I think every one of us would be much more aware if allegations are made in the future. . . . It's clear that the judiciary had to raise the awareness of their employees of their rights when they allege misconduct by federal judges. That said, the fact that Sam Kent is the only case in the history of the federal judiciary of this kind speaks well of us over time."[10]

McBroom felt sure Kent was not the only judge to abuse his power—and his employees.

CHAPTER 14

Another Encounter with Judge Kozinski

California, 2012–2017

Emily Murphy and other incoming law clerks gathered in September 2012 for a day-long orientation at the Ninth Circuit's main courthouse in San Francisco, a palatial Beaux Arts beauty designated a National Historic Landmark. The hundred or so novice clerks entered an enclave where the walls glistened with multicolored marble and walked down polished floors illuminated by golden light. Year-long clerkships with Ninth Circuit jurists were highly prized by law students (and their law professors) looking for valuable experience and seeking to enhance their reputations through courthouse connections. A clerkship with Chief Circuit Judge Alex Kozinski was especially coveted. And yet Murphy and some of her friends bypassed that particular opportunity because of things they'd heard or read about Kozinski, like how he'd squirreled away a collection of nudie pics and dirty jokes. Instead, she sought and obtained a clerkship with another judge.

Across the United States, about as many women as men were attending law schools in the 2010s, but most federal judges were men in their sixties or seventies, like Kozinski. These judges hand-picked and closely supervised much younger attorneys who worked as their clerks and who had far less experience and power. Some considered Kozinski a genius; others found him to be an oddball. He was known for requiring incredibly long hours of his clerks. But many men and women on the federal bench were type A workaholics who relied on clerks to help them keep up with crushing caseloads. Some federal judges earned reputations for being notoriously difficult, or for being screamers. Others were old-school sexists who expected young female clerks to fetch lunch, wear high heels and skirts, sit on their laps, wipe their mouths with a napkin, or kiss and hug them. One esteemed elderly jurist in New York for years required his female clerks to arrive early each morning to prepare his morning grapefruit.

It was difficult for prospective clerks to obtain reliable information in advance about federal judges and job conditions. To help graduates navigate the system, a smattering of student and alumni groups created informal lists or spreadsheets in law school communities—including at Stanford, Yale, and Harvard—where more candid confidential reviews were kept. According to former students who had consulted reviews, compliments to judges tended to be effusive and criticisms, veiled. Many ex-clerks had racked up $100,000 or more in student loans and knew that an incautious comment could prompt a backlash from a judge whose reference could build or destroy a law career. Few risked posting code phrases like "challenging work environment" or provided a phone number with "Call me." Some of Judge Kozinski's antics, though, had become well known since he so often appeared in the press.

Murphy sought and accepted a clerkship with Circuit Judge Richard Paez, a liberal who'd joined the Ninth Circuit in 2000 as a Bill Clinton nominee and was based at the courthouse in Pasadena, California. Paez had not been on the federal bench as long as Kozinski, his colleague, but he had been a well-known advocate for poor and rural Californians long before joining the judiciary. Paez had served both as a local jurist and as US District judge prior to joining the circuit court.

During the circuit orientation in San Francisco, Murphy and other digital-savvy millennials were told to safeguard court confidentiality and to stop posting anything on social media during their clerkships in 2012–2013. Clerks also were warned about potential dangers outside the San Francisco courthouse after dark, and instructed to seek an escort even for the two-block walk through the historic district to the downtown Bay Area Rapid Transit (BART) station, a stretch of urban streetscape that features a burlesque theater, the historic Oddfellows Hall, and a parade of homeless campers and travelers. After their sessions ended, Murphy walked with a group to the Parc 55 Hotel for a mixer and dinner intended to "build camaraderie" between incoming clerks and judges.

Murphy, thirty, was already married, a bit older and somewhat more self-assured than other clerks. She stood chatting with a group in an ultramodern hotel anteroom equipped with a cash bar and had a glass of wine in her hand when the topic of Kozinski came up. All of the clerks were supposed to sit with a judge they didn't know, but everyone had already heard "weird and creepy" stories about Kozinski. They weren't sure they wanted to sit at his table.

Murphy, who had been the coxswain of her rowing team in her undergraduate years at Harvard, remained lean and physically fit and enjoyed regular workouts. She and other clerks had moved on to discussing exercise routines when Kozinski walked up. Kozinski, as celebrity chief judge of the Ninth Circuit, didn't introduce himself, since he expected young lawyers to recognize him, and he immediately asked to know what they were discussing. He scoffed at their responses, declaring that exercise was a waste of life.

Murphy knew Kozinski, like Paez, was based at the circuit's smaller Pasadena courthouse, a former resort hotel with a cupola and formal gardens. She'd already spent a week working there and had spotted a tiny exercise room with a wall of mirrors and the limited equipment that seemed to be used only by courthouse guards. So, she attempted to make small talk. "Oh, the Pasadena courthouse gym is nice," she said. "There's never anyone there."

Kozinski suggested that Murphy take advantage of the vacant space "to work out naked." He waited for reactions, but no one joined in the joke. Instead, other clerks huddled around Murphy and tried to change the subject. The judge persisted. Murphy should exercise in the nude, he said again, adding that perhaps she should wear just her tennis shoes for safety and carry a towel to soak up the sweat.

As he spoke, Murphy felt his eyes roam her body. It seemed that this powerful man was mentally undressing her and inviting others to join him. "It was so awkward that everyone else just fell silent," Murphy later said. As Kozinski breezed away, she was left wondering, *Did that really just happen?*[1]

After orientation, Murphy returned to Pasadena to resume her clerkship with Paez. Before becoming an attorney, Murphy had studied to be a research scientist, spending hours in a lab examining the brains of rats before learning of her severe allergy to rodents. She had earned a PhD in behavioral neuroscience and psychopharmacology from Cambridge University and had gone on to a postdoctoral program at Stanford University from 2007 to 2009, where she "geeked out" over the intersections between brain science and law before enrolling as a law student from 2009 to 2012. She later embarked on explorations of the ways MRIs and other forms of neuroimaging were being used as evidence on how the neuroscience of addiction was being applied in courts.

Murphy remained excited about her clerkship, but when she returned to Pasadena from orientation in San Francisco, her own brain still seemed fixated on the awkward reception scene. It didn't seem like the best way to begin her new job, but she felt compelled to share the experience with Judge Paez.

Judge Paez regarded her carefully. Paez had become famous in legal circles for both patience and persistence. Though he was already a US district judge when nominated to be a circuit judge, Paez had been forced to wait more than a year to be confirmed because of congressional infighting over judicial nominations in the 2000s. He explained to Murphy that anyone can file a confidential misconduct complaint against a federal judge under the Judicial Conduct and Disability Act. Paez promised to support Murphy if she did so. But, Paez added, Kozinski in 2012 still served as the chief circuit judge, so her complaint would go right to him for initial review. Under the law, he explained, action would be taken only if a fellow judge was deemed to have committed "conduct prejudicial to the effective and expeditious administration of the business of the court."

Kozinski's chambers were located on another floor in the Pasadena courthouse, though he traveled frequently while serving his seven-year term as chief circuit judge from 2007 to 2014. All circuit judges travel to hear cases, but as chief, Kozinski also oversaw administrative gatherings and handled misconduct complaints against all jurists in the sprawling Ninth Circuit. In the 2010s the number of complaints filed against federal judges nationwide exploded to an average of more than 1,300 a year—nearly twice the volume of the 2000s. In the fall of 2012, Kozinski was investigating a high-profile complaint against Richard Cebull, the colorful and controversial Montana district chief judge. Cebull had made national news in March 2012 after forwarding a joke that implied that President Barack Obama's mother had committed bestiality and compared her famous offspring to a dog. The Ninth Circuit's investigation ultimately found that Cebull had circulated hundreds of emails containing jokes and remarks described as bigoted, sexist, or racist. (Cebull was publicly reprimanded in 2013 and retired.) In his years as chief judge, Kozinski also had been investigated and admonished in 2009, for the complaint Kozinski himself initiated after the *Los Angeles Times* published a story about his own online archive of jokes, nude pictures, and videos. Kozinski had requested that another circuit investigate that earlier complaint, but he and other chief circuit judges were not required to refer complaints about themselves or about their friends to other circuits.

Kozinski, like other federal judges, wielded tremendous powers. All rise when they enter a courtroom, and some attorneys still address them with the antiquated phrase "May it please the court." Kozinski and his colleagues collectively handled some ten thousand appeals annually, including reviews of executions. Defying such a powerful figure can be a risky and potentially career-ending move for a lawyer, law clerk, or federal employee. Murphy was just beginning her legal career. Under the most hopeful scenario, Murphy figured that if she filed a complaint, Kozinski would simply emphasize his ribald sense of humor. "And it probably would have just gone away, and I would have forever been the girl who couldn't take a joke," she later said.

Murphy decided she did not want one ugly experience to define her otherwise amazing year-long federal clerkship. Kozinski had publicly demeaned and humiliated her, but as an attorney she realized that his remarks likely didn't fit the definition of "conduct prejudicial to the effective and expeditious administration of the business of the courts." So for five years she tried to forget what had happened.

By 2017, Emily Murphy had left private practice to become an associate professor at the University of California Hastings College of the Law, located in downtown San Francisco. The busy streets and sidewalks around the college are shared by commuters pulling rolling briefcases to BART trains, pedestrians taking tokes from joints, and the occasional high-powered attorney or judge bound for the nearby main courthouse of the Ninth Circuit Court of Appeals. From her office tower window, Murphy can hear sirens, car alarms, and shouts from the streets below. She sometimes muses that her view offers insights into this city, with "the elite and the superrich, alongside the powerless and dispossessed." She keeps her office neat, though filled with stacks of research files, law books, and pictures of her daughter, born the year after her clerkship. Even in 2017 she still thought sometimes about what Kozinski had said and done at that clerks' welcome reception at the chic Parc 55 Hotel, only a five-minute walk from her office. She knew other attorneys who'd had odd experiences with Kozinski, but she'd never spoken out.

Murphy had never forgotten the negative experience she had after reporting another kind of sexual misconduct when she was a freshman at Harvard. During her second or third week of college, she had been sexually assaulted by a fellow student, someone she had previously trusted. At first she hesitated, then filed a formal complaint through the university after realizing the same man was approaching other friends. The results had been disappointing. The student she accused lost a leadership position in a freshman orientation group but remained on campus. Ultimately, she felt Harvard's administration chose to protect the institution's reputation over the risk her attacker posed. Murphy did not consider her own brief encounter with Kozinski to be as serious, but she worried that he might be using his authority and power to demean, harass, and abuse generations of clerks, including her own law students. The same kind of institutional failure to address cases of harassment and abuse that she'd found at Harvard seemed to infest the federal courts too. *The individuals are problematic, but institutional protection of harassers seemed to be a bigger problem,* she thought.

Her decision to go public about Kozinski came in the fall of 2017 after a member of a closed Facebook group for attorney moms to which she belonged posted a provocative invitation: "Let's all vent here and post all the times we've experienced sexual harassment in our jobs." The invitation was meant to encourage members to join the growing movement to share stories about sexual harassment and assault. Murphy quickly responded: "Oh yeah, the time a federal judge told me to work out naked in the gym of the courthouse. That was terrible."[2]

Soon another friend put Murphy in touch with Matt Zapotosky, a *Washington Post* reporter who at the time covered the US Department of Justice. Murphy told Zapotosky about Kozinski's comments at the reception, an incident she figured was part of a larger pattern of misbehavior. Murphy could provide little help in locating other whistleblowers. She suggested he contact women who had clerked for other Ninth Circuit judges based in Pasadena. She believed Kozinski had mistreated his own clerks, too, but figured any Kozinski clerk would feel too afraid and too bound by oaths to talk. Murphy didn't know that Heidi Bond, a former Kozinski clerk, was already thinking about contacting a reporter.

Bond, now an established best-selling romance novelist, had never forgotten Kozinski's stern insistence on loyalty and secrecy during her own year as his clerk from 2006 to 2007. Kozinski's own attitudes about the sacrosanct nature of the bonds between a federal judge and his or her clerks had been shaped by his own experience clerking for Chief Justice Warren E. Burger at the Supreme Court from 1976 to 1977, in an era when all justices and nearly all clerks were men. In 1979, not long after Kozinski completed his clerkship, Justice Burger was infuriated by what he considered a massive breach of court confidentiality when investigative reporter Bob Woodward, of Watergate fame, and Scott Armstrong published *The Brethren: Inside the Supreme Court.* Their investigation included details of confidential decision-making and debates that were far from complimentary to

Burger. The book unveiled the process behind high-profile cases, including *United States v. Nixon*, the matter in which President Richard Nixon had been required to turn over taped conversations about the break-in at the Watergate Hotel, the scandal that led to Nixon's resignation. Most sources spoke only "on background," but many were former Supreme Court clerks.

In the aftermath, Burger, a Nixon nominee, and others cracked down on requirements for clerk confidentiality. Kozinski hung a portrait of Burger on the wall in chambers after he became a federal judge. In 1998, Kozinski followed his mentor's lead, lashing out when attorney Edward Lazarus, another former Supreme Court clerk, authored a book called *Closed Chambers: The Rise, Fall, and Future of the Modern Supreme Court.* Though others praised Lazarus's book as an insightful analysis of political splits inside the high court, Kozinski, in a law journal article, excoriated Lazarus for violating court confidentiality and went so far as to put in telephone calls to some venues that had invited Lazarus to speak, urging them to reconsider.[3]

But Bond's own understanding of her duty as a law clerk shifted on June 5, 2016, when she received an email from Kozinski asking her to speak to a reporter about the experiences she'd had while clerking for Justice Anthony Kennedy. "A good friend of mine . . . is writing a book about the Supreme Court," Kozinski wrote in the email. "Think you might talk to him? I've known him for 25 years and he's 100 percent trustworthy. Ciao. AK."[4]

Bond was floored by that email. Her emotions roiled, flashing between anger, confusion, and betrayal. For a decade, she'd remained silent about how Kozinski had treated her as his clerk "because I had been told that judicial confidentiality protected the Judge—that it applied not just to chambers deliberations, but to his showing me porn in his office," she later wrote. And now, she thought, Kozinski seemed to be "asking me to breach my duty of loyalty to Justice Kennedy as if it were no big deal—as if I hadn't upended my life trying to escape the memories Kozinski had given me." Bond felt both "sick and angry" when Kozinski followed up with an email introduction to the journalist. *How dare he casually sell out the principle I'd been choking on for years?* she thought.

She never did the interview, and instead began to consider whether Kozinski's emails urging her to describe her Supreme Court clerkship had indirectly granted her the freedom to discuss personal aspects of her Kozinski clerkship. She had never spoken about that experience in any detail before, not even with her husband, best friends, or any therapist. For the first time she reached out to one close friend in confidence—a fellow writer with no connections to the field of law. It felt good to provide an outsider with an account of what had happened during that troubling year. But Bond spent many more months of 2016 and 2017 in anguished reflection. Gradually, she told several others about what happened. A few of them were attorneys. For Bond, the year of her clerkship had been an intensely painful experience that shaped the course of her life and her career. It was immediately clear to her confidantes that those experiences fell into the category of sexual harassment. Close friends tended to respond strongly with variations on "What? He did what?"

On the advice of attorney friends, Bond decided to consult legal experts to determine "the limits of judicial confidentiality." She first spoke with Jeffrey Minear, counselor to Chief Justice Roberts, and then, at Minear's suggestion, to Anthony J. Scirica, former chief judge of the Third Circuit Court of Appeals and the longtime chairman of the national-level Committee on Judicial Conduct and Disability.

Like Kozinski, Scirica was a powerful circuit judge and a Reagan appointee who'd served on the courts since the 1980s. Like Bond he is also a Michigan Law graduate (though he graduated forty years before her). Michigan, more than most law schools, had a tradition of fostering the careers of women attorneys, beginning with the first graduate way back in 1871. Bond remembers Scirica as being "warm, understanding, and kind," but Scirica offered only general advice. She recalls him telling her that "if what had happened was a matter of personal misconduct on the part of the judge, . . . I was not bound by the code of chambers confidentiality, and that whatever I needed to do for my own closure and healing was fine, so long as it wasn't about a judicial matter."

Bond still worried. She knew that some of the nude photos that Kozinski had shown her in chambers had been part of a larger archive he kept on a private server. After her clerkship, a *Los Angeles Times* story about the joke archive had led Kozinski to recuse himself from a pornography case, and a formal judicial misconduct complaint involving the contents of his web server had been initiated by Kozinski. Bond asked Scirica, "What if it's not about a matter that my judge decided, but if there's a nexus of facts that are relevant to another judicial matter? What then?"

Scirica likely guessed what Bond was talking about. As the former Third Circuit chief judge, Scirica had personally overseen the judicial misconduct investigation into complaints about Kozinski's website and archive of nude photos and videos. He'd also authored the public admonishment of Kozinski in 2009. Scirica told Bond he could not provide a specific answer about her obligations as clerk, especially if there was a potential connection to a misconduct complaint or federal court case. Then he added another cryptic comment that Bond jotted down: "I cannot think of any person, persons, or institution that can give you an answer on this."

As the #MeToo movement gathered strength in 2017, Bond began to consider telling her story to a newspaper reporter. She figured that Kozinski had so many other potential victims that eventually someone else would reveal things he'd said and done to so many women for so many years. She didn't want to be the first. Bond was still weighing options when she received an email from Zapotosky, the *Washington Post* reporter, who told her he was already working on a story about Kozinski and had interviewed others. One or two might be willing to go on the record, he said. Bond eventually decided to speak on the record too.

One of Kozinski's longtime critics, Cyrus Sanai, the Los Angeles attorney, later described Bond as the "perfect whistleblower," since as a novelist she no longer had clients, law students, or court cases to protect from retaliation from Kozinski or his powerful judicial allies. Bond disagreed. As a professional writer perhaps she risked less direct harm to her career, but "dealing with the long term emotional impact of making trauma public, of connecting with others who have been traumatized and experiencing vicarious trauma, has not exactly been conducive to my writing career, either," she later said, reflecting on the experience. Her only advantage as a whistleblower, she thought, was that she had often written about trauma suffered by women in her novels. She knew how to do it "in a way that accurately conveyed my experience in the clerkship."

Emily Murphy no longer practiced in federal courts in 2017, but as a new law professor, she knew that going public posed professional risks. She expected general support from law school colleagues, but feared a backlash in the greater academic community. Before agreeing to allow the *Washington Post* to publish her name, she sought input from a few faculty members and from David Faigman, dean of the UC Hastings College of the Law. She later wrote to the students in her contracts class that her decision was motivated by my "professional obligation to do whatever I can to make the legal profession better for the next generation. I was thinking of you all, my first batch of students, how hard you worked, and how earnest you are. I was thinking of the students who will come after you, and the people who came before and have endured some unconscionable things."

Bond and Murphy were the only two women who dared provide their names in Zapotosky's December 8, 2017, article "Prominent Appeals Court Judge Alex Kozinski Accused of Sexual Misconduct." They and four anonymous women described how Kozinski forced them to view nude photos, bestowed unwanted kisses and caresses, or made lewd comments. Five days later, Dahlia Lithwick added her prominent voice to the chorus in a commentary for *Slate* called "He Made Us All Victims and Accomplices." In the essay, Lithwick expressed regret: "For years, I've felt it was too early to speak up about Judge Alex Kozinski. Now I fear it's too late," she wrote.[5] Privately, Lithwick also reached out to Murphy and others to offer her personal support and dedicated one of her *Amicus* podcasts to the whistleblowers' cause. Over time, she became friends with the so-called Kozinski accusers and encountered many other people—men and women, some of whom were Article III judges—who never added their voices to the public debate but pulled her aside to express their solidarity.

When the first *Washington Post* story appeared, Leah Litman was still working as a law professor at UC Irvine, just an hour from

Kozinski's Pasadena power base. At the time she didn't know Bond or Murphy, though they had friends in common, and she recognized the type of behavior both described. She remembered how in only a few hours over dinner, Kozinski had made her feel demeaned and diminished, as if she were a doll or a toy. His technique had seemed polished and practiced. Litman contacted the *Post* and agreed to go on the record too. Litman appeared in a follow-up article that quoted nine more women. All fifteen women in the *Post* stories (sixteen if Lithwick's account is included) provided anecdotes that individually might perhaps be dismissed as an indiscretion, a slip in a social setting, or a distasteful joke. Taken together, their stories had the force of a multigenerational primal scream—long suppressed and therefore even more powerful.

It clearly came as a shock to Kozinski and to many of his friends that over the course of a few days in December his reputation as a colorful court celebrity and celebrated free thinker morphed into that of the best-known sexual harasser in the federal judiciary. Kozinski's successor as chief circuit judge, Sidney Thomas, announced a formal probe into the allegations before Litman's account even appeared. Kozinski, normally outspoken, fought back only briefly. As a former chief judge, Kozinski knew that even the most serious federal misconduct inquiry dies quietly when a federal judge leaves his post. Only four days after Thomas initiated a misconduct complaint, Kozinski announced his retirement, effective immediately. Kozinski thanked his judicial colleagues, the lawyers who practiced in his court, and the many young attorneys who had served as his clerks. In a statement, Kozinski said that although family and friends had urged him to defend himself, he did not think he could be both an "effective judge and simultaneously fight this battle."

Resigning was a wise economic move. At sixty-seven, Kozinski had enough seniority to collect a federal pension equal to his full pay. The accounts of Kozinski's alleged misconduct provided by sixteen women spanned decades, from Judge Christine O. C. Miller's ride in his car in the early 1980s to his 2017 dinner with Litman. Now none of those incidents would ever be investigated, since the judicial misconduct system did not apply to judges who retired or resigned. Kozinski's parting statement included no admission to committing any illegal or unethical act, though he did offer an apology of sorts: "I've always had a broad sense of humor and a candid way of speaking to both male and female law clerks alike. In doing so, I may not have been mindful enough of the special challenges and pressures that women face in the workplace. It grieves me to learn that I caused any of my clerks to feel uncomfortable; this was never my intent. For this I sincerely apologize."

A rapid resignation was not the outcome that Litman, Murphy, or Bond sought as whistleblowers. Without any real review, they feared there would never be a real inquiry into broader and systemic problems that they'd risked their reputations to expose: the decades-long pattern of sexual misbehavior by a prominent federal judge, the fear and reluctance of so many victims to report him, and other jurists' apparent willingness to tolerate or overlook his indiscretions.

Although in his retirement statement, Kozinski apologized to his clerks, a group that included Bond, he appeared to have deliberately excluded Murphy, Litman, and his former judicial colleague, Christine O. C. Miller. Litman and Murphy were both offended by their reading of his parting remarks. Indeed, they perceived an insult embedded in a part of his statement: Kozinski's regret that women with "special challenges and pressures" may have been unable to appreciate his "broad sense of humor."[6]

Bond, who knew Kozinski better than the others, had hoped that her former boss would engage in a broader public discussion that might over time educate others about the limits of acceptable behavior and the urgent need for better rules and training in the courts. Despite her negative experiences as his clerk, Bond said she knew Kozinski to be "capable of empathy and intelligence." She figured that if "someone out there was able to model what an appropriate rehabilitation and apology would actually look like; I had assumed it would be him. But he has no interest in playing that role, and so here we are."

Yet Kozinski's decision to retire did not usher in the quick resolution that he and perhaps other judges had desired. Instead, broader questions about sexual misconduct and sexual harassment within the nation's courts continued to be raised, in December 2017 and beyond. In January 2018, another of Kozinski's former clerks, Katherine Ku, wrote an op-ed in the *Washington Post* in which she shared troubling details of her own experience of sexual harassment by Kozinski. Ku, unlike Bond, worked at a private law firm and still practiced in federal courts, but Ku said she felt compelled to speak out anyway. She wrote that she feared that judicial leaders were in a way protecting harassers like Kozinski by pressuring them to retire or resign with the promise that their misconduct would never be investigated.

Kozinski's retirement was dramatic but hardly unique. He was the third federal judge in only two years who retired with full pay soon after allegations of sexual misconduct had been raised, though Kozinski's case received by far the most publicity. Back in 2014, Ty Clevenger, a whistleblowing conservative attorney, blogger, and ex-deputy sheriff, discovered that court leaders had failed to investigate a serious sexual harassment complaint lodged in 1998 by a young court employee against Judge Walter S. Smith Jr., of the Western District of Texas. Like Kent, Smith was king of his courthouse, the only district judge based in Waco. Clevenger, who had a Stanford Law degree and saw himself as a champion of underdogs, had clashed with Smith in court and documented his efforts to draw attention to allegations of Smith's misbehavior in blogs he called *DirtyRottenJudges* and *Lawflog*.[7] Eventually, Clevenger located the ex-clerk, who provided a sworn statement describing how she'd felt forced to abandon her federal job and had suffered a breakdown after Smith flirted with and propositioned her. "I laid out the evidence that Judge Smith forcibly groped and molested a female deputy clerk in his private chambers. Other female employees have described incidents of groping and sexual harassment at the hands of Judge Smith, but thus far none of them have gone public with their stories. I hope that changes soon," Clevenger wrote in one entry in 2014. On behalf of the former clerk who had been sexually harassed, Clevenger filed a new misconduct complaint against Smith, who was reprimanded in December 2015 by the Fifth Circuit Judicial Council. Clevenger appealed, alleging that Smith had more victims and deserved impeachment. Clevenger's effort to bring Smith to justice ended in September 2016, when Smith, too, retired with a full federal pension.

In March 2016, another federal judge who'd been accused of an older episode of sexual misconduct, Richard W. Roberts, then chief district judge in Washington, DC, was allowed to assume senior status early—give up his regular court duties and take a pension—because of a disability. Around the time of Roberts's request, the Utah attorney general filed a complaint alleging that Roberts in his years as a prosecutor had repeatedly coerced sex acts from a sixteen-year-old witness. There were no allegations that Roberts harassed women as a federal judge, but the Utah AG also claimed that Roberts had concealed his prior misconduct in 1998 when the FBI vetted him as a judicial nominee and later fabricated a disability claim to avoid a disciplinary review. A subsequent investigation conducted by the Denver-based Tenth Circuit Court of Appeals, however, found that the jurist's disability request was supported by medical evidence. Thus, Roberts, too, avoided disciplinary action and retained benefits equal to his full pay.

By tradition, the Supreme Court Chief Justice annually reflects on the events of the year in a brief speech to colleagues and selected members of congress. In December 2017, many court critics remained focused on Kozinski's recent retirement and the storm of #MeToo allegations levied against him and other judges. But Chief Justice John Roberts was understandably preoccupied with a violent spate of hurricanes and wildfires that had battered the nation and disrupted court business in Texas, Puerto Rico, the Virgin Islands, and beyond. The main focus of his year-end speech was the importance of a disaster response team for the federal courts, which had become a far-flung empire with thirty thousand employees across all US states and territories.

But at the end of his address, Roberts announced his intention to tackle what he called "a new challenge." Without mentioning Kozinski or other judges by name, Roberts said, "Events in recent months have illuminated the depth of the problem of sexual harassment in the workplace, and events in the past few weeks have made clear that the judicial branch is not immune. The judiciary will begin 2018 by undertaking a careful evaluation of whether its standards of conduct and its procedures for investigating and correcting inappropriate behavior are adequate to ensure an exemplary workplace for every judge and every court employee."

Meanwhile, congressional leaders like Sensenbrenner in the House of Representatives, Senator Chuck Grassley, and other longtime court critics began again to wonder aloud whether the secretive federal judicial complaint system was broken. If that was true, how many victims had likely remained silent? And how many other jurists with lifetime appointments and oversized egos had gotten away with decades of sexual harassment, and other forms of abuse?

CHAPTER 15

Calls for Reform—
and a Backlash

By 2018, romance novelist Heidi Bond and law professors Emily Murphy and Leah Litman had become known collectively in some circles as the "Kozinski accusers." They remained prime movers of an intensifying discussion about sexual misconduct and harassment in the federal courts. They and others kept pressing for more rights and protections for clerks and would-be whistleblowers. They still sought investigations of the allegations they had made against Kozinski despite his retirement, even though carrying on with that effort meant their own work suffered.

Bond's business of writing novels, under her nom de plume Courtney Milan, depended on a brisk pace of about two and a half books a year, but now her pace dropped to one book every two years. Litman was still teaching at UC Irvine, writing briefs in complex federal appellate cases, recording podcasts, and pondering a move back to Michigan, but also remained engaged in the fight.

Meanwhile, Murphy, a busy working mom, was struggling to juggle her demanding teaching schedule, ongoing research projects, and meeting the needs of her family. Only weeks after Kozinski's resignation, she'd become pregnant with her second child, and then tragically lost the baby in May 2018. Dealing with the pregnancy and then a personal tragedy on top of the national publicity vastly increased her level of stress. Murphy kept having to break from family time to take calls, offering her curious preschool daughter some version of the explanation that "Mommy is trying to keep bad men away from workplaces."

All three women continued to produce tweets, write op-eds, give campus speeches, and grant interviews in which they argued that Kozinski, along with other jurists who might have known about his misconduct and protected him, should still be formally investigated. Ninth Circuit leaders updated policies and conducted a survey of court employees but made no moves to open another misconduct inquiry. As the aftermath stretched on, Litman found the experience to be "a very painful reminder of how clubby the legal profession can be." The prevailing trend, she thought, was to "defend people in power, excuse their misbehavior and stick to your network or club."

Murphy became alarmed by Kozinski's efforts at what looked like a comeback attempt in the summer of 2018 when he published a tribute to the retiring Supreme Court justice Anthony Kennedy in the *Daily Journal*, an online legal publication, and granted a long interview on San Francisco public radio. Murphy gave a follow-up interview to the *Washington Post*, saying she feared that Kozinski's article and his talk-show appearance could be interpreted as a sign "that our profession doesn't actually care about harassment."[1]

But the grassroots movement whose progress a *New York Times* commentary headline heralded as "#MeToo Comes to the Federal Courts" continued to gain momentum as more attorneys, including current and former judicial employees, came together to write an open letter to Chief Justice Roberts and other court leaders in which the signatories demanded nationwide reforms, including stronger judicial policies on sexual harassment, better training, and improved reviews of misconduct complaints. The idea of the letter originated in December 2017, after Kozinski's resignation, with Deeva Shah, a recent Michigan Law grad who at the time was still clerking for another Ninth Circuit judge. Initially, four women attorneys took the lead, including Shah and Jaime Santos, an attorney based in Washington, DC, who had clerked in the Ninth Circuit in 2012–13, the same year as Murphy. By mid-2018, more than 850 people had added their names to that letter. Nearly all identified themselves as former law clerks for federal judges.

Soon, Shah, Santos, and others established a group they called Law Clerks for Workplace Accountability and launched a website and an active Twitter handle, @clerksforchange. The organization's mission is to "ensure that the federal judiciary provides a safe workplace environment, free of harassment for all employees and to assist the judiciary in reaching this goal."[2] Santos, an energetic former gymnast, mother of three daughters, and graduate of Harvard Law, had a strong professional interest in sexual harassment matters. Even though she was simultaneously representing clients in federal appellate courts, her firm was supportive of the time she dedicated as a leader of the new judicial reform group. And each leader of LCWA seemed to enjoy the tacit support of the judge for whom she'd clerked: the jurists' names appeared below theirs in their online letter; Santos's former bosses included George H. King of the US District Court for the Central District of California, and Judge Raymond C. Fisher, Kozinski's Ninth Circuit colleague. During her own clerkships, Santos made it clear that she'd experienced no harassment, but was dismayed to hear so many reports from other clerks who had. In 2018, Santos and other leaders of Law Clerks for Workplace Accountability were invited to meet with the Federal Judiciary Workplace Conduct Working Group, a new group formed by the courts to study sexual harassment in the courts and make recommendations. She and others hoped to convince the Working Group to boost accountability for judges, and enhance protections for victims of harassment and other whistleblowers.

The federal courts for years had maintained a standing disciplinary committee, which was led by Anthony Scirica, the white male circuit judge who had once investigated Kozinski. In contrast, three of the four judges initially tapped for the new Federal Judiciary Workplace Conduct Working Group in January 2018 were women. Though the group was chaired by James Duff, director of the Administrative Office of the US Courts, US District Judge Julie A. Robinson, an African American based in Kansas City, Kansas, took a particularly active role. Robinson already had dealt with judicial misconduct issues as a

member of the Tenth Circuit Judicial Council but had other reasons
for taking the issue seriously: in April 2016, one of her Kansas City
colleagues, US District Judge Carlos Murguia, had been quietly accused of sexually harassing a member of his own staff.

Murguia grew up in Kansas City's Argentine neighborhood and both
he and his family had a history of public service. In 1999, Murguia,
a Clinton nominee, became the first Mexican American judge in Kansas's federal district courts. His sister served as a federal judge on the
Ninth Circuit Court of Appeals and his wife was a longtime Wyan-
dotte County commissioner (they later divorced). In 2016, one of his
former judicial employees told two other judges that Murguia repeatedly sexually harassed her during and after working hours. Given the
seriousness of the allegations, the Kansas chief district judge, then
located in Wichita, contacted Timothy Tymkovich, chief judge of the
Tenth Circuit Court of Appeals in Denver in May 2016.

Tymkovich, a third-generation Coloradoan, was so conservative
that as the state's solicitor general he'd argued that Colorado should
deny Medicaid funding for abortions even for victims of rape and
incest. A federal circuit judge since 2003, Tymkovich had been chief
judge only about a year when he was first told about the court employee's complaint. Following tradition, Tymkovich privately spoke
with Murguia, who admitted to his misconduct and agreed to unspecified "treatment by a medical professional." The woman requested
confidentiality and never filed a formal complaint of her own; still,
it's unclear why Tymkovich failed to use his power as chief judge either to initiate a complaint or to form an investigatory committee.
Instead, in February 2017, Tymkovich agreed to keep the matter secret after Murguia finished "treatment." When even more tips about
Murguia arrived, circuit officials hired a retired FBI agent in December 2017 who discovered more problems. Finally, in August 2018,
Tymkovich initiated a formal complaint and formed an investigatory
committee. The confidential probe found that Murguia had harassed
three judicial employees and also carried out a years-long affair with
a convicted felon, a lapse of judgment that made him "susceptible
to extortion," according to a reprimand issued on September 30,

2019. In 2020, only after several congressmen complained that the case had been mishandled, Murguia announced plans to resign and the national Judicial Conduct and Disability committee released an unusual summary of the judicial misconduct investigation, explaining that the probe had dragged out so long in part because all three victims feared reprisals and requested anonymity.

To encourage people to participate in the 2018 national sexual harassment study, members of the Federal Judiciary Workplace Conduct Working Group set up an "electronic mailbox" to enable current or former employees to provide comments that could be anonymous if desired. Initially, Santos and other members of Law Clerks for Workplace Accountability were included in meetings and submitted comments, but they were never allowed to join. On June 1, 2018, the Working Group released its 144-page report and recommendations.[3] Among them: beef up the judicial code of conduct to emphasize judges' responsibilities to report other jurists' misconduct and revise handbooks to clarify that clerks and other employees could report harassment without being guilty of violating court confidentiality. (Most of the recommendations were subsequently adopted in March 2019 by the Judicial Conference of the United States.)

Still, Santos and other reformers expressed concern in 2018 that the report did not "effectively address the barriers to reporting harassment" that exist between judges who were virtual "titans" in the world of the courts and the employees who depended on their favor and were obliged to carry out judges' orders. "Judicial chambers are unlike any other type of working environment. Individuals lucky enough to be hired to work with judges are typically law students, for whom judges are more demigods than they are employers," Santos later testified to members of the Senate. "When a law clerk experiences or witnesses harassment, it can be devastating on a personal and professional level. And it is incredibly difficult to speak up against someone who has the unmatched power of a life-tenured federal judge."

Senator Grassley, the powerful Iowa Republican who chaired the Judiciary Committee from 2015 to January 2019, also thought the Federal Judiciary Workplace Conduct Working Group's final report fell short. On June 13, 2018, a few days after the report's release,

Grassley called a hearing to confront the issue of sexual harassment and other misconduct in the federal judiciary. In his opening statement, Grassley, a stern yet grandfatherly figure, singled out Heidi Bond for her bravery in publicly sharing her "harrowing" experiences as Kozinski's clerk. Looking down to read from a prepared statement, he quoted long passages aloud from Bond's online journal with details of how Kozinski had told her she'd be his slave and then subjected her to a barrage of dirty jokes and other forms of sexual harassment. Grassley said that Bond, and other clerks like her, felt they had "nowhere to go." Seeming moved, he glanced up through his glasses at faces of fellow senators and commented: "Just think of that!"[4]

In his speech, Grassley emphasized that of fifteen women who denounced Kozinski, Bond and law professor Emily Murphy had been the first to speak publicly. "Speaking out against powerful federal judges in a system that doesn't always protect victims takes tremendous courage," he said. "But because of these women's bravery, we can hopefully begin to make real, significant changes to these power imbalances that allow harassment to thrive."[5]

Grassley lambasted Chief Justice Roberts and his team of judicial leaders for failing to take advantage of a historic opportunity created by women whistleblowers and seize the "real chance to undertake reforms." Grassley said judicial leaders had failed to address obstacles to reporting misconduct despite the report produced by the Federal Judiciary Workplace Conduct Working Group. "In too many ways, this vague report kicks the can down the road. . . . It appears victims could be left wondering to whom they can report, with little instruction or transparency in the process."

Then Grassley delivered a long list of criticisms, and argued for the creation of a much stronger central mechanism to handle federal judicial misconduct complaints, instead of a system that forces employees to contact a variety of chief district or circuit judges, whom they might find intimidating. Those chiefs, he said, could still dismiss substantive complaints without ever disclosing their findings or methodology. "Finally, the report gave no apology for, or even acknowledgement of, what went wrong in the case of Judge Kozinski," he said. "And it didn't indicate how its recommendations will prevent similar scenarios from happening."

In the course of his nearly four decades as a senator, Grassley has enacted reforms to boost protections for whistleblowers and taken on Big Pharma and other powerful foes. He certainly seemed resolved to continue to help fight judicial misconduct and sexual harassment in the courts in June 2018. And yet, both he and Senator Dianne Feinstein, the senior committee members, gave the impression that they considered sexual misconduct to be a relatively new problem for the judiciary.

At the same hearing, Feinstein, a powerful Democrat from Kozinski's home state of California, declared her amazement that any federal judge ever dared commit sexual misconduct. "What is really surprising to me is that the problem exists in the federal judiciary," she said. "I don't think sexual harassment or misconduct can be tolerated in any workplace, but I'm really shocked to hear that we have to hold a hearing on harassment in the federal judiciary. The federal judiciary (now, I'm a non-lawyer) is the pinnacle of our laws and society. It's where all Americans go to have their rights protected. . . . So, I'm very concerned that this hearing is even necessary."

Grassley seemed to agree with Feinstein. He also remarked on how outrageous he found it that federal judges accused of sexual misconduct, like Kozinski and Smith, the Waco-based jurist, were able to retire with federal pensions. Grassley and Feinstein seemed to have a shared case of political amnesia. It seemed unlikely that both had truly forgotten the lessons of 1991, when Anita Hill testified about being sexually harassed by Clarence Thomas, who was confirmed to the Supreme Court despite lingering questions about whether he had lied under oath in response to Hill's allegations. If judicial misconduct complaints were filed against Thomas in relation to his testimony, their existence has never been publicly revealed. Grassley had already been a senator then and participated in other debates about gender bias and sexual harassment in the judiciary in the 1990s. Feinstein was elected to the Senate partly because voters actively backed women's congressional campaigns as part of the collective outrage over how the all-male Senate Judiciary Committee had treated Hill. Both senators also were in office in 2009, when Judge Kent was impeached for sexually assaulting his court employees and lying to conceal his crimes. And early in 2018, acting as leaders of the Judiciary

Committee, they'd cosigned a letter to the courts inquiring about a long string of sexual misconduct cases involving federal jurists, including Kozinski, Smith, and Kent.

But because the two senators, both in their eighties, seemed to have fading memories of other misbehaving judges, advocates wondered whether the Kozinski scandal as well might soon be forgotten. Reformers were dismayed when, three months later, Senator Grassley reconvened his committee to consider the nomination of a Kozinski protégé, Circuit Judge Brett Kavanaugh, a Trump appointee to the Supreme Court.

Kavanaugh, a circuit judge based in Washington DC, and Kozinski, based in California, had been closely allied for twenty-seven years. As a recent Yale Law School graduate, Kavanaugh had clerked for Kozinski from 1991 to 1992. In 1991 Kozinski wrote about how clerks and judges were "tethered together" in "Confessions of a Bad Apple," an article he wrote for the *Yale Law Journal*, where Kavanaugh had recently been a student editor. Kozinski wrote: "The law clerk is the judge's emissary to the world; although sworn to secrecy about the court's substantive work, clerks often comment, expressly or by knit of the brow, about the character, work habits, fairness, and generosity of the judges they clerked for. Mutual trust and respect are not merely desirable, they are essential."[6] Kavanaugh's clerkship with Kozinski helped him obtain a clerkship with Kennedy on the Supreme Court.

Later, Kavanaugh, as an associate independent counsel for the government, played a role in the Clinton impeachment and in 2001 joined the administration of George W. Bush, for whom in the 2000s he helped screen conservative judicial candidates such as Timothy Tymkovich. Because of controversy over his partisanship, Kavanaugh's first nomination to the Washington, DC, Circuit Court in 2004 was shot down. Kavanaugh was nominated again two years later and confirmed as a circuit judge on May 26, 2006. On that day, Kozinski formally introduced him to senators, saying: "I give Brett Kavanaugh my highest recommendation. I gave him my highest recommendation when he applied to Justice Kennedy, my own mentor. And I continue to give him my highest recommendation." Even as judges on opposite coasts, Kavanaugh and Kozinski remained in touch, contributing to each other's books and appearing on panels together. Then, in 2018, their mutual mentor, Kennedy, recommended Kavanaugh as his successor on the Supreme Court. It was a life-changing opportunity that Kavanaugh clearly owed, in part, to Kozinski.

But a close association with Kozinski was no longer desirable in September 2018, when Kavanaugh's nomination hearings began. Under questioning, Kavanaugh repeatedly denied knowing about his mentor's bawdy sense of humor, his Easy Rider Gag List, or any misconduct toward women. The 263-page congressional record of Kavanaugh's responses to senators' questions included seventy-one references to Kozinski. Among them:

> *Question:* During the entire course of your relationship with Judge Kozinski, did you ever witness him engaging in inappropriate behavior?
>
> *Response:* Judge Kozinski was known to be a tough boss, but I did not witness him engaging in inappropriate behavior of a sexual nature.
>
> *Question:* Did Judge Kozinski ever send you emails with sexually inappropriate jokes or pictures?
>
> *Response:* I do not remember receiving inappropriate emails of a sexual nature from Judge Kozinski.[7]

Heidi Bond, among others, publicly challenged Kavanaugh's answers as "baffling." In an article for *Slate,* she wrote, "I'm left wondering whether Kavanaugh and I clerked for the same man. Kozinski's sexual comments—to both women and men—were legendary."[8] Bond had met Kavanaugh just once, at a luncheon during her own Supreme Court clerkship. But she knew Kavanaugh and Kozinski had remained close. Even if Kavanaugh had never joined the Easy Rider Gag List, it seemed unlikely he'd never seen nor heard Kozinski's dirty jokes. One of the more lurid jokes Kozinski emailed to Bond involved a man bragging in a "love letter" to his estranged wife about the graphic details of extramarital sex acts with her kid sister. Bond said she figured the only way Kavanaugh could have forgotten Kozinski's off-color sense of humor "would be if he had amnesia about the clerkship in its entirety."[9]

Still, Kavanaugh's Supreme Court nomination seemed to be fast-tracked in hearings held September 4 to 7, 2018. Then another sexual misconduct complaint surfaced that directly targeted Kavanaugh's behavior as a teenager, decades prior to becoming a judge. That unexpected new round of testimony, broadcast live on September 27, 2018, focused on allegations from Christine Blasey Ford, the California psychology professor who reported that Kavanaugh had trapped her in a bedroom at a house party, and tried to rape her when both were teens. Over radio and TV broadcasts, Blasey Ford's high-pitched voice still sounded a lot like an adolescent's, though she used clinical language to explain how memories can be affected by traumatic experiences. She could recall neither the precise address nor the date. Yet when she testified, Blasey Ford described in detail how she'd been pushed into a bedroom, held down on the bed, and pawed by an attacker whose efforts were thwarted partly by the one-piece bathing suit she'd worn under her clothes that day.

When Bond read about Blasey Ford's allegations she wrote again to Grassley, first thanking him for reading her own statement about a misbehaving federal judge to other senators. Bond asked Grassley to seriously consider Blasey Ford's testimony too. "Coming forward about harassment was one of the hardest things I ever did," Bond wrote. "I pride myself on being a strong and independent woman; publicly exposing the fact that I had been vulnerable in the past was something I did not do for myself, but because I hoped that doing so would pave the road to a better future, one where women did not need to stay silent about harassment. Today I write to you to beg you to treat Dr. Christine Blasey Ford with the same respect." Still, Grassley and others seemed more persuaded by Kavanaugh's vigorous denials than by Blasey Ford's tearful testimony about attempted rape.

As debate over the nomination continued, some of Kavanaugh's former Yale classmates also publicly challenged his testimony. Several gave interviews or wrote op-eds complaining that Kavanaugh had made misleading or false statements under oath about his behavior and his drinking. Deborah Ramirez alleged that he'd exposed himself to her while drunk at a college party at Yale, and she and others challenged his denial. Later, dozens of people—described as "lawyers, doctors, professors and concerned citizens" but whose identities were never revealed—began to file what eventually totaled eighty-three misconduct complaints against Kavanaugh, including allegations that he made "false statements" during nomination hearings for the DC Circuit Court in 2004 and 2006, and for the Supreme Court in 2018. The first fifteen complaints went directly to the chief judge of the DC Circuit Court, where Kavanaugh was still serving as circuit judge at the time of the hearings.

No rule prevents chief circuit judges from reviewing complaints against their colleagues or even against themselves. But at the behest of DC Circuit leaders, Chief Justice Roberts later transferred responsibility for the review to Tymkovich in the Tenth Circuit in Denver, to avoid the appearance of a conflict of interest. Tymkovich was still reviewing complaints against Murguia, the Kansas jurist accused of sexually harassing an employee, when dozens of misconduct complaints against Kavanaugh arrived between October and December 2018.

Ultimately, the judicial misconduct system again proved itself incapable of dealing with the investigation of high-profile allegations against a powerful sitting judge. On October 6, 2018—only nine days after Blasey Ford's testimony—Kavanaugh was confirmed by a 50–48 vote as an associate justice of the US Supreme Court. Two months later, all of the complaints against him were dismissed. The Tenth Circuit Judicial Council concluded that the Judicial Conduct and Disability Act of 1980 does not apply to Supreme Court justices, like Kavanaugh, who are immune from both investigation and disciplinary action by their peers. "The Act covers individuals only while they are circuit, district bankruptcy or magistrate judges, even if the alleged misconduct occurred during the time the judge was covered," the Tenth Circuit Judicial Council's December 12, 2018, order stated. Members of the council acknowledged that "allegations contained in the complaints are serious," but claimed they were forced to dismiss them anyway.

Kavanaugh won his seat on the Supreme Court, but simultaneously earned a reputation as a federal judge publicly accused of making "false statements" and other "serious allegations" of misconduct, as the Tenth Circuit Judicial Council order said. Those complaints remain uninvestigated. Members of the House of Representatives wield the authority under the Constitution to investigate allegations of misconduct by a sitting Supreme Court justice through their impeachment powers, but they have not impeached any member of the high court since President Jefferson's time.

Although no longer as a sitting judge, Kozinski soon resumed a prominent place in public life in Southern California. One San Francisco radio show host invited Kozinski for a friendly hour-long chat about his career as a federal judge, without mentioning the reasons behind his sudden retirement. He published articles and appeared on the radio and onstage as moderator of a political debate in a glittering Beverly Hills theater (the topic of sexual harassment was mentioned, but the allegations against Kozinski were not). He also appeared as counsel in a case in the Ninth Circuit Court of Appeals, an opportunity to address his former colleagues.

Some federal judges thought the leaders of Law Clerks for Workplace Accountability and other reformers had gone too far by continuing to insist Kozinski be investigated for misconduct even in retirement. In late July 2018, Senior US District Judge Richard Kopf—known in his home state of Nebraska as a rabble-rouser—launched barbs on social media aimed at leaders of LCWA. In a string of tweets, Kopf acknowledged that Kozinski likely misbehaved, but Kopf said the group's "desire to revisit the Kozinski matter and perhaps other past sins by other judges looks inquisitorial to me."[10] To underscore the point, Kopf posted a drawing of a man tied and tortured on a medieval rack. Kopf insulted Santos and others by name by tagging their Twitter handles and described them as "uninformed busybodies."[11] Kopf had previously proved himself unafraid of negative attention. In blog entries he'd told the Supreme Court to "STFU," described himself as a "Dirty Old Man," and advised female attorneys to wear short skirts and revealing blouses in court.[12] Santos never filed a complaint, but in days Kopf deleted his tweets, saying only that others had told him they were "inartful" and "lacked nuance."[13]

There was plenty of turmoil inside the lovely Ninth Circuit courthouse in Pasadena, where Kozinski still appeared in a group portrait of circuit jurists displayed in an alcove for years after his retirement. Jurists there remained divided over the issues surrounding Kozinski's retirement. Several Ninth Circuit judges appeared to back

Law Clerks for Workplace Accountability—their clerks were among the group's cofounders. Two of the most outspoken leaders, Santos and Deeva Shah, both clerked for Judge Fisher. Whistleblower Emily Murphy had clerked for Judge Paez. In 2018, both Judges Fisher and Paez were based in Pasadena. But other Ninth Circuit jurists were openly angry about Kozinski's retirement and the #MeToo debates, including Judge Stephen Reinhardt, a 1979 Carter nominee known as the Ninth Circuit's "liberal lion." He also happened to be one of Kozinski's close friends.

In February 2018, Leah Litman was reluctantly adjusting to life as one of the so-called "Kozinski accusers" when she received an invitation to yet another UC Irvine Law School dinner with a prominent federal judge. The gathering was part of an annual guest lecture honoring Judge Reinhardt and his third wife, Ramona Ripston, the retired executive director of the American Civil Liberties Union of Southern California. The lecture series, according to the law school's announcement, honored two "legendary advocates" who "fought for and preserved civil liberties for decades, inspiring and influencing thousands of attorneys and activists."

Reinhardt arrived early and alone. His wife of twenty-seven years was so ill with dementia that he'd begun working from home at times to keep a close watch over her. Behind the scenes, he also had been struggling with the loss on the court of Kozinski, with whom he still spoke regularly. Kozinski had sparred with Reinhardt over their ideological differences, but the two intellectuals forged a friendship over three decades based on alliances in cases involving social issues and the First Amendment, as well as a shared appreciation for jokes and for films.

Both men grew up in Los Angeles: Kozinski was the son of a Hollywood grocer and Reinhardt, the stepson and adopted grandson of famous Hollywood directors. Though Reinhardt was older and had more seniority on the court, both men were educated in decades—Reinhardt in the 1950s; Kozinski in the 1970s—when most American universities remained majority white. Reinhardt had just one Black classmate during his years at Pomona College: an African exchange student from Liberia. Reinhardt had gone on to graduate in 1954 from Yale Law School, an elite bubble also dominated by white men.

But over the decades, Reinhardt had aggressively employed his considerable legal and intellectual powers to help America's workplaces and universities become more diverse and equitable. In a 2015 commencement speech, Reinhardt told recent Pomona graduates: "Your generation must work and work hard to bring an end to the continuing discrimination in the justice system, in law enforcement and in society in general. Your generation must strive—you must strive—to bring about the society we have not yet reached . . . a truly post-racial society. One that is fair to all and one in which all are truly equal."

By 2018, Reinhardt was struggling with stress and isolation, friends thought. He was slowly losing his beloved wife, and he missed Kozinski, whose departure from the Pasadena courthouse had significantly diminished his opportunities to laugh or to win arguments on civil liberties cases in a circuit that increasingly tilted to the right.

In February 2018, Reinhardt was greeted at the UC Irvine dinner by newly appointed Dean L. Song Richardson, who according to her university biography was then the only woman of color to lead a Top 30 law school. Richardson introduced Litman, a rising star on her faculty, to Reinhardt. Reinhardt, an eminence grise with a double chin and a regal air, turned his stern gaze on Litman, whom he knew to be a Kozinski accuser. He turned his back on her and walked out of the room, reentering the room only after several former law clerks and other attorneys he knew had joined the gathering, Litman later recalled. Reinhardt could be socially awkward, but Litman saw his move as a snub. The small group included several former clerks, including the evening's guest lecturer, Jeffrey L. Fisher, a Stanford law professor. Fisher, codirector of Stanford's Supreme Court litigation clinic, was a Michigan Law graduate, like Litman, though more than a decade older. All dined together around one table.

At dinner Litman didn't expect Reinhardt to speak to her, but he took time to single her out. Reinhardt mused in his dry way that he'd had several excellent clerks from Michigan Law, and counted on them to identify the best in each class. Her name had never come up, he said, adding that Litman must "not have been very smart" or a "very good student or particularly liked by them," Litman recalled.

Litman did not respond or mention Kozinski. That would, she later said, have "seemed rude, given that [Reinhardt] was an honored guest at the dinner that my law school was hosting." She knew from courthouse whisper networks that some Ninth Circuit judges worried aloud that they could not trust any female clerks after what had happened to Kozinski. Litman was acquainted with Olivia Warren, one of Reinhardt's clerks from 2017 to 2018. She'd briefly met Warren during her year as a fellow at Harvard Law and knew her as a feminist. If Reinhardt had been so openly hostile toward her, a law professor, how might he be privately treating Warren?

Litman sent off an email to Warren's Harvard.edu account. "I had dinner with your judge and I wanted to see how you were doing and how your year was going," she wrote. Litman told Warren that Reinhardt had pointedly and publicly insulted her, a known "Kozinski accuser," and she worried he might be "misbehaving elsewhere." Warren responded with thanks, but little else. Litman suggested they stay in touch.

Liv Warren first met Reinhardt when he visited Harvard in 2015 and recruited her, then a first-year law student, to be his clerk upon her graduation. She shared the judge's passion for defending the rights of indigent defendants and felt "thrilled" to begin in May 2017. Warren, a dance major at her liberal arts college, now dreamed of being a capital defense attorney. Warren knew that Reinhardt was also well known for his pro-choice opinions. For decades he'd been married to Ripston, one of Southern California's most outspoken advocates for reproductive rights. Still, one former clerk warned Warren that Reinhardt exhibited signs of what he called "your grandfather's sexism."

Nationwide, dozens of Reinhardt's former clerks played prominent roles in nonprofit organizations, public defender offices, and law schools. Together they formed a powerful band, which Warren wanted to join. Despite his quirks, Reinhardt was venerated by former clerks who praised him as a supportive mentor and civil rights advocate, though Reinhardt could be both stern and caustic, and like Kozinski, demanded long hours of his staff. Reinhardt often hired women as clerks, but sometimes asked them to fetch coffee or made remarks they considered sexist. He told one female clerk that he preferred clerks with out-of-town boyfriends or girlfriends so they had no distractions. He told another, Michele Landis Dauber, that he would never hire any other clerks who were working moms, like her, because they were too much trouble. Dauber, who later became a Stanford Law professor, respected her mentor for his positive qualities, but as far as she knew, he'd kept his word: he never hired another mom as his clerk.[14]

One of his last female clerks, Warren was married, without children. After her clerkship began in 2017, Warren quickly learned that Reinhardt was angry with the accusations and demands made by members of the burgeoning #MeToo movement. Reinhardt told Warren that he thought women who accused the film producer Harvey Weinstein of sex crimes had "wanted it" and later changed their minds. His fury only intensified when his close friend Alex Kozinski resigned after being publicly accused of sexual misconduct by Litman, Murphy, Bond, and others. He told Warren he planned to confront Litman when he visited UC Irvine.

Privately, Reinhardt took out his frustrations on Warren, she later said, though in her time as clerk, Warren shared nothing with outsiders about what she considered verbal abuse and sexual harassment. Warren had already proved she could adapt to difficult conditions, having taught in a remote Cambodian village as an undergrad. She listened, shared her point of view as a woman, and responded to his attacks on the #MeToo movement, but her efforts only seemed to make him angrier. After Reinhardt died suddenly of a heart attack on March 29, 2018, she cried at his funeral. She stayed on at the Ninth Circuit until June 2018 to finish her clerkship. Only after leaving the Ninth Circuit, where Reinhardt was revered, did she attempt to report problems she'd experienced. Nothing happened. Later, Warren accepted a job as staff defense attorney at the nonprofit Center for Death Penalty Litigation in Durham, North Carolina. She remained concerned, but hesitated to publicly criticize Reinhardt or federal court officials about the lack of response to her complaints.

Litman stayed in touch. By 2020, Warren still had confided little to Litman about her clerkship, but she had begun consulting other attorneys about options. Litman told Warren that her own experience of denouncing sexual harassment by a federal judge had complicated her life. Some friends she'd expected to support her had not, and dealing with the fallout of being a "Kozinski accuser" had consumed tremendous time and energy. But Litman won the 2019 Professor of the Year award at UC Irvine Law School. Later that year she accepted a new teaching position at her alma mater, Michigan Law. She continued her appellate legal work, started a podcast, *Strict Scrutiny*, about the Supreme Court, and adopted a puppy she named Stevie. And yet Litman also had begun to reluctantly conclude that some people would always overlook her other accomplishments and judge her merely on the basis of her decision to denounce Kozinski's misbehavior.

In 2020, James Sensenbrenner and other congressmen began to ask why the federal judiciary still seemed to be struggling with reports of sexual harassment so long after Kozinski's retirement. Sensenbrenner and other lawmakers thought jurists had botched the Murguia case and had failed to adequately assist employees who'd been harassed. During a hearing of the House Appropriations Committee, Representative Norma Torres, a California Democrat, confronted a Kansas-based federal judge (whose chambers had been in the same courthouse as Murguia's) and a senior federal court administrator: "One of the most troubling things for me is that no one—no one— came forward" to assist staff members who reported Murguia, Torres told them. The victims were "too afraid," she said, and yet other witnesses and federal judges with inside information failed to support them or to take action. Torres suggested that other judges, through hesitation and inaction, were "also party to that harassment."

A hearing specifically to discuss several recent cases of federal judicial misconduct was set for February 13, 2020 by Sensenbrenner and other leaders of the House Subcommittee on Courts, Intellectual Property, and the Internet (part of the House Judiciary Committee). Santos and Shah, the cofounders of Law Clerks for Workplace Accountability, attended, as did Lithwick, who came down from New York. And at the last minute, Liv Warren agreed to testify, driving more than 250 miles from Durham on a workday. Litman, now teaching in Ann Arbor, also traveled to Washington for the hearing.

Warren began her testimony by telling congressmen she had decided to speak out, not because she wanted "to destroy Judge Reinhardt's significant contributions to the law or to condemn him."[15] Instead, she had reluctantly decided that testifying to Congress might be the best way to expose weaknesses in reforms aimed at reducing sexual harassment in the judiciary. Warren was adept at controlling performance jitters from her days as a dance major. She kept her voice steady as she read from a written statement that would echo across social media in a series of tweets distributed by Litman, Bond, Santos, @clerksforchange, and former Reinhardt clerks, many of whom reacted swiftly in outrage.

She introduced her clerkship experience by describing an unusual drawing she spotted on her first day at work. The diagram, taped to a computer, looked like one of her middle-school algebra assignments: "a sine chart, which resembles two hills drawn on an x-axis." But someone had added dots to make the hills look like nipples. Another clerk "noticed me staring and explained that he had sketched the chart . . . and the judge himself had added the nipples."[16] A male clerk had laughed off the incident. Warren still felt uncomfortable, especially after Reinhardt later asked if she liked his drawing. That was only a harbinger of the type of behavior that would make her increasingly ill at ease.

Reinhardt's wood-paneled office in Pasadena was lined with bookshelves that held framed portraits and snapshots of family, friends, dignitaries, and former clerks. Reinhardt often hired women he considered both smart and pretty and displayed pictures of his favorites on a special shelf. The judge made it clear that Warren's photo would never be displayed there. Instead, he "routinely and frequently made disparaging statements about my physical appearance, my views about feminism and women's rights, and my relationship with my husband," she testified.[17] "Often, these remarks included expressing surprise that I even had a husband, because I was not a woman who any man would be attracted to. In that vein, Judge Reinhardt often speculated that my husband must be a 'wimp,' or possibly gay. Judge Reinhardt would use both words and gestures to suggest that my 'wimp' husband must either lack a penis, or not be able to get an erection in my presence. He implied that my marriage had not been consummated." Warren said similar insults were delivered in almost daily doses.

As Reinhardt's clerk Warren never considered complaining about Reinhardt to the Ninth Circuit Judicial Council, though its leaders enacted their own reforms after Kozinski's retirement. "After carefully reviewing the applicable procedures for reporting harassment, Ms. Warren did not feel that she could safely report to the Ninth Circuit," Warren's attorney, Zainab Ahmad, later said in a statement. "Although the procedures technically allowed her to report anonymously, the substance of her complaint would have made her identity obvious. . . . She also worried that these procedures would not protect her from retaliation—something she had already witnessed and something she feared deeply."[18]

But after her clerkship ended on June 1, 2018, Warren made two attempts to report her experiences, she told the house committee. She went first to the dean and other leaders at Harvard Law. She also contacted a new office at the Administrative Office of the US Courts in Washington, DC, the Office of Judicial Integrity, a one-person operation set up specifically to provide confidential advice to clerks and other current and former judicial employees navigating workplace misconduct issues and considering the possibility of pursuing formal or informal complaints. She thought the federal court's new advisor, a former circuit court official appointed to the new role in December 2018, provided only confusing and unhelpful information. As she finished her 2020 testimony, Warren reemphasized that her goal was to raise awareness about the judiciary's continuing failure to adequately address complaints. "The federal courts' reform efforts were clearly incomplete," she told congressmen. "I hope that my testimony today will result in law clerks (both current and former) and judiciary employees feeling less silenced and more capable of seeking accountability and redress for any harassment or other misconduct." Warren added that she worried about long-term consequences for the legal profession if victims continued to feel unheard and alienated. Warren feared that women and people of color, already underrepresented in the federal judiciary and other elite legal circles, would suffer most.

At the hearing, Deeva Shah, cofounder of Law Clerks for Workplace Accountability and another newly minted attorney, added her voice to amplify Warren's. Through dozens of conversations with current and former clerks and externs, her group had uncovered many others who had been "demeaned," "belittled," and "humiliated" while working for federal judges. "People shared stories about being asked sexual questions unrelated to work, hearing their judges or other employees speak about female attorneys in objectifying terms, and being groped in public and in private," Shah said. Then she repeated the call for better protection for whistleblowers, and for improvements in the reporting system and in the disciplinary statute. No judge should be allowed to escape disciplinary action or the disclosure of the findings of a formal judicial misconduct investigation simply by retiring or resigning. Other judges who knew about a colleague's misconduct and failed to report it or covered it up should also be held accountable, she said.

Chief Justice Roberts never publicly responded to the allegations raised at the 2020 congressional hearing, but the Administrative Office of the US Courts immediately issued a statement that said: "No judiciary employee should suffer the kind of harassment described by former law clerk Olivia Warren today." It promised that court leaders were taking her testimony seriously and that work on reforms continued. "We are committed to addressing this new information and continuing to refine our processes and procedures for protecting our employees and addressing misconduct." Roberts soon became consumed by the COVID-19 pandemic and didn't mention sexual harassment or judicial misconduct in his 2020 year-end address.

Harvard Law leaders never issued any public response to Warren's testimony at all. Perhaps that was no surprise: law school rankings depend in part on the number of clerkships that star students land with federal judges. Individual students from both Yale and Harvard—the two law schools that supply a third or more of all Supreme Court clerks—also appeared at the hearing to support the call for reforms. Law professors and prominent alums who belong to Law Clerks for Workplace Accountability have testified too. But some advocates believe that pressure to reform misconduct reviews and improve conditions for law clerks and other employees may be possible only if more powerful federal judges and deans actively engage in the fight.

In the end, perhaps the strongest statement of support for Liv Warren came from seventy-three former clerks of Judge Reinhardt, an effort organized by Michele Landis Dauber, the Stanford Law School professor. Some had spotted signs of "your grandfather's sexism" in their mentor; others had not. All signed a letter, published online, that called the conduct Warren described "totally unacceptable in any workplace." It was "particularly unfortunate that this conduct occurred in the chambers of a preeminent judge who made pursuing justice his lifelong goal and who wrote countless opinions advancing the cause of gender equality, civil rights, and labor rights."[19] One signer was Heather Gerken, who identified herself only as Reinhardt's clerk from 1994 to 1995. She is also the dean of the Yale Law School.

Publicly, Warren said no more. Instead, she returned to her "dream job" in North Carolina, where she labors at a nonprofit defending legal rights of death row inmates whose lives are literally on the line. In a way, her efforts to eliminate sexual harassment were a form of the civil rights activism that Reinhardt, in his better days, had long expected from former clerks. Her testimony, like Shah's, has provided compelling evidence that the next generation of young lawyers will no longer silently accept such misbehavior, even if federal judges fail to take adequate steps to stop it.

The Quilter

Texas, 2017–2020

Cathy McBroom's story was constantly on my mind when the #MeToo movement began to hit the federal courts in 2017. I called and we agreed to meet at a Starbucks in the Houston suburb of Deer Park, and caught up over coffee. Unfortunately, we both agreed, attitudes about sexual misconduct by members of the federal judiciary did not appear to have changed enough in the decade since she reported Kent's misconduct, though these days many more women were beginning to speak out. When McBroom had first denounced Judge Kent, she felt frightened and totally alone. "When I came out, I didn't know of anyone who had done that at all. I kind of felt like I was 'Small Town' trying to do something big and I didn't have a support system," she said, sipping from a cup of iced latte.

The only role model she had was a woman she'd never met: Anita Hill. Back in 1991, the year Hill took on a federal judge, McBroom had been a divorced working mom in her early thirties—not yet a federal court employee. McBroom watched Hill testify on TV about sexual misconduct allegedly committed years before by Thomas, then a Supreme Court nominee (and a DC Circuit judge). In some ways, Hill's testimony before the Senate Judiciary Committee anticipated Christine Blasey Ford's in 2018, twenty-seven years later.

McBroom told me she'd watched a documentary about Hill's life, *Anita*, soon after its release in 2014. Told mostly through a series of compelling interwoven interviews, the film recounts Hill's life as the youngest child in her close-knit family, her subsequent struggle as a young African American woman attorney in Washington, DC, and her disturbing encounters with her boss, Clarence Thomas. After testifying about Thomas, Hill had been attacked in hundreds of telephone calls and threatening letters and eventually had left her job at the University of Oklahoma. Subsequent waves of retaliation against Hill continued long after Thomas assumed his Supreme Court seat—yet many victims of sexual assault also wrote or called to thank her. In the opening of her autobiography, *Speaking Truth to Power*, Hill writes that "more than anything else, the Hill-Thomas hearing . . . was about finding our voices and breaking the silence forever."[1]

McBroom told me that she cried through much of the ninety-five-minute film. Hill's pain and the pattern of abuse she had suffered felt so familiar. At times, McBroom had fallen into a pit of depression and anxiety. To protect herself, she had sometimes retreated, disappearing for days and not answering phone calls, even from her children.

In my years as an investigative reporter, I had seen other whistleblowers break or descend into mental illness. Several I knew had lost their jobs and marriages during long fights to seek justice. I later met up with Cathy's oldest daughter, Evelyn, for lunch at a Houston mall to talk about her mother's ordeal. She told me that at times, she feared her mother was "going crazy," acting in ways that seemed self-destructive. Evelyn, a busy working mom who gave birth to two girls in the years McBroom's fight continued against Kent, felt compelled to temporarily cut off contact at one point until her mother eventually regained self-control. "She was made out to be the villain; they were working against her," she told me. "And if it wouldn't have been for the people who finally heard her—I think it could have completely destroyed her."

McBroom's personal and professional life began to turn around as Kent served his prison term. She grew closer to Kent's other victim, Donna Wilkerson. That was a piece of her own recovery. She kept in touch off and on with Rusty Hardin. And I knew from surprising posts on Facebook that she had reconciled with her husband, Rex.

In the four years since his wife had hurled a vase that shattered their bathroom mirror, Rex McBroom had never given up on Mc-Broom. Rex remained her friend even after she filed for divorce. He had never dated, even after she got engaged and seriously considered marrying someone else. They continued to raise their son, Caleb, together, buying houses near each other in the Clear Lake area, and amicably sharing custody. Then one day in 2011, McBroom was taking a shower at the Seabrook house, where she lived alone, when she had an epiphany: "The man you need to be with is your husband and he's out there waiting for you." She got out, dried herself off, and called him. The two quietly began dating again. Her daughter and others in the family were skeptical, so they kept their remarriage secret at first. These days, they celebrate their original anniversary, November 21, 1991, as if the divorce had never happened.

McBroom feels less satisfied with changes in her longtime workplace, the federal courts. She told me she sometimes wonders, *What was it all for? I did succeed in getting [Judge Kent] off the bench, but I guess I wanted to see more reforms. I wanted to send a message to people that this should stop.* Broader awareness and changes in training, policies, and attitudes that McBroom had hoped to see about sexual harassment and misconduct following Kent's conviction never materialized—not even at the Sugar Cube in Houston. Some federal judges McBroom worked with from 2010 to 2015 in Houston and in Galveston openly expressed dismay with her role as a whistleblower, even after Kent went to prison. One told McBroom that he'd heard she was "belligerent" and "disrespectful." Another seemed angry when she received an award from an attorney group honoring her bravery; he asked her to turn it down. (She accepted anyway.)

US District Judge Lynn Hughes, a white-haired freewheeling libertarian, reminded McBroom a little too much of King Kent. From late 2009 and into 2010, McBroom worked as deputy case manager for Hughes, a Reagan appointee who has been on the bench since 1985 and relishes his reputation as an outspoken eccentric. He "had no filter, liked being surrounded by his staff members and being the center of attention," she told me. All judges entered their courtrooms with a certain degree of ceremony, but Hughes, then sixty-eight, insisted on a particularly elaborate ritual of being "knocked in." Before any hearing, someone on staff was required to physically knock loudly on the door between the chambers and the courtroom and then "do the cry," asking all to rise for the entrance of the Honorable Judge Lynn Hughes. Hughes had a designated pecking order on his staff that determined who could do what part of that ceremony. "And then there was a procession. It was like a royalty thing," McBroom said.

I and other *Chronicle* reporters had written stories about lawyers who had complained that the outspoken judge sometimes made blatantly sexist or racist comments in court. But the Fifth Circuit chief circuit judge, Carl Stewart, a Clinton nominee who served as chief from 2012 to 2019, never took any public action on a misconduct complaint that an attorney for the Texas Civil Rights Project filed in 2013 that criticized Hughes for remarks and rulings that seemed racist. Later, Hughes also kept publicly referring to women in his courtroom as "girls"—including female FBI agents—though he denied being either racist or sexist in interviews. He banned a woman prosecutor from his court after she included his remarks about "girls" in an appeal.

Behind the scenes, McBroom told me that Hughes demanded that female employees wear heels and skirts. He told McBroom to tuck in her blouse one day, and then ogled her, seeming to notice instantly how it became tighter across her breasts. Once when they were alone in his office, the judge summoned her to his computer to show off a risqué photo of a model wearing a mesh shirt that revealed nipples, and asked McBroom for her opinion.

Hughes cracked jokes in chambers during his review of a 2009 civil dispute over a seventy-five-year-old Japanese inventor's claim that others were infringing on his patent for a medical massage device, in *High Island Health v. Libertybelle Marketing (also known as Pleasure2me)*. Jiro Takashima and his daughter argued that his invention had been intended for prostate problems, but sales took off after it became popular as a sex toy and inspired illegal imitations.[2] In a private behind-the-scenes discussion that had nothing to do with that case, McBroom said, Hughes made a hand gesture and referred to a crude sex act in front of McBroom and several other female court employees. McBroom tried to ignore Hughes; a young law clerk immediately walked out. Later, McBroom told me she wondered why she never told Hughes, "That's inappropriate." Even after everything she had gone through, she still wondered, *Where's my voice? I still felt like he had power and I didn't.* She never considered filing a judicial misconduct complaint. Instead she applied for another job.

In response to an email, Hughes said he could not discuss any disciplinary matters and had "no recollection" of making jokes, gestures, or remarks like those described by McBroom when he was asked about them about a decade later. "Cathy McBroom worked for Judge Hughes for about a year. . . . He has no recollection of the events described in your email," his secretary wrote.[3]

In late 2010, McBroom accepted a promotion and returned to the Galveston Division, where in one of those odd circle-of-life moments she took over as deputy-in-charge, the position previously held by her former boss Marianne Gore. "It was bizarre going back there," she told me in another one of our conversations. Some of the same court security guards who'd seen her flee from Kent remained at their posts. As part of the move, McBroom became Donna Wilkerson's supervisor.

Wilkerson had not immediately been reassigned after Kent's prosecution. Instead, she languished inside his empty Houston office before being transferred to a low-level clerk's office position in Galveston, though as a crime victim, she successfully fought a proposed 25 percent pay cut. Wilkerson subsequently applied for other judicial secretary jobs, but never got an offer. At one point McBroom worried that Wilkerson might have a nervous breakdown. Over the five years that she served as Wilkerson's boss, from 2010 to 2015, McBroom did her best to assist with the other woman's recovery. Still, McBroom felt that the Kent case "followed me and it still follows Donna."

As a distraction, she took up quilting.

McBroom smiled with pleasure on February 10, 2020, as she showed me inside Painted Pony 'n' Quilts, a store filled with shelves lined with bright bolts of cloth in the bayside town of La Porte. She favored batiks and bold palettes created by modern designers over the calicos or the brown and cream-colored fabrics of the 1800s. McBroom stopped sharply in one aisle to extract and inspect a bolt with a particularly striking pattern featuring indigo hydrangea blossoms set off by scarlet leaves, magenta roses, and flashes of jade. "What do you think?" she asked me. "Isn't this beautiful?" She already was envisioning how to blend this fabric with swatches collected in previous forays. Not yet satisfied, she replaced the bolt and continued to scan, like a skilled hunter-gatherer, swooping in to examine other potential prizes before returning to collect yardage needed for her latest project. Everywhere, she saw patterns and possibilities.

Following her long fight with Judge Kent, McBroom took solace and found solidarity in quilting, a tradition born of women's collective need to exchange stories, survive harsh winters, and reuse what had been discarded. She started small, sewing the first patches on an old sewing machine when she returned home from the courthouse after work. In 2011, inspired by her visit to the enormous Houston International Quilt Festival, McBroom tore down a wall in her small Seabrook house to make room for a $12,000 quilting machine that enabled a pace of three thousand stitches per minute. She took it as a promising sign that after she and Rex reconciled, he never protested sharing space with a machine that weighs five hundred pounds and is mounted to a platform larger than their dinner table.

In 2015, McBroom left behind the pomp and paperwork of her federal court career, retiring a little earlier than planned. By then she had survived a series of revolving judges assigned to the Galveston Division with differing demands. Although she was younger than the standard retirement age, she confirmed she was vested in federal retirement. "I got to the point where I thought I'd rather be quilting," she says.

Bright quilts of many colors decorate every room of the home she now shares with Rex in a tree-lined neighborhood in Beaumont. On a bench near the entryway, she displays a quilted pillow that depicts their life together. It features a series of patchwork houses, a triangular pine, and a turquoise and magenta RV with a button wheel for the couple that seems constantly on the go. "Home is wherever we are together" reads red lettering stitched on one patch. Rex is still working, but these days, they split their time between Beaumont and a condo on the beach in Belize.

In the process of many moves—after she retired, after Rex changed jobs, and after the floods of Hurricane Harvey—McBroom purged many things she felt she no longer needed: the business suits and dresses she used to wear to work at the courthouse; the blue pullover sweater she wore when Kent last assaulted her; the computer files of emotional memos and emails written in days and nights of panic. She joined a close-knit quilting club and began attending weeklong retreats. She's become a master of the way generations of women have reassembled fabrics and scraps of their own lives into art. In retirement, McBroom gradually remade her life in a world filled with creative circles of women. Yet she knows there are pieces of the Kent story she will never let go.

Cathy McBroom has discovered in quilting a solidarity that eluded her when she first stood up to a powerful judge. McBroom watched closely when other women started to stand up and speak out in 2017. Partly through the skills she developed in this folk art, she began to see how the threads of her struggle tie her to other women and whistleblowers who also have taken risks, revealed problems, and fought for change in federal courts in California, in Texas, in Washington, DC, in Colorado, in Kansas, and elsewhere across the United States. The longer she stares at each patch of this story, the more patterns emerge.

She knows that more work remains before federal court culture is truly altered and the patterns of sexual harassment and abuse finally change. There are still too many holes in the fabric. And yet—she has hope.

ACKNOWLEDGMENTS

Thanks to Cathy McBroom, Leah Litman, Emily Murphy, Heidi Bond, Donna Wilkerson, and many others who shared stories, time, and expertise over the ten years it took to put together this book.

I appreciate the invaluable support of valued friends and mentors, including Rosie Schaap, Katie Iles, Maggie Galehouse, Kema Geroux, Skip Hollandsworth, Mimi Swartz, and Andrea White, all of whom read draft chapters or offered advice. More help came from Schaap and other members of Fairleigh Dickinson University's Creative Writing faculty: René Steinke, Renee Ashley, Rebecca Chase, Donna Freitas, and Minna Proctor.

Profound thanks to Krys Doerfler, whose scholarship in the name of her husband Ron contributed to this work. Wonderful writer friends Leigh Hopper and Lourdes Cardenas provided companionship and support on out-of-town research trips. I'm very grateful to George Getschow, founder of the Mayborn Literary Nonfiction Conference, and veteran Texas columnist Rick Casey, who provided early encouragement.

More thanks go to attorneys Joe Larsen and to David Smallman for their support and legal advice. I appreciate insights from law professor Arthur Hellman on the judicial disciplinary system, from author Barbara Radnofsky on impeachment, and from author Linda Hirshman on sexual harassment law. All mistakes are my own.

This story may never have been published at all without the strong support and hard work of my original *Houston Chronicle* colleagues and editors: Harvey Rice, George Haj, Jacquee Petchel, and Jeff Cohen.

This book became a reality thanks to my agent, Susan Canavan, at Scott Waxman & Associates; and to my editor, Joanna Green; managing editor Susan Lumenello; and the team at Beacon Press.

Above all, thanks to my family: Ron, Jeremy, and Gabriel.

NOTES

Much of the information in this book comes from court and congressional records, as well as from more than one hundred interviews conducted from 2007 to 2020 in person, by phone, and via emails with people involved directly in the Kent case and in other misconduct matters involving Judges Kozinski, Porteous, Smith, Murguia, Roberts, and Nottingham. Cathy McBroom was particularly generous with her time, granting eight in-person interviews and numerous follow-ups. Others interviewed include Heidi Bond, Tony Buzbee, Charlene Clark, Ty Clevenger, James Cobb, Susan Criss, Valorie Davenport, Dick DeGuerin, Patrick Fanning, Raphael Goyeneche III, Anthony Griffin, George Haj, Rusty Hardin, Richard L. Hasen, Arthur Hellman, Mark Lindow, Dahlia Lithwick, Leah Litman, Laurie Lyons, Tony Mauro, Rex McBroom, Emily Murphy, Jaime Santos, Randy Schaffer, Lynn Hecht Schafran, Arthur Schechter, Mary Ann Schopp, James Sensenbrenner, Mark Stevens, and Donna Wilkerson. Retired Judge Christie O. Miller provided an email; US District Judge Lynn Hughes spoke via phone in 2019 and in a 2020 email; Samuel Kent responded via letter in 2008; comments from other judges are from public documents, or statements provided through spokespersons. Other federal officials and attorneys provided information on background. The talented Skip Hollandsworth shared additional information and encouragement. Many thanks to all. Unless otherwise noted, quotes attributed to people in this book came from interviews, emails, court transcripts, court opinions, congressional proceedings, or misconduct complaint orders and related records in possession of the author. Some conversations in the book are based on documents; others were recreated based on the recollections of one or more participants.

CHAPTER 1: AN AWKWARD ENCOUNTER

1. Matt Zapotosky, "Nine More Women Say Judge Subjected Them to Inappropriate Behavior," *Washington Post*, December 15, 2017.
2. Zapotosky, "Nine More Women Say Judge Subjected Them to Inappropriate Behavior."
3. Judge Christine O. C. Miller, email to author, November 2, 2018.
4. Matt Zapotosky, "Prominent Appeals Court Judge Alex Kozinski Accused of Sexual Misconduct," *Washington Post*, December 8, 2017.
5. Maura Dolan, "9th Circuit Judge Alex Kozinski Is Accused by Former Clerks of Making Sexual Comments," *Los Angeles Times*, December 8, 2017.
6. Zapotosky, "Prominent Appeals Court Judge Alex Kozinski Accused of Sexual Misconduct."

Additional information in this chapter is from Litman, Hasen, Murphy, statements issued by Kozinski (who did not respond to interview requests), and author visits to the Canaletto and the US circuit courthouses in Pasadena and San Francisco.

CHAPTER 2: FLIGHT

1. The proportion did not reach 50 percent until 2016. For more on historic ABA law school enrollment data, see Richard K. Newman Jr., "Women in Legal Education: What the Statistics Show," *Hofstra Law Faculty Scholarship* (September 2000), https://scholarlycommons.law .hofstra.edu/cgi/viewcontent. cgi?article=1882&context=faculty_scholarship.
2. Lynn Hecht Schafran, "Will Inquiry Produce Action? Studying the Effects of Gender in the Federal Courts," *University of Richmond Law Review* 32, no. 3 (1998): 615–45, https://scholarship.richmond.edu /cgi/viewcontent.cgi?article=2285&context=lawreview. Schafran also spoke to the author and provided a copy of the testimony she gave on January 1993 to the National Commission on Judicial Discipline and Removal.
3. Code of Conduct for Judicial Employees, effective March 12, 2019, https://www.uscourts.gov/sites/default/files/code_of_conduct_for _judicial_employees_effective_march_12_2019_0.pdf.

CHAPTER 3: KINGS OF THE COURTS

1. "Appointed Forever," lyrics 1997 by the Bar & Grill Singers, used by permission. See https://www.singers.com/group/Bar-Grill-Singers.

2. Christine Biederman, "Temper, Temper," *Dallas Observer*, October 2, 1997.

3. Scott Greenfield, "Texas: Where Decisions Are Decisions and Lawyers Are Nervous," *Simple Justice* (blog), August 30, 2007, https://blog .simplejustice.us/2007/08/30/texas-where-decisions-are-decisions-and -lawyers-are-nervous.

4. Steven Lubet, "Bullying from the Bench," *Green Bag Law Review* (Autumn 2001), www.greenbag.org/v5n1/v5n1_articles_lubet.pdf.

5. Lise Olsen, "Amid Difficult Times, Kent Talks of His Struggles," *Houston Chronicle*, January 13, 2008. Additional quotes from Kent's 2008 letter to author are used elsewhere in this chapter.

6. Collins Fitzpatrick, "Building a Better Bench: Informally Addressing Instance of Judicial Misconduct," *Judges' Journal* 45, no. 1 (Winter 2005).

7. Olsen, "Amid Difficult Times, Kent Talks of His Struggles."

8. Mary Flood, "Houston Federal Judge Removed from 85 Cases," *Houston Chronicle*, August 24, 2001.

Additional information in this chapter is from author interviews with Hellman, Schafran, Schopp, and McBroom. McBroom's March 27, 2007, request for an emergency transfer and her May 21, 2007, complaint of judicial misconduct against Kent are in the possession of the author.

CHAPTER 4: CHAMBERS AND SECRETS

1. *A Handbook for Law Clerks to Federal Judges* (Grand Rapids: Michigan Legal Publishing, 1989) has gone through several editions. This quote is taken from the original 1989 version. See also the 2017 and 2020 versions on the Federal Judicial Center website, https://www.fjc .gov/content/345912/law-clerk-handbook-handbook-law-clerks-federal -judges-fourth-edition.

2. Heidi Bond, journal entry posted on Courtney Milan author blog, December 2017, http://www.courtneymilan.com/metoo/kozinski.html. Other dialogue between Bond and Kozinski is from the journal. Additional details are from Bond's interview with and emails to author.

3. Amanda Taub, "The #MeToo Moment: How One Harasser Can Rob a Generation of Women," *New York Times*, December 14, 2017.

4. Tony Mauro, "Corps of Clerks Lacking in Diversity," *USA Today*, March 13, 1998.

5. Tony Mauro, "Supreme Court Clerks Are Overwhelmingly White and Male. Just Like 20 Years Ago," *USA Today*, January 8, 2018. Additional information from Mauro's interview with author.

6. Alex Kozinski, foreword to *Sexual Harassment in Employment Law*, ed. Barbara Lindemann and David D. Kadue (Arlington, VA: Bureau of National Affairs, 1992), vii.

7. Catherine Crump, "Clerkships Are Invaluable for Young Lawyers; They Can Also Be a Setup for Abuse," *Washington Post*, December 15, 2017.

8. Joanna Grossman, @joannagrossman, December 9, 2017, https://twitter.com/JoannaGrossman/status/939542418638147584.

9. Procter Hug Jr., Marilyn L. Huff, and John C. Coughenour, "Ninth Circuit: The Gender Bias Task Force," *University of Richmond Law Review* 32, no. 3 (1998), http://scholarship.richmond.edu/lawreview/vol32/iss3/10.

10. Alex Kozinski, "Federal Judge Alex Kozinski's 1996 Slate Diary," *Slate*, July 21, 1996, https://slate.com/news-and-politics/1996/07/alex-kozinski-s-slate-diary-10.html.

11. Dahlia Lithwick, "He Made Us All Victims and Accomplices," *Slate*, December 13, 2017, https://slate.com/news-and-politics/2017/12/judge-alex-kozinski-made-us-all-victims-and-accomplices.html.

12. Lithwick, "He Made Us All Victims and Accomplices." Additional quotes from Lithwick's interview with the author.

13. Katherine Ku, "Pressuring Harassers to Quit Can End Up Protecting Them," *Washington Post*, January 5, 2018.

14. Alex Kozinski, "Confessions of a Bad Apple," *Yale Law Journal* 100 (1992): 1708, https://digitalcommons.law.yale.edu/cgi/viewcontent.cgi?article=7349&context=ylj.

15. Heidi Bond, "Some Things About Heidi," undated journal entry, www.qiken.org/heidi.html.

16. Bond, December 2017 entry.

17. Heidi Bond, "I Received Some of Kozinski's Infamous Gag List Emails. I'm Baffled by Kavanaugh's Responses to Questions About Them," *Slate*, September 14, 2018. Additional information from Bond's emails to and interview with the author.

18. Alex Kozinski, "Kozinski Strikes Back," *The Recorder*, September 23, 2005; comments emailed from Cyrus Sanai to US Courts on November 13, 2018, https://www.uscourts.gov/sites/default/files/cyrus_sanai-l._ralph_mecham_public_comment_proposed_changes_code_rules.pdf.

19. Scott Glover, "9th Circuit's Chief Judge Posted Sexually Explicit Matter on His Website," *Los Angeles Times*, June 11, 2008.

20. Cyrus Sanai, email to Honorable Ralph R. Erickson, chair, Committee on Codes of Conduct, and to Honorable Anthony J. Scirica, chair, Committee on Judicial Conduct and Disability, Judicial Conference of the United States, October 25, 2018, https://www.uscourts.gov/sites/default/files/cyrus_sanai_witness_statement_proposed_changes_code_rules_0.pdf.

21. See petition in Sanai v. Kozinski, a 2019 federal civil lawsuit in the Northern District of California, https://turtletalk.files.wordpress.com/2020/03/sanai-v.-kozinski.pdf.

CHAPTER 5: THE RELUCTANT WHISTLEBLOWER
The events described and conversations in this chapter are based on author interviews with McBroom, Clark, Schopp, Williams, Wilkerson, Cobb, Buzbee, Wells Davenport, DeGuerin, Hardin, and others. Kent's assaults are also described in McBroom's March 27, 2007, transfer request and her

May 21, 2007, complaint of judicial misconduct against Kent. Documents in possession of the author.

CHAPTER 6: THE COMPLAINT

1. Henry Weinstein, "Panel Votes to Censure U.S. Judge," *Los Angeles Times*, December 23, 2006, https://www.latimes.com/archives/la-xpm -2006-dec-23-me-real23-story.html.
2. Lara A. Bazelon, "Putting the Mice in Charge of the Cheese: Why Federal Judges Cannot Always Be Trusted to Police Themselves and What Congress Can Do About It," *Kentucky Law Journal* 97 (2009): 439; Lara A. Bazelon, "Putting the Mice in Charge of the Cheese: Why Federal Judges Cannot Always Be Trusted to Police Themselves and What Congress Can Do About It," Loyola-LA Legal Studies Paper No. 2012–41, SSRN: https://ssrn.com/abstract=1676956, last revised October 26, 2012.
3. Bazelon, "Putting the Mice in Charge of the Cheese," Loyola, 2.

Additional information and context are from author interviews with Weinstein, Bazelon, Hellman, and court officials, as well as from court documents.

CHAPTER 7: HER HONOR

1. Edith Hollan Jones, dismissal orders, Fifth Circuit archives, New Orleans. Other quotes from complaints in this chapter from Jones's dismissal orders.
2. Susanna Dokupil, "Hon. Edith H. Jones," *Independent Women's Forum*, July 2, 2012, http://www.iwf.org/modern-feminist/2788377/Hon .-Edith-H.-Jones.
3. See also Linda Hirshman, *Reckoning: The Epic Battle Against Sexual Abuse and Harassment* (New York: Houghton Mifflin Harcourt, 2019), for detailed background and explanation of sexual harassment case law in landmark cases such as *Meritor v. Vinson* and others mentioned in this chapter. Additional information from author interview with Hirshman.
4. Comments attributed to Jones and other judges: Laurie Lyons, author's interview; Paul Schneider, "The Verdict on Edith Jones," *Mirabella*, March 1991. Additional details from the author's interview with Lyons.
5. Linda Hirshman's books *Reckoning* and *Sisters in Law* explore the evolution of these rulings and O'Connor's and Ginsburg's roles in detail. Louis Dubose, "Naked City off the Desk," *Austin Chronicle*, February 2, 2001; Louis Dubose, "Left Field," *Texas Observer*, February 16, 2001.
6. Hirshman, *Sisters in Law*, 161.

Additional information gathered from author's visits to the Fifth Circuit Court of Appeals archives in New Orleans and to the archives of disciplinary orders at the Administrative Office of the US Courts in Washington,

DC; reviews of yearbooks and law journals from the 1970s at the UT School of Law; and reviews of Jones's speeches on YouTube.

CHAPTER 8: A BOTCHED INVESTIGATION

1. Summary of witness statements gathered in 2007 by Hardin and Associates, in possession of the author.
2. Judith L. Herman, "Justice from the Victim's Perspective," *Violence Against Women* 11, no. 5 (May 2005): 571–602, http://nrs.harvard .edu/urn-3:HUL.InstRepos:34961943..
3. Herman, "Justice from the Victim's Perspective."
4. Arthur Hellman, "Judges Judging Judges: The Federal Judicial Misconduct Statutes and the Breyer Committee Report," *Justice System Journal* 28, no. 3 (2007): 426–35.
5. Bazelon, "Putting the Mice in Charge of the Cheese," Loyola, 2.
6. Lise Olsen, "Secrecy May Help Misbehaving Judges; Does Secret Process Let Errant Judges Get Away with Breaking the Law?," *Houston Chronicle*, December 14, 2009.
7. Lise Olsen, "Accused Judge Enlists Help of Dick DeGuerin," *Houston Chronicle*, December 12, 2007.
8. Bazelon, "Putting the Mice in Charge of the Cheese," Loyola, 22.

INTERLUDE: THE EXPOSÉ

1. Lise Olsen and Harvey Rice, "Judge Disciplined for Sexual Harassment," *Houston Chronicle*, September 28, 2007.
2. Lise Olsen, "Details Emerge in Judge Kent Scandal; How Far Did This Federal Judge Go?," *Houston Chronicle*, November 11, 2007.

Additional information from author interviews with Haj, Rice, Hardin, De-Guerin, Williams, and other former court officials and attorneys.

CHAPTER 9: A CORRUPT JUDGE

1. Borkin, *Corrupt Judge*, 141–86.
2. Reynolds's complaint was described both in the author's interview with Rafael C. Goyeneche III and in House Report No. 111–427, "Impeachment of G. Thomas Porteous Jr. of the US District Court of the Eastern District of Louisiana," March 4, 2010.
3. The MCC's written summary of the meeting in possession of the author. Additional information from author's interview with Goyeneche. See also *House Report on the Impeachment of Porteous*; Goyeneche's September 14, 2010, Senate Impeachment Trial testimony, https://www.c-span.org/video/?295450-6/judge-porteous-impeachment-trial-rafael -goyeneche-testimony.

Information on Porteous's testimony before the investigatory committee is taken from a transcript released in 2007 by the Fifth Circuit Court of Appeals (in possession of the author), as well as author interviews with Patrick Fanning and others with knowledge of the closed proceeding.

CHAPTER 10: THE KEEPER OF SECRETS

1. For more details, see Susan Criss, "I Know First Hand It's Hard to Report Sexual Harassment by a Powerful Man," *Houston Chronicle*, September 28, 2018, https://www.houstonchronicle.com/local/gray-matters /article/reporting-sexual-harassment-christine-blasey-ford-13266776.php.

Additional information in this chapter is based on interviews with McBroom, Wilkerson, and Criss and with other attorneys and court and government officials. Additional details from statements Wilkerson and McBroom gave on June 3, 2009, to the House Impeachment Task Force and in federal court. See also Skip Hollandsworth, "Perversion of Justice," *Texas Monthly*, December 2009, https://www.texasmonthly.com/articles /perversion-of-justice.

CHAPTER 11: A CRIMINAL PROBE

1. John Council and Brenda Sapino Jeffreys, "Harassment Claims Against Federal Judge Involve High-Profile Lawyers on Both Sides," *Texas Lawyer*, December 21, 2007.
2. Herman, "Justice from the Victim's Perspective."
3. Judith Herman, *Trauma and Recovery: The Aftermath of Violence—from Domestic Abuse to Political Terror* (1992; New York: Basic Books, 1997).
4. Duff Wilson, "Entertainer and Fighter Is Clemens's Lead Lawyer," *New York Times*, December 28, 2007.
5. Meeting described in interviews with author and separately summarized by Alan Baron, special impeachment counsel for the House Judiciary Committee, in the June 3, 2009, *Hearing Before the Task Force on Judicial Impeachment of Samuel Kent.*

Additional information for this chapter from interviews with McBroom, Wilkerson, Hardin, Roden, DeGuerin, and government and court officials who spoke on background only. Author covered January 2008 protest.

CHAPTER 12: PERSON B

1. Lise Olsen, "Feds Broaden Sex Misconduct Investigation of Kent, Justice Department Broadening Investigation. Sale of Home and Gift Reporting Being Examined," *Houston Chronicle*, July 20, 2008, https:// www.chron.com/news/houston-texas/article/Feds-broaden-sex -misconduct-investigation-of-Kent-1671098.php.
2. Olsen, "Feds Broaden Sex Misconduct Investigation of Kent."
3. Accounts of Donna Wilkerson's experiences described in this chapter from author interviews with Wilkerson and her statements in Kent's 2009 sentencing hearing and in the House Task Force June 3, 2009, hearing on Kent's impeachment.
4. Quotes from McBroom, Wilkerson, DeGuerin, and Judge Vinson during Kent's May 11, 2009, sentencing (federal court transcript.)

Additional information from interviews with Schaffer, McBroom, Buzbee, and DeGuerin, as well as records of the house sale.

CHAPTER 13: THE PATH TO IMPEACHMENT

1. New Hampshire Historical Society, "Pickering, John (1737–1805)," https://nhhistory.org/object/251789/pickering-john-1737–1805.
2. Lynn Turner, "The Impeachment of John Pickering," *American Historical Review* 54, no. 3 (April 1949): 490.
3. Turner, "The Impeachment of John Pickering."
4. To Thomas Jefferson from Albert Gallatin, January 31, 1803, Jefferson Papers, https://founders.archives.gov/documents/Jefferson/01-39-02 -0363.
5. See also "The Impeachment and Trial of John Pickering," Precedents of the House of Representatives, available from the Government Printing Office, https://www.govinfo.gov/content/pkg/GPO-HPREC-HINDS-V3 /pdf/GPO-HPREC-HINDS-V3-20.pdf.
6. William J. Eaton, "House Votes Impeachment of Federal Judge in Florida," *Los Angeles Times*, August 4, 1988, https://www.latimes.com /archives/la-xpm-1988-08-04-mn-10225-story.html.
7. See also House report on Kent's impeachment.
8. Cathy McBroom, full statement to the House Impeachment Task Force, June 9, 2009, https://blog.chron.com/newswatch/files/legacy /McBroom090603.pdf.
9. Brenda Sapino Jeffreys, "Former Judge Sam Kent Serving Sentence in Home Confinement," *Texas Lawyer*, August 8, 2011.
10. John Council, "Truth and Consequences: Cathy McBroom's Bravery Alters Federal Judicial Disciplinary Procedure," *Texas Lawyer*, December 21, 2009.

Additional information from author interviews with Sensenbrenner in Washington, DC, on the day of Kent's impeachment in 2009; with Barbara A. Radnofsky, author of *A Citizen's Guide to Impeachment* (Brooklyn, NY: Melville House, 2017); and with McBroom and Wilkerson on the day of Kent's release from prison. See also Lise Olsen, "Fifth Circuit Backs Impeachment for Judge Kent," *Houston Chronicle*, May 27, 2009, https:// www.chron.com/neighborhood/baytown-news/article/5th-Circuit-council -backs-impeachment-for-Judge-1739080.ph.

CHAPTER 14: ANOTHER ENCOUNTER WITH JUDGE KOZINSKI

1. Murphy's account of her conversation with Kozinski is based on interviews with the author. See also Zapotosky, "Prominent Appeals Court Judge Alex Kozinski Accused of Sexual Misconduct"; Ray Suarez, "Federal Judge Retires amid Allegations of Sexual Misconduct," interview of Emily Murphy, *All Things Considered*, December 18, 2017, transcript at https://www.npr.org/2017/12/18/571735676/federal-judge -retires-amid-allegations-of-sexual-harassment.
2. Irin Carmon and Amelia Schonbek, "Was It Worth It? Is It Still? Will It Ever Be?," *The Cut* (*New York* magazine), September 30, 2019, https:// www.thecut.com/2019/09/coming-forward-about-sexual-assault-and -what-comes-after.html.

3. Alex Kozinski, "Conduct Unbecoming," *Yale Law Journal*, 1999. See also Tony Mauro, "Supreme Court Tightens Secrecy Rules for Clerks," *USA Today*, November 9, 1998. Additional information from Mauro's interview with author.

4. Bond's description of her email from Kozinski and her conversation with Scirica are from Bond's December 2017 journal entry, courtney milan.com, and her emails and interviews with the author.

5. Dahlia Lithwick, "He Made Us All Victims and Accomplices," *Slate*, December 13, 2017. Additional information from Lithwick's interview with author.

6. Quote from Kozinski's 2017 resignation statement. See also Leah Litman, Emily Murphy, and Katherine H. Ku, "Opinion: A Comeback but No Reckoning," *New York Times*, August 2, 2018, https://www .nytimes.com/2018/08/02/opinion/sunday/alex-kozinski-harassment -allegations-comeback.html.

7. Ty Clevenger, "The Beginning of the End for U.S. District Judge Walter S. Smith, Jr.," September 11, 2014, https://lawflog.com/?p=472, is one of many examples of the blog entries penned by Clevenger.

Additional information from interviews with Clevenger and with the former court employee who reported that Smith sexually harassed her, as well as from judicial disciplinary orders, including the Fifth Circuit Judicial Council's "Order of Reprimand and Memorandum of Reasons" of Walter Smith, December 5, 2015.

CHAPTER 15: CALLS FOR REFORM—AND A BACKLASH

1. Matt Zapotosky, "A Los Angeles Federal Judge, Once Accused of Sexual Misconduct, Returns to the Public Eye," *Los Angeles Times*, July 24, 2018.

2. Law Clerks for Workplace Accountability, mission statement, http:// clerksforaccountability.org/#mission, retrieved May 20, 2020.

3. *Report of the Federal Judiciary Workplace Conduct Working Group to the Judicial Conference of the United States* (June 2018), https://www .uscourts.gov/sites/default/files/workplace_conduct_working_group _final_report_0.pdf.

4. Statements from Grassley, Feinstein, and Santos are from the written records and video of the June 13, 2018, hearing of the Senate Judicial Committee.

5. "Prepared Statement by Senator Chuck Grassley of Iowa, Chairman, Senate Judiciary Committee, Hearing on Confronting Sexual Harassment and Other Workplace Misconduct in the Federal Judiciary," June 13, 2018, www.judiciary.senate.gov/imo/media/doc/06-13-18%20 Grassley%20Statement.pdf.

6. Kozinski, "Confessions of a Bad Apple," 1709.

7. From "Kavanaugh Responses to Questions for the Record," Senate Judiciary Committee, September 10, 2018, https://www.judiciary.senate .gov/download/kavanaugh-responses-to-questions-for-the-record.

8. Bond, "I Received Some of Kozinski's Infamous Gag List Emails."

9. Bond, "I Received Some of Kozinski's Infamous Gag List Emails."

10. Richard Kopf, @JudgeKopf, tweet posted July 20, 2018. Deleted. Screen grab in possession of the author.

11. Richard Kopf, @JudgeKopf, tweet posted July 21, 2018. Deleted. Screen grab in possession of the author.

12. Billy Kelly, "Nebraska Federal Judge Ends Controversial Blog; Will Remain on Bench," interview with Judge Richard Kopf, NET News, July 10, 2015, video at http://netnebraska.org/article/news/981511/nebraska -federal-judge-ends-controversial-blog-will-remain-bench.

13. Associated Press, "Nebraska Judge Apologizes After Backlash over Tweet," July 27, 2018, https://apnews.com/ba2101e3066344aeba5715 08c456ab28/Nebraska-judge-apologizes-after-backlash-over-tweet.

14. Debra Cassens Weiss, "Over 70 Former Reinhardt Clerks Urge Judiciary to Change Reporting Procedures and Training," *ABA Journal*, February 21, 2020, https://www.abajournal.com/news/article/former -reinhardt-clerks-urge-judiciary-to-change-reporting-procedures-and -training.

15. Olivia Warren, "Hearing on Protecting Federal Judicial Employees from Sexual Harassment, Discrimination and Other Workplace Misconduct, House Judiciary's Subcommittee on the Courts, Intellectual Property, and the Internet." Warren's testimony: https://docs.house.gov /meetings/JU/JU03/20200213/110505/HHRG-116-JU03-Wstate -WarrenO-20200213-U2.pdf; full record: https://judiciary.house.gov /calendar/eventsingle.aspx?EventID=2791.16. Warren, testimony.

16. Warren, testimony.

17. Liv Warren, in a statement emailed to the author by Warren's attorneys, Greta B. Williams and Zainab Ahmad, of Gibson, Dunn & Crutcher, May 5, 2020. See also Jacqueline Thomsen, "'Failures of the System': Law Students, Advocates Push for Protections at the Judiciary," *National Law Journal*, March 25, 2020.

18. Jacqueline Thomsen, "'Failures of the System': Law Students, Advocates Push for Protections at the Judiciary," *National Law Journal*, March 25, 2020. Warren's statement also provided via email to the author.

19. Michele Landis Dauber et al., "Reinhardt Clerk Letter Press Release," February 20, 2020, https://docs.google.com/document/d/1d6Xvp2Fu RAaSI-W7c2nX-qfIppB5N38xzSoHWlmd15g/edit.

Additional quotes and other information from the testimony Warren and Shah provided in the February 2020 House subcommittee hearing and from interviews with Bond, Litman, Santos, Lithwick, and Warren's attorneys. Other former law clerks who knew Reinhardt spoke on background. Additional details about Murguia came from his September 30, 2019 reprimand, https://www.ca10.uscourts.gov/ce/news/judicial-council -order-10-18-90022.j, and from information released by the Judicial Conference's Judicial Conduct and Disciplinary Committee on March 3,

2020, https://www.uscourts.gov/sites/default/files/c.c.d._no._19-02 _march_3_2020_0.pdf.

EPILOGUE: THE QUILTER

1. Hill, *Speaking Truth to Power*, 7.
2. Mary Flood, "Inventor in Sex Toy Court Battle Targets Copies of Device, Inventor Pursues Sex Toy Battle in Court; He Says Copies Violate His Patent and May Be Harmful," *Houston Chronicle*, June 4, 2010.
3. Judge Lynn Hughes's email response to author, sent via Hughes's secretary, Kathy L. Grant, September 17, 2020. Hughes previously spoke with the author about remarks he made in court about "girls." See also Olsen and Gabrielle Banks, "Houston Federal Judge Bars Female Prosecutor from Court, Sparking Standoff with U.S. Attorney's Office," *Houston Chronicle*, February 12, 2019.

Additional information from interviews with McBroom and Evelyn Baldwin, as well as visits to McBroom's home and to a quilt shop in 2019 and 2020.

SELECTED BIBLIOGRAPHY

Federal judicial misconduct orders and other documents related to Code of Silence have been posted at https://www.documentcloud.com /codeofsilence.

BOOKS

Borkin, Joseph. *The Currupt Judge: An Inquiry into Other High Crimes and Misdemeanors in the Federal Courts*. New York: Clarkson N. Potter, 1962.

Hill, Anita. *Speaking Truth to Power*. New York: Doubleday, 1997.

Hirshman, Linda. *Sisters in Law: How Sandra Day O'Connor and Ruth Bader Ginsburg Went to the Supreme Court and Changed the World*. New York: HarperCollins, 2015.

———. *Reckoning: The Epic Battle Against Sexual Abuse and Harassment*. New York: Houghton Mifflin Harcourt, 2019.

Lobel, Orly. *You Don't Own Me: How Mattel v. MGA Entertainment Exposed Barbie's Dark Side*. New York: W. W. Norton, 2018.

Pogrebin, Robin, and Kate Kelly. *The Education of Brett Kavanaugh: An Investigation*. New York: Portfolio/Penguin, 2019.

Radnofsky, Barbara. *A Citizen's Guide to Impeachment*. Brooklyn, NY: Melville House, 2017.

Rehnquist, William H. *Grand Inquests: The Historic Impeachments of Justice Samuel Chase and President Andrew Jackson*. New York: Morrow, 1992.

Simpson, Alex, Jr. *A Treatise on Federal Impeachments*. Wilmington, DE: Scholarly Resources, 1973.

Volcansek, Mary. *Judicial Impeachment: None Called for Justice*. Urbana: University of Illinois Press, 1993.

CONGRESSIONAL AND COURT RECORDS

Associate Justice Stephen Breyer et al., *The Implementation of the Judicial Conduct and Disability Act of 1980: A Report to the Chief Justice*, September 2006. https://www.supremecourt.gov/publicinfo/breyer committeereport.pdf.

Federal Judicial Center. "Biographical Directory of Article III Federal Judges, 1789–Present." https://www.fjc.gov/node/7946.

Federal Judicial Center. "Impeachments of Federal Judges." https://www .fjc.gov/history/judges/impeachments-federal-judges.

Hearing Before the Task Force on Judicial Impeachment, House Judiciary Committee, June 3, 2009. https://www.govinfo.gov/content/pkg/CHRG -111hhrg50067/html/CHRG-111hhrg50067.htm

House Report No. 111–159, "Impeachment of Judge Samuel B. Kent," June 17, 2009. https://www.congress.gov/111/crpt/hrpt159/CRPT-111hrpt159 .pdf. House Report No. 111–427, "Impeachment of G. Thomas Porteous, Judge for the Eastern District of Louisiana," March 4, 2010. https://www.congress.gov/111/crpt/hrpt427/CRPT-111hrpt427.pdf.

Hearing Before the Senate Judiciary Committee: Confronting Harassment and Other Workplace Misconduct in the Federal Judiciary, June 13, 2018. https://www.judiciary.senate.gov/meetings/confronting-sexual -harassment-and-other-workplace-misconduct-in-the-federal-judiciary.

Hearing Before the House Subcommittee on Courts, Intellectual Property, and the Internet: Protecting Federal Judiciary Employees from Sexual Harassment, Discrimination, and Other Workplace Misconduct, February 13, 2020. https://docs.house.gov/Committee/Calendar/ByEvent .aspx?EventID=110505.

Report of the Federal Judicial Workplace Conduct Working Group to the Judicial Conference of the United States, June 1, 2018. https://www .uscourts.gov/sites/default/files/workplace_conduct_working_group _final_report_0.pdf.

US Courts. "Public Comment on Proposed Changes to Code of Conduct for US Judges and Judicial Conduct and Disability Rules." Statements from Sanai, Law Clerks for Accountability, and others posted here: https://www.uscourts.gov/rules-policies/judiciary-policies/proposed -changes-code-and-jcd-rules/public-comment-proposed.